The Television
Crime Fighters Factbook

ALSO BY VINCENT TERRACE
AND FROM MCFARLAND

*Radio Program Openings and Closings,
1931–1972* (2003)

*Crime Fighting Heroes of Television:
Over 10,000 Facts from 151 Shows,
1949–2001* (2002)

*Sitcom Factfinder, 1948–1984:
Over 9,700 Details from 168 Television Shows* (2002)

*Television Sitcom Factbook: Over 8,700 Details
from 130 Shows, 1985–2000* (2000)

*Radio Programs, 1924–1984:
A Catalog of Over 1800 Shows* (1999)

*Experimental Television, Test Films, Pilots
and Trial Series, 1925 through 1995:
Seven Decades of Small Screen Almosts* (1997)

*Television Specials: 3,201 Entertainment
Spectaculars, 1939 through 1993* (1995)

*Television Character and Story Facts:
Over 110,000 Details from
1,008 Shows, 1945–1992* (1993)

The Television Crime Fighters Factbook

Over 9,800 Details from 301 Programs, 1937–2003

Vincent Terrace

McFarland & Company, Inc., Publishers
Jefferson, North Carolina, and London

Library of Congress Cataloguing-in-Publication Data

Terrace, Vincent, 1948–
  The television crime fighters factbook : over 9,800 details from 301 programs, 1937–2003 / by Vincent Terrace.
    p.   cm.
  Includes index.

  ISBN 0-7864-1533-9 (softcover : 50# alkaline paper)

  1. Detective and mystery television programs — United States — Miscellanea. 2. Cop shows — United States — Miscellanea. I. Title.
  PN1992.8.D48T47   2004
  791.45'6556 — dc21   2003020315

British Library cataloguing data are available

©2004 Vincent Terrace. All rights reserved

No part of this book may be reproduced or transmitted in any form or by any means, electronic or mechanical, including photocopying or recording, or by any information storage and retrieval system, without permission in writing from the publisher.

Cover art ©2003 EyeWire

Manufactured in the United States of America

McFarland & Company, Inc., Publishers
  Box 611, Jefferson, North Carolina 28640
  www.mcfarlandpub.com

Contents

Preface 1

Angel Street 5
B.A.D. Cats 5
Baywatch Nights 6
B.J. and the Bear 7
B.L. Stryker 10
Boston Blackie 10
Bourbon Street Beat 11
Broken Badges 13
The Brothers Brannagan 14
Buddy Faro 15
Burke's Law 15
Cagney and Lacey 16
The Cases of Eddie Drake 18
Charlie's Angels 18
Chase 25
CHiPs 26
Columbo 27
The Commish 29
The Cosby Mysteries 29
Crime Photographer 30
Crossing Jordan 31
C.S.I.: Crime Scene Investigation 33
Danger Theater 37

Decoy 38
Dellaventura 39
Department S 39
Diagnosis Murder 40
Dick Tracy 42
The District 43
Dog and Cat 45
Downtown 45
Dragnet 46
The Eddie Capra Mysteries 48
Ellery Queen 49
Eye to Eye 50
Fastlane 51
Father Dowling Mysteries 52
Gallery of Mme. Liu Tsong 55
Get Christie Love 56
The Great Defender 57
Griff 58
Hack 58
Hardball 59
Hardcastle and McCormick 60
The Hardy Boys 61
Harry O 64
Hart to Hart 65
The Hat Squad 66

Contents

Haunted 67	Murder, She Wrote 111
Hawaiian Eye 70	Murphy's Law 114
Heart of the City 71	Naked City 115
Honey West 72	Nancy Drew 117
Hudson Street 74	Nash Bridges 120
Hunter 74	Nero Wolfe 122
I Had Three Wives 77	Over My Dead Body 124
In the Heat of the Night 77	Partners in Crime 125
Jake and the Fatman 78	Pete Kelly's Blues 126
The Job 79	Peter Gunn 128
John Doe 80	Picket Fences 129
Johnny Midnight 82	Police Squad 131
Just Cause 82	Police Woman 131
Kate Loves a Mystery 84	Pros and Cons 133
Kojak 85	P.S. I Luv U 134
Lady Blue 87	Quincy, M.E. 135
The Last Precinct 87	Raven 136
The Law and Harry McGraw 88	Remington Steele 137
Leg Work 89	Richard Diamond 139
MacGruder and Loud 90	The Roaring 20's 141
Magnum, P.I. 90	Robin's Hoods 142
Martin Kane, Private Eye 93	The Rockford Files 143
Matlock 94	Serpico 145
Matt Helm 96	77 Sunset Strip 146
Matt Houston 97	She Spies 149
McMillan and Wife 98	She's the Sheriff 152
Me and Mom 99	Silk Stalkings 153
Miami Vice 99	Sledge Hammer 155
Michael Shayne 100	Snoops 156
Mike Hammer 101	Sons of Thunder 157
Mr. and Mrs. North 103	Spenser: For Hire 158
The Mod Squad 105	Starsky and Hutch 159
Monk 107	Street Justice 160
Moon Over Miami 109	Strike Force 161
Moonlighting 110	The Strip 162
	Sue Thomas, F.B.Eye 163

SurfSide 6   166
Sweating Bullets   167
Switch   168
Ten Speed and Brown Shoe   169
Tequila and Bonetti   169
The Thin Man   172
Thunder in Paradise   174
Tightrope   175
T.J. Hooker   175
Total Security   176

21 Beacon Street   178
21 Jump Street   179
Unsub   180
The Untouchables   181
Walker, Texas Ranger   184

Appendix A: Television's Experimental Crime Fighters   187
Appendix B: Pilot Films   189
Index   201

Preface

Did you know that detective Adrian Monk (*Monk*) is afraid of milk? or that Pinky's real first name on *The Roaring 20's* is Delaware? Were you aware that Mary Tyler Moore played Sam, the Hi Fi Answering Service girl on *Richard Diamond*? or that on *Charlie's Angels*, Sabrina was the only Angel who was never seen in a bikini or swimsuit? These are only a few of the more than 9,800 facts that you will find in *The Television Crime Fighters Factbook*.

This sequel to *Crime Fighting Heroes of Television* (McFarland, 2002) chronicles the work of television's ordinary law enforcers — from cops and private eyes to sheriffs and amateur sleuths who risk their lives to solve crimes and bring criminals to justice. Detailed information is presented on 134 network, syndicated and cable series broadcast from 1948 to 2003. There are also two appendices of basic program information. Appendix A lists the five experimental, crime-related programs broadcast from 1937 to 1946; Appendix B lists the 204 unsold pilot films dealing with law enforcers broadcast from 1948 to 1996 (the last year in which the networks broadcast 30 and 60-minute failed series ideas).

Many of the 134 series chronicled here include TV movie update information as well as the proposed spinoffs (pilots) that were broadcast as part of a series (for example, Sharon Stone played detective Dani Starr on the "Hollywood Starr" episode of *T.J. Hooker*). Where applicable, entries also contain related project information (the series and/or pilots that used a similar format before a chronicled entry; for example, the 2002 entry *Haunted* contains all the prior projects that dealt with ghosts helping a private detective solve crimes).

All entries are listed alphabetically and relate factual information regarding characters, addresses, names of pets, telephone numbers and license plate numbers to name a few; in short, anything and everything that adds interest to a program and its characters. As with prior volumes in this series, all

Preface

information is compiled from the actual episodes of the series listed. There is also an index of performers who appear in each of the programs.

The author would like to thank James Robert Parish and Jennifer Mormile for their help in making this book possible.

THE SHOWS

1. **Angel Street** (CBS, 1992)

The Roll Call is the local watering hole for the detectives attached to the Homicide Division of the Violent Crimes Unit of the Chicago Police Department. It is a place where detectives Anita Wellman King (Robin Givens), Dorothy Paretsky (Pamela Gidley) and Ken Brannigan (Ron Dean) find a haven from the gruelling and often gritty aspects of their jobs.

Anita and Dorothy first met when they were teamed by the department. Anita, a glamorous black woman, "overdresses for the job" (as Dorothy says). She wears skirts and heels and gets rather upset when she ruins her expensive, $15 a pair, pantyhose chasing suspects. She is a Catholic and grew up on the poor South Side of Chicago. She now lives in a better neighborhood at 311 Ashford Drive; 555-6616 is her phone number and her car license plate reads M9 640. Anita is also ambitious and has set her goal to become a lieutenant.

Dorothy, called Dotty, is a street-wise cop who began her career with the narcotics department (Anita had previously worked with Internal Affairs). She is satisfied where she is and refuses to work with Anita on cases that do not involve murder ("We're homicide — no body, no case"). Dotty is Catholic (attended Francis Xavier Elementary School) and grew up in the Polish Hill section of Chicago, a posh area that is also called Angel Street. Dotty has a bad habit of smoking (she is seen smoking Marlboro cigarettes) and lives at 9034 Mid-Valley Road. Her phone number is 555-1310 and her car license plate reads 609 703A. Dorothy is a single mother and lives with her daughter Jennifer (Christina Robinson) and her grandfather, "Pobby" (Everett Smith, Jan Rubes). Dorothy refuses to talk about Jennifer's father or whether she was married to him or just had an affair.

Ken is the senior detective in the unit. He has an unseen wife named Marjorie whom he calls Mrs. B and "Blonde in the Pond" was his first case, a still unsolved Jane Doe (a girl was found in a lake. No one claimed the body; no suspects). The series was originally titled "Polish Hill." Anthony Marinelli composed the theme "Angel Street."

Angeles *See* Charlie's Angels

Angels '88 *See* Charlie's Angels

2. **B.A.D. Cats** (ABC, 1980)

Samantha Jenson (Michelle Pfeiffer), Nick Donovan (Asher Brauner) and Ocee James (Steven Hanks) are undercover officers with the B.A.D. Cats

(Burglary Auto Detail, Commercial Auto Thefts) Division of the L.A.P.D. Samantha, called Sunshine, has the car code Cat-2; she lives at 701 Figueroa Street and 555-3113 is her phone number. Nick and Ocee share a car and have the code Cat-1 (also given as Stray Cat-1). Nick resides at 1324½ Los Palmas and Ocee in an apartment on Bergen Street; his car license plate reads 938 LYN. Ma's Place, a restaurant owned by a woman known only as Ma (La Wanda Page), is their favorite eatery and hangout. Eugene Nathan (Vic Morrow) is their captain, a stern man who has the nickname Skip; 264 PPA is his license plate number. Barry DeVorzon composed the theme "B.A.D. Cats."

3. Baywatch Nights (Syndicated, 1995–1997)

When he was eight years old, Mitch Buchannon saw what he considered to be the ultimate private detective movie, *The Maltese Falcon*. The movie so inspired Mitch that he wanted to become a private eye when he grew up. He even had a subscription to *True Detective Magazine*. Fate, however, intervened, and Mitch (David Hasselhoff) became a lifeguard and eventually head of the Los Angeles County Lifeguards at Baywatch (from the series *Baywatch*, from which *Baywatch Nights* is a spinoff).

Garner Ellerbee (Greg Alan Williams), a beach patrol cop and friend of Mitch's, is unhappy with his job and yearns to become his own boss by opening a private detective agency. Ryan McBride (Angie Harmon) is a beautiful young private eye, newly arrived in Santa Monica from New York, who purchases the bankrupt Pine Detective Agency at 2000 Beach Boulevard above a nightclub called Nights.

Garner takes the first step by moonlighting as a private detective. When he needs help solving a crime involving a stolen jade, he asks Mitch to assist. During their investigation they meet Ryan, who became involved in the same case when she discovered the Pine Agency was a front for a smuggling ring. They join forces, solve the case and decide to remain a team, forming the Buchannon-Ellerbee-McBride Detective Agency. After countless arguments about what to call the agency, they decided to do it alphabetically.

The program has limited trivia information. Ryan, a former Miss Texas, lives in a trailer at the Malibu Cliffs Trailer Court. She paid $25,000 for the Pine Agency, was born in Texas and earned her P.I. license in New York City. She is also a computer whiz and uses the password "Butthead" to access the office computer information. Mitch, who attended Palisade High School, drives a car with the license plate 3KKL 263. Garner's car license plate reads SHAFT 7 after his favorite movie hero, Shaft. Mitch, Ryan and Garner charge $50 an hour for their services. Singer Lou Raymond (Lou Rawls) owns and performs at Nights. Destiny (Lisa Stahl) is the local beach tarot card reader who helps out at the office. She also confuses Mitch with her predictions and Mitch wishes she would come with a set of instructions so he can understand her.

Midway through the first season, Destiny and Lou were dropped. The glamorous and wealthy D.J. Marco (Donna D'Errico) became the new owner of Nights and Griff Walker (Eddie Cibrian) became the agency's new helper. He is the owner of the Griff Walker Photography Studio opposite the agency in Room 102. D.J., whose real name is Donna, says she uses the initials because it makes business easier. Her car license plate reads 3NPG 622.

The second season dramatically changed the series concept. Typical cases were dropped in favor of the team investigating crimes associated with the unnatural (from mutants to ghosts to genetically engineered beings). The change in focus was devastating: unbelievable stories coupled with bad directing (constant rocking and swaying of cameras to produce unsteady images) simply turned viewers off. The series was abruptly cancelled shortly after. During this time, Garner was also dropped in favor of a mysterious figure named Teague (Dorian Gregory) who hired the team (Ryan, Mitch and Griff) to investigate strange happenings. Angie Harmon's character name, Ryan McBride, is taken from the agency Frank MacBride and Peterson T. Ryan ran on the 1975–1978 CBS series *Switch* (MacBride-Ryan Investigations).

David Hasselhoff sings the theme "Baywatch Nights."

4. **B.J. and the Bear** (NBC, 1979–1981)

Bear Enterprises is an unusual business at 800 Palmer Street in Hollywood, California. It is located above Phil's Disco, a bar-restaurant, and run by Billie Joe McKay (Greg Evigan), a big rig trucker who named the business after his simian traveling companion, Bear. B.J. (as Billie Joe is called) established the business as an independent trucking company, but he and his associates are more like private detectives as the jobs they acquire involve them with shady characters and crimes they must solve. A scale model of B.J.'s truck, which doubles as a lamp, is on his desk; 555-7993 is the office phone number.

B.J. was originally (1979–1980) an independent trucker who would haul anything legal anywhere for $1.50 a mile plus expenses. His red with white trim Kenworth 18-wheeler is registered in Milwaukee (his hometown) and the following license plates can be seen on the truck: UT 3665, 806-356,

635-608, and 4T-3665. The Milwaukee Kid is his C.B. handle and the Country Comfort Truckers' Stop in Bowlin County is his favorite watering hole.

B.J. named Bear after Paul "Bear" Bryant, whom B.J. considers to be the greatest football coach of all time (for the University of Alabama). B.J. was a chopper pilot during the Vietnam War when he first met Bear. B.J. was a P.O.W. and Bear would bring him food to help him survive. When B.J. was rescued he took Bear with him. B.J. plays piano and sax and sang in a band called Ghettoway City. B.J. often calls Bear "Kid" or "The Kid."

When B.J. established Bear Enterprises in 1980, seven beautiful female truckers were added to the cast to assist him: Jeannie Campbell (Judy Landers), Samantha Smith (Barbra Horan), Callie Everett (Linda McCullough), Cindy Grant (Sherilyn Wolter), Angie Cartwright (Sheila DeWindt) and twins Geri and Teri Garrison (Candi and Randi Brough).

Jeannie, nicknamed Stacks, measures 37C-24-36. She is very sweet and very feminine and somewhat of a dumb blonde. Perilous situations do not phase Stacks until she thinks about what is happening to her. It is then that her senses kick in and she becomes a totally different person—logical and intelligent. While not totally vain, Stacks knows she is a beautiful girl and loves to have cheesecake pictures taken of herself, especially if she is wearing a bikini or low cut blouse. Stacks is always dreaming about getting married but falls for shady characters who shatter those dreams. She drives an 18-wheeler with the license plate 4JJ 0162.

Callie is Stacks direct opposite. Though pretty, she dresses in jeans and is the toughest and most physically violent of the girls. She can handle herself in a fight (although B.J. prefers that she not fight) and, as B.J. says, "has a smart mouth." Callie has a secret crush on B.J. and believes "B.J. sees me only as a girl who can drive a rig and fix a flat tire." Her 18-wheel rig license plate reads 1XT 403.

Geri and Teri are identical twins who also work as waitresses at Phil's Disco. Geri is impatient and likes to take matters in her own hands. Teri calls her a hot head. Teri is patient and prefers to take things slow and easy. They drive an 18-wheeler with the license plate UJJ 4004. Angie, the least active of the girls (and the only black member of the cast) spends most of her time moonlighting as a radio disc jockey called "The Nightingale." Her truck license plate reads 040 3777. Samantha and Cindy share a truck with the license plate XTR 7162. Samantha is another sweet girl, not prone to violent confrontations, who looks after Bear when she and B.J. are on assignments together. Cindy is easily upset and a bit irrational. She has knowledge of criminal law and often warns B.J. that what he is about to do to crack a case could be construed as breaking the law. Circumstances often force B.J. to break the rules to get the job done. Cindy's father is Rutherford T. Grant (Murray Hamilton), the corrupt head of S.C.A.T. (the Special Crimes Action Team), Southern Division of the L.A.P.D. Grant has made it his top priority to put B.J. behind bars. He feels that B.J. and his truckers are a threat to his illegal activities. Cindy is always caught in the middle but realizes her father is wrong and often sides with B.J.

"Where there is money, there is Grant," says B.J., as he caters to the mob, unscrupulous characters and uses blackmail to get people to do his dirty work. He is assisted by Lieutenant Jim Steiger (Eric Server), a man who is not as dishonest as Grant, but follows his orders. "Close the door as you leave, Steiger" is Grant's catchphrase as he tells Jim to leave his office. When Grant makes the wrong move and embezzles $947,000 from S.C.A.T. and tries to frame B.J., B.J. and the girls, with the help of Steiger and the Feds, end Grant's reign of corruption. Steiger is promoted to captain and warns B.J. to stay clean—"or I'll pick up where Grant left off."

First season episodes depict B.J. as a clean cut kid attempting to do his job and mind his own business but always encountering shady characters. His friend at this time was Snow White (Laurette Spang), a trucker who was head of the all-girl Piston Packin' Mamas. His enemies were Elroy P. Lobo (Claude Akins), the corrupt sheriff of Orly County, Georgia; J.P. Pierson (M.P. Murphy), head of the organized (but corrupt) High Ballers Trucking Company who opposed independents like B.J. taking their business; Jason T. Willard (Jock Mahoney), head of the corrupt Trans-Cal Trucking; Captain John Sebastian Cain (Ed Lauter), an honest cop who believed B.J. was corrupt; and Beauregard Wiley (Slim Pickens), the corrupt Deputy Sheriff of Winslow County.

Greg Evigan sings the theme "B.J. and the Bear."

Proposed Spinoffs (Unsold Pilots)

1. *The Eyes of Texas* (November 10, 1979). Texas International is a small, Dallas, Texas-based private detective organization owned by Mort Jarvis (Roger C. Carmel). Heather Fern (Rebecca Reynolds) and Caroline Capoty (Lorrie Mahaffey) are his operatives, two beautiful girls who call themselves "The Eyes of Texas." The story finds Heather and Caroline seeking a con man who preys on wealthy, older women.

2. *The Eyes of Texas* (February 23, 1980). A reworking of the prior pilot that finds Heather Fern (Rebecca Reynolds) and Caroline Capoty (Heather Thomas) as investigators for Texas International, a two-bit private detective organization now run by Helen Jarvis (Eve Arden), the late Mort's wife. The

story, titled "The Girls on the Hollywood High," finds Heather and Caroline helping B.J. McKay find his sister Shauna (Deborah Ryan), who disappeared after witnessing a murder.

3. Detective Finger, I Presume (May 2, 1981). Police drama with comical overtones as Fred Finger (Greg Mullavey), a detective lieutenant with the San Francisco Police Department, sets out to solve crimes — by accident. He is assisted by Sergeant Williams (Paul Tulley). The pilot story finds Detective Finger solving the theft of a valuable painting.

5. B.L. Stryker (ABC, 1989–1990)

Buddy Lee Stryker (Burt Reynolds), called B.L., is a private detective and owner of Stryker Investigations at 62 Palm Drive in Palm Beach, Florida. He is assisted by Oz Jackson (Ossie Davis), a former world-famous boxer, and Lyynda Lennox (Dana Kaminski), his slightly flighty secretary. B.L. was a former police officer with the New Orleans P.D. He liked to take chances and used considerable violence to achieve his goals. Constant reprimands forced him to quit the force. He returned to his hometown and established his own company to help people in trouble — but do it by whatever means possible within (or just above) the limits of the law.

B.L. has a parrot named Gilbert and drives a classic Cadillac. He lives on a houseboat called the *No Trump*, which is docked at 22 Ocean Park Marina. It was first called Maxie's Marina, then Oliver's Marina. B.L. is divorced from Kimberly (Rita Moreno), who is now married to the wealthy but elderly Clayton Baskin (Abe Vigoda). Lyynda, who spells her name with two y's "because I want to be different," has a dog named Fred. Oz's license plate reads OZ II and Kimberly's Rolls Royce license plate is CII 86R. Mike Post composed the theme.

Booker *See* 21 Jump Street

6. Boston Blackie (Syndicated, 1951–1953)

Boston Blackie (Kent Taylor) is a former thief and safecracker who turned his life around and now uses his knowledge of the underworld to fight crime. He has established himself as a private detective in Los Angeles and lives at the Brownstone Apartments. Andy's Luncheonette (also called Andy's Lunch Room) is his favorite eatery. Blackie, as he is called, claims "I can open any vault with these fingers" and he knows it's not ethical to open a safe "but who's ethical," he says.

Mary Wesley (Lois Collier) is a beautiful nurse who is also Blackie's girlfriend and the only person who actually looks out for him, "because he won't." Mary lives at 712 Walden Avenue and is very independent and gutsy much in the same manner as Lois Lane on *Superman*; it's not unusual to see Mary get punched or knocked out as she attempts to help Blackie. Miraculously, she never gets a bruise. Blackie is very protective of Mary and becomes jealous if anyone makes goo goo eyes at her. "Before you get any ideas," he would tell an admirer, "Miss Wesley is my girl. Got it?" Mary is also a bit worried about Blackie's roving eye for beautiful women; although jealous, she accepts Blackie's excuse — "If I didn't have a roving eye for beauty, I couldn't appreciate you."

Blackie has a dog named Whitey. Whitey also comes to Blackie's aid when he senses danger, but he has a bad habit. He barks when he hears the words *bone* or *stake* (for example, "I've got a bone to pick with you" or "There's a lot at stake here"). Inspector Faraday (Frank Orth) is the L.A.P.D. homicide detective who believes he is assisting Blackie, but it's actually Blackie who assists him.

The program opens with a figure walking in the shadows of an alleyway. An announcer's voice is then heard: "Danger. Excitement. Adventure. Boston Blackie — enemy to those who make him an enemy; friend to those who have no friends."

7. Bourbon Street Beat (ABC, 1959–1960)

Randolph and Calhoun — Special Services is a private investigative firm owned and operated by Rex Randolph (Richard Long) and Cal Calhoun (Andrew Duggan). The firm is located next to the historic old Absinthe House, a nightclub on Bourbon Street in the French Quarter of New Orleans. Express 7123 is the firm's telephone number.

Rex, an Ivy league man, was born in New Orleans and loves to cook. He will not give up on a case until he uncovers the who, where and how of a crime. Rex originally ran a company called Randolph and Jelkins — Special Services. When his original partner, Sam Jelkins, disappears while investigating a case in a town called Pelican Point, Rex begins an inquiry. He befriends Police Lieutenant Calhoun ("people call me Cal") and together they solve the mystery: Sam was killed when he tried to muscle in on a blackmail scheme to extract money from a wealthy woman. Shortly after Rex returns to his office, Cal walks in and says, "I kissed Pelican Point goodbye."

The company sign is changed to Randolph and Calhoun. Cal (no other first name given) was raised in the bayou country where his parents worked as sharecroppers. Rex's parents were wealthy business executives. Cal is untidy while Rex is neat and orderly. Since Rex's hobby of cooking was a part of the show, a book called *Recipes from Bourbon Street Beat* was released in 1959.

Kenny Madison (Van Williams) is the firm's part-time investigator. He is from an oil-rich Texas family and is attending Tulhane University, where he is studying to become a lawyer. While he doesn't need the money, he works for Rex for the experience he hopes to acquire in apprehending law breakers.

Melody Lee Mercer (Arlene Howell) is the firm's attractive receptionist, secretary and file clerk. She was born in Shreveport, Louisiana and was Miss U.S.A. in the 1958 Miss Universe Pageant. Melody Lee was previously the runner-up as Miss Sazu City in the Miss Mississippi Pageant. She claims she lost "because the judges were northerners." When Melody Lee took the job "I knew there would be gunplay and such" and "puts up with Rex and Cal and all the violence." She hopes to one day become a detective and is thrilled when she is asked to do investigative work on a case. She likes to be called Melody Lee and not Melody ("I don't like it when people leave off part of my name").

Lusti Weather (Nita Talbot) is a beautiful singer and dancer at the Racquet Club in the French Quarter. She also plays the bongo drums and says, "The bongos keep my torso from becoming more so." She often exposes too much skin and is not only suspended but "busted by the police," says Cal. Rex calls her Lusti Love and she has such colorful, unseen friends as Sunset Strip and Midnight Frenzy. Lusti also has a language all her own (for example, "magnesia" is amnesia; "hot shot on the rock" is a martini). Lusti also yearns to be a detective and enjoys helping Rex and Cal. It is at this time that Melody Lee becomes extremely jealous — "I'll show that female Sherlock Holmes who does the detective work around here," says Melody Lee, who often plunges unthinkingly into a case only to be rescued by Lusti in the end.

The Baron (Eddie Cole) is the leader of the jazz group that plays nightly at the Absinthe House. In the pilot episode, they are seen playing and singing the show's theme song. Beauregard O'Hanlon (Kelton Garwood) is the painter who runs an art objects business next to the Absinthe House called Beauregard O'Hanlon's World Renowned Treasure Chest.

Mack David and Jerry Livingston composed the theme "Bourbon Street Beat."

8. Broken Badges (CBS, 1990–1991)

Beau Jack Bowman (Miguel Ferrer) is a former Cajun sergeant with the Louisiana Police Department who now heads a special division of the Bay City, California, Police Department called the Rubber Gun Squad (officers on psychiatric leave who are "broken and unstable"). The unit consists of Judy Tingreedies (Eileen Davidson), Stanley Jones (Jay Johnson) and Toby Baker (Ernie Hudson). Police Chief Sterling (Don Davis) is their superior.

Jack calls his team the Cobra Squad. They perform limited, non-specific assignments and are officially called T.A.R.P. (Temporary Assignment of Restricted Personnel Cops). The squad's car license plate reads 2ME A471. Jack is 37 years old and proud of his Cajun heritage. He uses violent and unorthodox methods to achieve his goals and makes up the rules as he goes along. He prefers his Cajun cuisine and says, "A Cajun will eat anything that won't eat him first." Jack drives a car with the license plate N39E 467 and there is a sign next to his house that reads "Cajun Jack's Hospitality House."

Judy, an officer with the nickname Bullet, is, as she calls herself, a street bitch with an attitude. She is a motorcycle cop and because of her addiction to danger she was removed from the force due to extreme psychosis. Judy is pretty, always eager for action and constantly asking Jack, "When are we gonna go out and kick some butt?" Judy loves her motorcycle (a Harley) and wears leather and tops that accentuate her ample bosom; however, she says, "I don't like guys staring at my chest — it makes me angry." And, as Jack says, "You don't want to get Judy angry."

Stanley, now a sergeant, was a street cop for three years. Due to the pressures of his job, he retreated to a world in which he is now a ventriloquist and all communication is made through his dummy, Officer Danny, whom Stanley believes is a real person. He claims that if he and Danny were to have a fist fight, Danny would win. Stanley is street smart, has a talent for throwing his voice and has the nickname Whipusall. No one can explain what it means. Jack believes it is a variation of "Whip Us All" because Stanley uses the steel plate in his head like a battering ran and can whip anybody in a fight. Stanley has written a book of poems called *The Forest* under the pen name L.S. Jones. He is also sensitive about his height and gets violently upset if he is called Little Guy. Officer Danny has a severe attitude problem and is an escort with the All Male Mahogany Escort Service. He and Stanley live at 134 Meadow Lark Drive. Stanley's car license plate reads 2ME BOH.

Toby, a sergeant, is a forensics expert who suffers from fits of depression and self-hatred. He is also a kleptomaniac and when assignments become stressful, he believes he is an old west Texas Ranger named Cactus Cole Watson. Eleanor Hardwicke (Teresa Donahue), a lieutenant under Chief Sterling, is the team's computer expert and department contact. Actually, she is the only assistant the Chief has; she calls herself a member of the Chief's Special Staff. Eleanor has a Ph.D. from the University of Chicago and did her dissertation on police department procedures. She hopes to implement her research in the department and make it operational based on her beliefs of what a police department should be. Dr. Priscilla Mathers (Charlotte Lewis) is the psychologist assigned by Chief Sterling to watch over Jack's team. Mike Post composed the theme.

Related Project (Unsold Pilot)

The Rubber Gun Squad (NBC, September 1, 1977). The title refers to misfit police officers who are removed from active duty and reassigned to non-hazardous work until they can prove themselves worthy again. The proposed series was to focus on Chopper (Andy Romano) and Eddie (Lenny Baker), N.Y.P.D. officers who have been reassigned to patrol Central Park.

9. The Brothers Brannagan (Syndicated, 1960)

Brannagan and Brannagan is a Phoenix, Arizona-based private detective agency owned by Bob and Mike Brannagan (Mark Roberts, Steve Dunne), brothers who are as different as night and day. The agency is located at 72 Kato Avenue and the brothers do agree on one thing: "We're great detectives," says Bob. People claim the brothers have good deductive powers and are hired by clients who do not want to involve the police in a matter.

Although Bob and Mike try to do things in a non-violent way, the situations in which they become involved often call for fists or gunplay. Bob appears to be the more intellectual of the two. He sets the pace for each case. He scrutinizes the clues before acting and hopes the impetuous Mike will follow his game plan. If plans are followed, Mike usually stays behind as the backup while Bob probes the situation. While both Brannagans have an eye for the ladies, it is Mike who is the most romantic and more often the one who gets his face slapped by a girl he is trying to impress. He has a little black book that appears to be filled with pick up lines and sweet snatches of poetry rather than addresses. Mike has all the wise cracks (people often say, "I hope your brother here is a straightman") while Bob tries his best to read suspects and outwit them. Bob tries to be more like himself (laidback) while Mike puts on airs to impress people. The series is filmed on location in Arizona and does encompass a great deal of outdoor filming.

The program opens with a scene of Bob and Mike walking forward with their backs to the camera. The only lyric in the theme "Hey Brannagan" is heard. The brothers turn to the camera and respond with, "Which one?" The theme music plays and both credits appear at the same time — Steve Dunne and Mark Roberts. Sally Ross, the Brannagans' secretary, is played by Rebecca Wells. Alexander Courage composed the theme "Hey Brannagan."

10. Buddy Faro (CBS, 1998)

Buddy Faro (Dennis Farina) was said to be the best private detective in the business. He knows everything about finding missing people. He invented modern detective techniques in the 1960s and even wrote a book called *I, Private Eye*. His methods were copied by everyone. In 1978, a case went bad and Buddy skipped town. The legend was gone, but the man embarked on a twenty year drinking binge in the hope of forgetting his past. In 1998, Buddy is found by novice private detective Bob Jones (Frank Whaley) in a Mexican gutter and brought back to Los Angeles to clean up his act. Now sober, Buddy joins forces with Bob and they establish Buddy Faro Investigations — and Bob Jones on the Sunset Strip. Bob was hired by Buddy's niece to find him when he inherited a large sum of money.

Buddy has been out of touch with reality and is culturally displaced. For example, he is unaware of the O.J. Simpson murder trial; he still looks for the long cancelled *Tonight Show Starring Johnny Carson* on late night TV. Buddy is tough when he has to be and often disputes what people say about him — "I get the job done, but I'm not the sharpest knife in the drawer." Buddy has style and knows how to sell himself. He attributes this to his success. But he also has several problems. He drinks and becomes depressed if he can't solve a case. The Neon Martini is his favorite bar; IFD 318 is his car license plate number. Bob, who previously ran AAAA Investigations, is not as forceful as Buddy and prefers to rely on his wits rather than his fists.

11. Burke's Law (ABC, 1963–1965; CBS, 1994–1995)

Amos Burke (Gene Barry; both versions) is a multi-millionaire with a job — police captain of the Metropolitan Division of the L.A.P.D. He resides in a mansion at 109 North Milbourne and has a Rolls Royce (his police car) with the plate JZG 063 (also seen as JEB 495. In CBS episodes, his car is a

1961 Silver Ghost II Rolls Royce with the plate 36E GH92). His office phone number is Madison 6-7399.

Amos is handsome, suave, witty, clever and rich, and does not need to work but does so because it is what he does best — solve crimes. Amos strictly follows the book while investigating a crime and does not use unorthodox methods to achieve his goal. The title refers to his words of wisdom; for example: Never turn your back on a beautiful woman — Burke's Law; Money is worthless unless you can enjoy it — Burke's Law; It's never easy — Burke's Law; Never bet against a sure thing — Burke's Law; Never make fun of an older woman — one day you'll be married to one — Burke's Law. While mostly elusive about how he actually acquired his wealth ("My grandfather died and left me a fortune"), Amos claims he dabbled in the stock market and invested in real estate. In ABC episodes, Amos is a ladies' man and single; he is a widower and the father of Peter (Peter Barton) in the CBS version. Amos, now a police chief, mentioned he met his late wife, Sarah, on the dance floor of the Coconut Grove Club in Los Angeles. Peter is a brilliant detective who works under his father's supervision. Amos calls him "The Big Wonder" for his ability to perceive what others want. Vinnie's Restaurant By-the-Sea is Amos's favorite eatery.

In the ABC version, Leon Lontoc played Henry, Burke's houseboy/chauffeur. Gary Conway was Detective Tim Tillson; Regis Toomey was Detective Sergeant Lester Hart, who lived at 106 Essex Drive; 676-4882 was his phone number. Eileen O'Neill was the sexy Sergeant Ames. In addition to Peter, the CBS version featured Bever-Leigh Banfield as Lily Morgan, the forensics detective; and Danny Kamekona as Henry, Amos's chauffeur/houseboy. Dick Powell played Amos Burke in the pilot episode, "Who Killed Julie Greer," which aired on *The Dick Powell Show*. In the episode of January 21, 1994 ("Who Killed Nick Hazzard?"), Anne Francis played Honey Best, a takeoff on her role as TV's *Honey West* detective character, the pilot for which aired on *Burke's Law* in 1965. See *Honey West* for additional information.

Herschel Burke Gilbert composed the original theme (ABC); John E. Davis, the revised CBS theme.

12. Cagney and Lacey (CBS, 1982–1988)

Christine Cagney (Meg Foster, Sharon Gless) and Mary Beth Lacey (Tyne Daly) are best friends and police officers with the Manhattan 14th Precinct in New York City. Christine, a sergeant, and Mary Beth, a detective, worked undercover as prostitutes on the John Squad of the 23rd Precinct before being transferred to Homicide to solve a series of call girl killings.

They became the 14th Precinct's first female detectives. Both girls despise posing as ladies of the evening. "Cops' feet aren't made for hookers' shoes," says Mary Beth. Each has a bad habit: Mary Beth smokes and Chris drinks; Chris is trying to break her habit and attends AA meetings. She is also urging Mary Beth to give up cigarettes.

Chris and Mary Beth approach each case with motivation and opportunity based on what a subject would do. Mary Beth is a stickler for the details of a case while Christine is satisfied with gathering the obvious evidence. They ride in an unmarked car with the code 312 (later 27, then 394) and socialize at Flannery's Bar, later called O'Malley's Bar.

Christine, called Chris, is single because "I understand about commitments and responsibilities," something she can't handle since a psychic told her she was going to get married, live on a farm and have four children. Chris lives in Manhattan at 11 West 49th Street and drives a car with the license plate 562 BLA, later 801 FEM; her badge number is 763. Chris is a member of the precinct's Community Board, where she oversees minor cases like a missing dog or slashed tires, and hates to lose at anything. She becomes angry and has to punch or kick something. Loretta Swit played Chris in the pilot episode.

Mary Beth is married to Harvey (John Karlen) and the mother of Harvey, Jr. (Tony LaTorre), Michael (Troy Slaten) and Alice (Donna and Paige Bardolph). They first live in Manhattan (Apartment 9) then Jackson Heights, Queens, at 7132 West 46th Street; 555-1519 is their home phone number; 340 is Mary Beth's badge number. In Meg Foster episodes, Mary Beth and Harvey are living in Manhattan, Apartment 4E in a building with the street number 333. Harvey works as the building's super and in construction when he can; he has an inner-ear infection and tends to lose his balance when working at great heights. In Sharon Gless episodes, Mary Beth and Harvey are living in Jackson Heights for 15 years according to Mary Beth. Harvey is said to be in construction. As a kid, Harvey raised pigeons and he and Mary Beth have a philosophy about cars: "Drive 'em till they die." Harvey calls Mary Beth "Babe," and "Lucks 'n' Bucks" is his favorite TV game show, wherein people dress in outlandish costumes to answer questions. For an undercover assignment to see if the show was rigged, Chris dressed as a pineapple and Mary Beth as a tomato. Harvey becomes upset when Chris and Mary Beth discuss police matters over dinner and hates it when Mary Beth is assigned to a missing person's case. She gets moody and takes it personally; her father is missing. He disappeared when she was a child and Mary Beth is not sure if he is dead or alive. Tuesday is Harvey's bowling night and they order pizza from Luigi's. In the fifth grade, Mary Beth was called Mary Number Two by her teacher to distinguish her from Mary Beth Number One — Mary Beth Lazonne.

Lieutenant Albert Samuels (Al Waxman) is Chris and Mary Beth's superior. Victor Isbecki (Martin Kove) and Mark Petrie (Carl Lumbly) are detectives who work with Cagney and Lacey. Marie Cain sings the theme "Ain't That the Way," in Meg Foster episodes; "The Theme from Cagney and Lacey" by Bill Conti is used for the Sharon Gless episodes.

Proposed Spinoff (Unsold Pilot)

The Bounty Hunter (April 23, 1984). Brian Dennehy as Mike Mac-Gruder, a ruthless bounty hunter. The story finds Mike locking horns with Cagney and Lacey, both of whom are seeking a Michigan bail jumper for armed robbery in New York.

13. The Cases of Eddie Drake (DuMont, 1952)

The Drake Detective Agency at 130 West 45th Street in Manhattan is owned by Eddie Drake (Don Haggerty), a private investigator who has a remarkable affinity for crime and violence. Dr. Karen Gayle (Patricia Morison, Lynn Roberts) is a private practice psychiatrist who assists Eddie for research material ("I want to know all about criminals, what they say, how they act and why they do the things they do").

Eddie is personable, intelligent and honest. He does carry a gun and he does use it. While most of his clients are walk-ins, he does get some referrals from an agency called Jenny's Bail Bonds. Eddie drives a car with the license plate 3C-26-53 and his office phone number is 346-1621.

Karen has an office at 64 Park Avenue. She considers herself a student of all the abnormal behavior of the human mind. She is writing a book on criminal behavior and in order to get material that is fresh and stimulating, she has retained Eddie as her personal library. While Karen does find herself becoming actively involved in solving crimes, she objects to one thing — the violence — and wishes Eddie could guarantee a minimum of shooting. Karen's office phone number is 346-7112. Theodore Von Eltz plays Lieutenant Walsh, a detective with the Homicide Bureau of the N.Y.P.D., whom Eddie and Karen help and vice versa.

14. Charlie's Angels (ABC, 1976–1981)

Townsend Investigations is a Los Angeles-based private detective organization owned by the never seen (only heard) Charles Townsend (John Forsythe), a man of mystery who knows many people and has many connections. He is represented by his lawyer, John Bosley (David Doyle) and, although he has offices in Los Angeles, Paris and Hawaii, only three operatives, called Angels by Charlie, are ever seen — Sabrina Duncan (Kate Jackson), Jill Munroe (Farrah Fawcett) and Kelly Garrett (Jaclyn Smith). Jill was replaced by her sister, Kris Munroe (Cheryl Ladd), Sabrina by Tiffany Welles (Shelley Hack) and Tiffany by Julie Rogers (Tanya Roberts).

Charlie's agency is also called the Townsend Detective Agency; Charles Townsend, Private Investigations; the Townsend Agency; and Townsend Associates. The Hawaiian branch is located at 4376 Kalahai Avenue; only the street number, 193, is seen for the Los Angeles agency. Dollar figures for services are not mentioned, only "You're paying a great deal of money for our services" or "a substantial fee." The agency receives ten percent of the value of stolen items they recover. Charlie also owns the all-girl Venus Trucking Company although he does not refer to these employees as Angels. Charlie has an aquarium of tropical fish in his office — Mildred is his favorite fish — and is plagued by a number of perplexing problems; for example, "I've just been served tea and crumpets by my new English maid. Should I dunk or not dunk the crumpet so as not to offend her?" While very rich and apparently a man of leisure, Charlie does do work for the team — via computer checks and using his numerous contacts to help solve crimes.

It was revealed that Charlie was in the military during World War II and has many important connections throughout the world. He does complain about the Angels' knack for damaging the company cars and it was said that Charlie loves figures — girls' figures. He is often seen in plush settings with a beautiful girl or two by his side.

The girls are not really angels. They lie, steal and cheat to accomplish their goals. The Angels have one wish — to see Charlie. Charlie promises the girls he will join them on a case but something always comes up to deter that; for example, relaxing in a pool, getting a massage. Jill believes the reason why Charlie chooses to remain anonymous is due to the fact that he has sent many people to prison; people who will be getting out sooner or later and may seek revenge. Not revealing himself to the Angels is his way to protecting them in the long run. Kelly is the only Angel who believes she saw Charlie. In the last episode, "Let Our Angel Live," Kelly is seriously injured when she is shot in the head. During her operation, Charlie was by Kelly's side, disguised in hospital greens. In the recovery room, as Kelly awakens, she believes she sees Charlie, but can't be sure as she is in a dazed state.

Bosley is called Boz by the Angels. He is apparently the only operative who has ever seen Charlie and constantly tells the Angels, "Ladies, you know I can't divulge anything about Charlie." While Bosley is careful to conceal

Charlie's identity, he does let them see photographs of Charlie — as a baby, as a boy, or in bad light from the back of the head. Bosley hates paperwork, but always gets stuck with it, and has an untraceable, direct phone line to Charlie — 555-9626; the agency's phone number is 213-555-0267. Bosley mentioned that he once appeared with the Gilbert and Sullivan Acting Troupe while in college and that Jill and Kris have a peculiar sense of humor. Charlie is heard through the white and tan speaker phone in the office. "When Charlie says he will call, you can count on Charlie to be punctual at all times," says Bosley.

The Mother Goose Toy Company produced action figures of Sabrina, Kelly and Kris as seen in the episode "Mother Goose Is Running for His Life." Sabrina favors standing behind the bar in the office; Kelly and Kris are seen seated on the sofa next to the bar.

Sabrina, Jill and Kelly are former police officers with the Los Angeles Police Department, Division 28. They were introduced by Charlie via narration in the opening theme: "Once upon a time there were three little girls who went to the police academy. And they were each assigned very hazardous duties [Sabrina handing out parking tickets; Jill typing files; Kelly as a school crossing guard]. But I took them away from all that and now they work for me; my name is Charlie." The silhouette seen during the theme places Sabrina in the middle; Kelly to the left of the screen and Jill on the right.

Sabrina, called Bree by the other Angels, tends to think like Charlie and often comes up with the same ideas. She is loyal and cares about people but is sometimes too uptight. She promises to loosen up and be carefree because "I've got a guardian angel who keeps an eye on me." Sabrina is an expert with fingerprint dusting and appreciates law officers who go by the book although she says, "So do I, but I use a different book," when she does things her way.

Sabrina was the only one of the Angels who was married — to Bill Duncan — but is now divorced. She is prim and proper, always a lady, always stylishly dressed and most always receives the glamorous undercover assignments. Her most unusual assignment was acting as a mime in a circus. Sabrina is the only Angel who admits they have a fault — "We're the biggest chauvinists of them all. Who says the murderer can't be a woman?"

Jill is blonde and gorgeous and has the ability to distract others so Sabrina and Kelly can get their jobs done. She is the more aggressive one of the group and ready to put her nose where it doesn't belong to help someone in trouble. Jill is caring and supportive and loves skate boarding. "It's dangerous," says Bosley. "So is working for Charlie," says Jill. Jill lives in a house on the beach and drives a white Cobra II with the license plate 861 BMG.

Jill meditates to relax and carries in her purse an old fashioned pocket watch that was given to her by her father. Jill is 24 years old and says, "In my tomboyish youth I was a real Roy Rogers freak." She calls herself, Bree and Kelly a team like the Supremes. Jill's most unusual undercover assignment: sexy waitress at the Feline Club, then model for *Feline* magazine.

Kelly is concerned and caring and has the ability to sing and dance; she was lead alto in a glee club. She is brilliant at figuring out complex clues and is an expert shot. She is also a master at bugging devices and picking locks. Guido's Italian Diner is her favorite eatery and Tequila straight up with a lime chaser is her favorite drink. In an early episode, Kelly mentioned she was raised in Texas and learned to shoot from her father. A later episode reveals that Kelly was born in San Diego in August of 1955. She was lost as an infant when her mother was killed in a 23-car pile up on a Texas highway. In a rush to get victims to hospitals, Kelly was misplaced. When no one claimed the infant girl, she was sent to the St. Agnes Home for the Orphaned in Dallas. It is not revealed how the infant received her first name of Kelly, but her last name, Garrett, was the family name of one of the sisters of the orphanage who cared for her. Kelly was adopted in 1964 and raised by foster parents. Kelly now lives in a private house — street number 10426 — and drives a car with the license plate 129 UBO. While Kelly does go undercover as a singer and/or dancer, her most unusual undercover assignment was as a motorcycle daredevil.

When Jill left the series at the end of the first season to pursue her car racing career (she hopes to become the first woman to win Le Mans), a new girl (Kristine Munroe) is hired and new opening theme dialogue is used: "Once upon a time, there were three little girls who went to the police academy — two in Los Angeles [Sabrina and Kelly], the other in San Francisco [Kris]. And they were each assigned very hazardous duties [Sabrina, writing parking tickets; Kelly, a school crossing guard; Kris, a switchboard operator]. But I took them away from all that and now they work for me. My name is Charlie."

Kris is Jill's equally gorgeous sister, a graduate of the San Francisco Police Academy. Jill had been paying for Kris's college education and believed she was studying to become a teacher. For reasons that are not explained, Kris chose to become a police officer. When Sabrina and Kelly first learned that Charlie had replaced Jill with another girl, they objected: "We don't need another girl." "Trust Charlie," Bosley told them. Sabrina and Kelly welcomed Kris when they learned she was the new Angel. Although Kris was never mentioned during the Jill episodes, Bree and Kelly apparently knew her as they were close to Jill and her family.

Kris is an expert at distraction and cares about people. She carries two special items with her when she travels: A Raggedy Ann doll she had as a child and the book *Hansel and Gretel* that was given to her by her mother. She considers the book a good luck charm. In the book there is a picture of Kris as a girl with her mother. Kris mentioned she was the first one in her high school class to learn pig latin. Her favorite drink is Scotch on the rocks and she drives a white Cobra with the license plate 590 VGG. When Kris went undercover as a big rig trucker, she used the C.B. handle "Angel Eyes." Her most unusual undercover assignment was posing as a lifesize Raggedy Ann doll at the Mother Goose Toy Company to find a killer.

Sabrina left at the end of the second season to marry for a second time. Charlie mentions to Kelly and Kris that she is expecting a baby and is quite thrilled about the whole thing. New opening theme dialogue is used to introduce the newest Angel, Tiffany Welles: "Once upon a time there were three little girls who went to the police academy: one in Los Angeles [Kelly], one in San Francisco [Kris], and one in Boston [Tiffany], and they were each assigned very hazardous duties. But I took them away from all that and now they work for me. My name is Charlie." Kris and Kelly have the same hazardous jobs as previously described; Tiffany is seen filing papers.

As Kelly and Kris anxiously await to meet the new Angel, Charlie tells them, "I hope you'll like Miss Welles; her father is an old friend of mine, a detective lieutenant in Boston. She graduated from the police academy there, top in her class. She's something special, as you'll see when you meet her." The girls meet. Kris and Kelly tell Charlie, "We like her."

Tiffany, the soft-spoken Angel, is a crusader for women's rights. She is called Tiff by the other Angels and was a nurse's aide in high school. She was president of the Kappa Omega Society sorority house at Whitney College in California. She was a resident of Tracy Hall (her dorm room) and during one summer she worked with Hans Kemper, a famous ghost hunter. Tiffany learned she was a sensitive and could communicate with spirits. She had a brief period when she became involved with the occult and conducted seances. Tiffany appeared to be the most fragile and delicate of the Angels and so sophisticated that she seemed out of place as a detective or police officer. Her stunning good looks were also her greatest weapon as she could fool even the most brilliant criminal.

Tiffany left a year later to pursue a modeling career in New York City. Kris and Kelly learn from Charlie that Tiffany decided to stay East for a while. Her replacement is Julie Rogers, a beautiful girl with a troubled past. Again, the opening theme dialogue changes: "Once upon a time there were three beautiful girls. Two of them graduated from the policy academy [Kelly and

Kris], the other graduated from a top school for models [Julie]. And they each reaped the rewards of their exciting careers. But I took them away from all that and now they work for me. My name is Charlie." The "rewards," as Charlie calls them, were the same hazardous duties previously described for Kelly and Kris; for Julie, it was modeling Joggerade Health Juice on a treadmill. As a model, Julie also appeared on the cover of *Elite* magazine.

Julie was born in New York City and raised street tough. Her father split when Julie was too young to remember him. Her mother died in 1978 in a charity hospital of acute alcoholism. In Los Angeles, Julie was arrested for shoplifting a dress. She was broke and needed a new outfit for a job interview. After serving time in jail, she was released on parole and assigned to Harry Sterns (Vic Morrow), an officer with the L.A.P.D. Shortly after, Julie acquires a modeling job at the Woodman Agency. When Julie notices an exchange of drugs between the models and clients, she informs Harry. Harry investigates, using Julie as a spy, but is killed when Julie is exposed. Julie is bitter and determined to find Harry's killer. In the meantime, Angels Kris and Kelly have been hired to find the killer of a young model. They are working undercover as models when they meet Julie. The girls join forces and solve both crimes. Julie becomes the newest Angel when Charlie tells Kris and Kelly that he talked with the police commissioner about Julie's work. Because Charlie needs another operative, Julie is issued a temporary investigator's license and given special permission to work for Charlie.

The series was originally conceived under the title "Harry's Angels" with Gig Young slated to provide the voice for Harry. Many actresses were interviewed to replace Jill and Sabrina. Cheryl Ladd was chosen over Kim Basinger for the role of Kris while model Shelley Hack was chosen over strong contenders Barbara Bach, Catherine Bach (no relation), Shari Belafonte and Connie Sellecca. *Charlie's Angels* is famous for initiating what is called "Jiggle TV"—the actresses not wearing bras and plots that cause the Angels to trot. Much publicity surrounded this, but it appears that only Farrah Fawcett was actually braless through most of her scenes. This is especially apparent in the episode "Angels in Chains" where Farrah, who measures 33½B-23-34, accidentally exposed part of her right breast and nipple when her mostly unbuttoned blouse exposed more than it should have. And, with the exception of one obvious scene in which Kelly models a dress without a bra, the other Angels appear to be wearing bras under their dress clothes. Bikinis and swimsuits were another matter. The figures of all the Angels, except Sabrina, were blatantly displayed in skimpy swimwear whenever the opportunity arose, mostly in episodes set in Hawaii.

The *Charlie's Angels* pilot film aired on ABC on March 21, 1976. Kate

Jackson, Farrah Fawcett and Jaclyn Smith were Angels Sabrina Duncan, Jill Munroe and Kelly Garrett but they had not yet taken on the qualities they possessed in the series. The Angels are a bit more reckless and do not carry guns; they rely on their wits and experiences as police officers to deal with situations. John Forsythe is heard as their unseen boss, Charlie Townsend; David Doyle is John Bosley, Charlie's representative; and David Ogden Stiers is Scott Woodville, Charlie's lawyer (dropped from the series). The pilot story finds the Angels seeking the killer of a vineyard owner.

Jack Elliott and Allyn Ferguson composed the theme "Charlie's Angels." See also *She Spies*.

Proposed Spinoff (Unsold Pilot)

Toni's Boys (April 2, 1980). Originally broadcast under the title "The Male Angel Affair." The series was to focus on Antonia "Toni" Blake (Barbara Stanwyck), a widow who runs a private detective company called the Blake Agency at 612 Essex Road in Los Angeles. Toni is a friend of Charlie's and took over control of the company after the death of her husband. Toni claims she has the best private detective agency in the business. Cotton Harper (Stephen Shortridge), Matt Parrish (Bruce Bauer) and Bob Sorenson (Bob Seagren) are her operatives.

Cotton is a former rodeo rider, roper and tracker; Bob is a former U.S. Olympic champion; and Matt is a master of disguises and weapons. Toni is assisted by her butler, Rolph (James E. Broadhead). When she meets with a client Toni says, "I'm Toni and these are my boys." The pilot story finds Toni's boys attempting to protect Charlie's Angels (Kelly, Kris and Tiffany) from an assassin.

Other Versions

1. *Angels '88.* In 1988 a nationwide search was begun to find a quartet of Angels for an update of the series that was to be called *Angels '88*. The Fox network had scheduled the series for the fall of 1988 but preproduction problems forced a title change (to *Angels '89*) then a complete shutdown of the project. Other than screen tests, it is difficult to determine if a pilot episode was filmed. There have been no such reviews and no newspaper or *TV Guide* listings. Some sources say the project was never filmed; others claim a pilot was produced. Based on press information, the new Angels were to be Sandra Canning as Pamela Ryan; Karen Kopins as Trisha Lawrence; Tea Leoni as Bernice "Bernie" Colter; and Claire Yarlett as Connie Bates.

2. *Angeles.* A Spanish version of *Charlie's Angels* that was broadcast by the Telemundo network for 13 episodes in 1999. Adriana Vega (played by Patricia Manterola), Elena Sanchez (Sandra Vidal) and Gina Navarro (Magali Caicedo) are the Angels of the title — three beautiful girls who work as private detectives for the never seen Charlie, head of Angeles Investigaciones in the coastal town of Costa Rosa, California. They are assisted by David Bose (Mauricio Mendoza), their only link to the mysterious Charlie. Adriana, Elena and Gina are based on the original Charlie's Angels (Sabrina, Jill and Kelly), but resemble them only in their passion for apprehending criminals. Gina, Elena and Adriana are stronger, more forceful women with special talents and abilities, which they are forced to rely upon for their survival. Adriana was an undercover police woman with a talent for disguises. She was dismissed from the force for exposing a corrupt group of fellow officers. She now carries a chip on her shoulder and is eager to prove she did the right thing. Elena is the mysterious one of the group. She is a brilliant computer expert and a former FBI agent who can access any system in the world. Elena Sanchez is an alias and she refuses to reveal her true name and identity. Gina is an outspoken, sassy ex-cat burglar who now uses her skills to help the team achieve their goals. Like John Bosley, David Bose is the man who watches over the Angels for Charlie. The series is broadcast in the U.S. on Telemundo stations in Open Captioning (Spanish dialogue; English subtitles).

3. *Charlie's Angels.* John Forsythe reprised his role as the voice of Charles Townsend for a theatrical version of the original *Charlie's Angels* series. The film, released on November 3, 2000, features a new trio of beautiful Angels: Drew Barrymore as Dylan Sanders; Cameron Diaz as Natalie Cook and Lucy Liu as Alexandra "Alex" Munday. Bill Murray became the new John Bosley. Dylan, called "The Wild Angel," is not only alluring, but reckless and tough. Natalie, "The Scientific Angel," is the brains of the outfit, all work and no play. And Alex, "The Sexy Angel," is the daring one of the group and well versed in the martial arts.

4. *Charlie's Angels: Full Throttle.* A second theatrical film (released in June of 2003) that reunites Drew Barrymore, Cameron Diaz and Lucy Liu as Angels Dylan Sanders, Natalie Cook and Alex Munday. John Forsythe again provides the voice of Charles Townsend, but Bosley, Charlie's link with the Angels, is now played by black comedian Bernie Mac. The story finds the Angels seeking a rogue FBI agent. The film was originally called *Charlie's Angels 2.*

15. Chase (NBC, 1973–1974)

Chase Reddick (Mitchell Ryan) is a captain and head of Chase, a special unit of undercover police agents who tackle the cases left unsolved by the homicide, burglary and robbery divisions of the L.A.P.D. His code name is Chase Control.

Members of the Chase team are: Sergeant Sam MacCray (Wayne Maunder); 628 DVE is his license plate number and Chase One is his car code. Officer Fred Sing (Brian Fong) has the mobil car code Chase 17. Chase 43 is the mobile car code for Officer Tom Wilson (Craig Gardner), and Officer Ed Rice (Gary Crosby) has the car code Chase 2; his license plate reads QVZ 725. Fred and Tom are also co-pilots of the unit's helicopter, Chase 3 (also its air code). Ed feels he gets the worst assignments, such as a janitor or gas station attendant, because he looks the part. The team's German Shepherd, who rides with Sam, is Fuzz, a narc dog. The actual energy crises at the time plagues the team. The lights are dimmed at headquarters, and car chases are curtailed due to the gasoline shortage. Oliver Nelson composed the theme.

16. CHiPs (NBC, 1977–1983)

CHiPs (the small *i* and *s* added for pronunciation purposes) stands for the California Highway Patrol. Francis "Ponch" Poncherello (Erik Estrada), Jonathan "Jon" Baker (Larry Wilcox), Bonnie Clark (Randi Oakes) and Robert "Bobby" Nelson (Tom Reilly) are officers attached to the unit. With the exception of Bonnie, who drives a patrol car, the officers ride Kawasaki motorcycles. Their supervisor is Sergeant Joe Getraer (Robert Pine). The precinct's favorite charity is the Children's Liver Foundation and 555-7374 is the phone number for C.H.P. headquarters. The motorcycles are equipped with Motorola radios.

Ponch, born in the barrio, has badge number 2140 (also given as B-600). His mobile codes were given as 7-Mary-3, LA-15-Mary 2 and LA-15-Mary 6. His car license plate reads 8003 IF and Marinino's Restaurant is his favorite eatery.

Jon, Ponch's first partner, has badge number 5712. His mobile codes were given as 7-Mary-4 and LA-15-Mary-3; 16A60 is his cycle license plate. Jon was born in Wyoming and was replaced by Bruce Nelson (Bruce Penahll) in last season episodes when Larry Wilcox left the series. Bruce's mobile code is LA-15-Mary-7.

Bonnie, a highway patrol car officer, has the mobile code 7-Charles and the license plate 999001. She is part of the C.H.P. Deaf Liaison Program (she took sign communications at Cal State) and is called "Bon Bon" by Ponch. Sindy Cahill (Brianne Leary) is a patrol officer with the bike code LA-15-Mary-23. Kathy Linehan (Tina Gayle) is an officer assigned to the C.H.P.

headquarters building where she works as the computer operator in the Report Room. She lives in a beachhouse at 153½ Malibu Road and when on assignments, her bike code is LA-15-Mary-10. MERV (Maximum Efficiency Robotization Vector Series 1) was an attempt by the C.H.P. to introduce efficiency into the department via a robotics program. It failed when MERV short circuited and became dangerous.

Two attempts were made to introduce a female motorcycle unit. The first occurred with recurring characters Emily (Melody Anderson) and Sylvia (Debbie Evans), two beautiful motorcycle-riding girls who were called The Highway Angels. The girls helped C.H.P. by spotting lawbreakers and calling in the crime. "They're our streets, says Emily. "We don't want to see them turn into a battlefield. If just one driver slows down because of the Highway Angels, then we are accomplishing something." The second attempt was a failed pilot called "Ponch's Angels" (February 28 and March 1, 1981) wherein Melanie Mitchell (Trisha Townsend) and Paula Wood (Barbara Stock) become the first C.H.P. female unit assigned to Ponch for training, hence the title.

In 1998, the Nashville Network presented a TV movie called *CHiPs '99* that reunited the cast in a story that finds Ponch and Jon attempting to solve a series of car thefts. Larry Wilcox was now Captain Jon Baker; Erik Estrada, Officer Frank Poncherello; Robert Pine, C.H.P. Commissioner, Joseph Getraer; and Bruce Penhall, Sergeant Bruce Nelson.

Proposed Spinoff (Unsold Pilot)

Force Seven (NBC, May 23, 1982). Fred Dryer as John LeGarre, an L.A.P.D. lieutenant who organizes Force Seven, a group of undercover martial arts experts to battle the growing crime rate. The pilot story finds John's three operatives, Cindy Miwa David (Donna Kei Benz), Sly Angeletti (Tony Longo) and Rick Nicholls (Tom Reilly) seeking a renegade engineer who has stolen a deadly short range missile.

17. Columbo (NBC, 1971–1978; ABC, 1989–1991)

Lieutenant Columbo (Peter Falk) is a homicide detective with the Hollenbeck Division of the L.A.P.D., later Central Division. Columbo rarely uses his gun and attributes his becoming a police officer to the James Cagney, Humphrey Bogart and Edward G. Robinson gangster pictures of the 1930s and '40s that he watched as a child. They instilled in him a passion for justice. Columbo, first name mentioned as Philip in one episode, is rarely in his office due to his field investigations. He often neglects his yearly required firing range tests and when it comes to dancing he said, "I have two left feet." He is married to the never seen Mrs. Columbo; her first name is Kate, but he refers to her as "the wife"; and has a dog, a basset hound, called both Fang and Dog — "He's a dog, so we call him Dog." It's Columbo's job to take the dog to the park for his run. Sometimes duty calls and the dog accompanies Columbo on his investigations. The dog usually waits in the car; if possible, Columbo gives him ice cream as a reward. Columbo mentioned that the dog goes swimming every morning since the neighbors installed a pool.

Columbo drives a rundown 1952 Peugeot, plate 448 DBZ. Even though people say the car is in bad shape, Columbo parks it in the shade; the sun wrecks havoc with the paint. Columbo, badge number 436, wears a rumpled raincoat virtually every place he goes. He is a master of deductive reasoning but claims to have a bad memory. He slouches, is always early for appointments and studies peoples' faces for their reactions to his questions. He is fascinated by the evidence he finds and is persistent. Little insignificant details bother him and he will not rest until he can tie up every loose end. He believes there is something wrong with him because "I seem to bother people and make them nervous," especially when he approaches a suspect and says, "Oh, just one more thing." Columbo taught a criminology course at Freemont College and has a bad habit of smoking cigars. When people complain about the cigar smoke he says, "I know it's a filthy habit and that I should have given it up years ago. Even my wife complains and sends me out to the porch." He also claims that his wife prefers that he smoke a pipe "but that's too much for me to carry around." According to Columbo, the wife wears lingerie made by Maidenform, likes marmalade, flowers and painting. "Although they're the paint-by-number canvases, they come out pretty good." He also says she loves shopping; she is a great cook and housekeeper and that her favorite musical piece is *Madame Butterfly*. For additional information, see the spinoff series, *Kate Loves a Mystery*. Columbo and the wife have been married for 25 years in 1991.

Columbo appears to always be working on a case. He would like Saturday nights off but "I can't take it off if duty calls." He enjoys a hot cup of tea — "I don't like luke warm tea" — and hot, strong black coffee — "no decaf for me." He enjoys variety and comedy programs when he has time to watch television and gave up listening to the radio — "Perry Como and Louis Armstrong I understand, but those rock groups give me an earache."

Bert Freed first played the Columbo character on the "Enough Rope" episode of *The Chevy Mystery Show* (NBC, July 31, 1960). Peter Falk first played the role in the TV movie, *Prescription Murder* (NBC, February 20, 1968). The series was first broadcast as part of *The NBC Mystery Movie*, then

The ABC Mystery Movie. Mike Post and Pete Carpenter composed the ABC theme version; Dave Grusin, Billy Goldenberg and Henry Mancini composed the various NBC versions of the theme.

18. The Commish (ABC, 1991–1995)

Tony Scali (Michael Chiklis) was a former New York City street cop who is now the Police Commissioner of Eastbridge, a suburban New York community. He lives at 1209 Beach Street with his wife, Rachel (Theresa Saldana) and their children David (Kaj-Eric Erikson) and infant Sarah (Justine and Dayna Cornborough). Tony and Rachel previously lived in Manhattan and came to Eastbridge in 1988 when Tony was asked to head the Eastbridge Police Department. Tony and Rachel bank at the Liberty Trust Company. Tony is a Catholic. Rachel, a teacher at Eastbridge Grammar School, is Jewish. They are raising David in the Jewish faith; Sarah as a Catholic.

Tony is based in the Eastbridge Municipal Building; C-1 then X-Ray-4 are his car codes. "The Great Pretender" is his favorite song and baseball legend Yogi Bera was his hero as a kid. Tony was born in Brooklyn, New York, and attended Saint Mary's High School. He obtained a law degree from Fordham University in the Bronx but chose law enforcement as a career. He is hard on criminals but a softie at heart and is affectionately called The Commish by his fellow officers. Tony studies the reactions to questions he asks of suspects and always says "Got ya" when he apprehends a criminal. In the opening theme, Tony is seen reading the book *Tissue Decomposition: A Homicide Primer*. His car license plate reads HCM 1971; Rachel's plate is LLQ 118. Mike Post composed the theme.

Proposed Series Spinoff (Unsold Pilot)

Off Broadway (May 13 and 20, 1995). Lisa Vidal as Consuela "Connie" Muldoon, a tough, dedicated N.Y.P.D. homicide detective who prefers to work alone. Connie is single and the mother of 13-year-old Julianna (Christina Vidal). The pilot story finds Connie traveling to Eastbridge to help Tony solve the murder of his goddaughter.

19. The Cosby Mysteries (NBC, 1994–1995)

When there are no obvious clues, no suspects and no leads in a homicide case, forensic scientist Guy Hanks (Bill Cosby) is called in to investigate. Guy combines his keen sense of deductive reasoning with the latest lab equipment to determine the facts about a crime.

Guy was born in Philadelphia. He is a widower and lives at 610 West 110th Street, Apartment 3F, in Manhattan. His telephone number is 555-3434 and he is with the 15th Precinct of the N.Y.P.D. Gus is studying the bass clarinet and every Wednesday morning he buys a lottery ticket. After playing the game for 19 years (the amount of time he was on the force) he wins a multi-million dollar jackpot. The money enables Guy to retire, but he soon becomes bored and returns to the force "because I can't resist the urge to solve crimes." Guy began working for the department in 1972. He recalled his first case as being "The Olivia Bellini Murder Case," wherein he solved the murder of an unpopular co-ed found dead in a car.

Oona David (Alice Playten) is Guy's housekeeper. Oona has been working for Guy for 20 years and longs to be an actress. Her biggest claim to fame is a part she played in *Henry IV, Part 2*, at the SoHo Theater Company in Manhattan. Adam Sully (James Naughton) is a detective with the 15th Precinct who works with Guy. VGP 418 is his license plate number. Barbara Lorenz (Lynn Whitfield) is the physical therapist Guy visits after he is wounded (shot in the arm). Barbara is from Whitestone, Queens, N.Y., and had planned to become a dance teacher. One day, while in a dance class, a student fell and broke her hip. Barbara helped the girl regain the use of her legs and found her true calling as a physical therapist. She and Guy eventually became romantically involved.

William E. Cosby, Jr., David Black and Craig Hardy composed the theme.

20. Crime Photographer (CBS, 1951–1952)

The Express Building in New York City is home to the *Morning Express*, a crusading newspaper. John "Jack" Casey (Richard Carlyle, Darren McGavin) is the paper's top photographer who covers the crime news of a great city. Casey, as he is called, lives in an apartment at 110 Mulberry Street and works like a detective to uncover the headline making stories. He develops his own pictures at the paper and even during simple assignments, Casey's lens captures things he sometimes doesn't see. He is most often assisted by Ann Williams (Jan Miner), the paper's gutsy crime reporter. She lives in an apartment on 56th Street. Ann, like Casey, finds trouble wherever she goes. Casey, unlike Ann, hates covering social functions — especially weddings — but does so to be near Ann.

Casey's hangout is the Blue Note Cafe, a mid-Manhattan club where he finds relaxation and a place to think. His information man is the club's bartender, Ethelbert (John Gibson), a man who knows everything about everything and everybody. Casey says, "He reads the *Atlantic Monthly* and he's tough; sometimes he has to be a bouncer." Bill Logan (Bernard Lenrow) is the homicide detective with the N.Y.P.D. who arrests the criminals Casey and Ann uncover. The Tony Mottola Trio perform as the Blue Note Cafe Musicians; Morton Gould composed the theme.

The series is also known as *Casey, Crime Photographer* and *Casey, Press Photographer* and is based on the radio series *Flashgun Casey, Press Photographer* (also titled *Casey, Crime Photographer* and *Crime Photographer*). CBS adapted the radio series to television in 1945 as *Diary of Death* with Oliver Thorndike as Casey, Ruth Ford as Ann and John Gibson as Ethelbert.

21. **Crossing Jordan** (NBC, 2001)

Dr. Jordan Cavanaugh (Jill Hennessy) is a medical examiner for the Commonwealth of Massachusetts, Office of the Chief Medical Examiner. "I cut up dead people for a living," she says. Jordan is opposed to injustice ("That pisses me off") and has a commendation from the Chicago Police Department for solving five murders. She has extraordinary skills, is compassionate about her work and an excellent diagnostician. She also has one serious problem — insubordination. She constantly clashes with her superiors and has an obsessive desire to solve crimes.

Jordan is the daughter of Max Cavanaugh (Ken Howard), a former cop with the Boston Police Department (now retired after 38 years on the force). When Jordan was a child she would sneak out of her room at night to spy on her father as he sat at the kitchen table with a glass of scotch and all the evidence in a case he was investigating laid out on the table. Max would stare at the evidence and envision himself as both the killer and the victim in an attempt to solve the crime. Max always knew Jordan was watching him and one night asked her, "Would you like to be the victim or the killer?" "And that's how it started," says Jordan. "It was like our very own game of Clue, only it wasn't Colonel Mustard in the drawing room with a knife."

Max was forced into early retirement when he became obsessed with finding the man who killed his wife and Jordan's mother. The case is still unsolved. He now helps Jordan through their game of role playing and with the contacts he has in the police department. When Jordan and Max play their game, the audience sees a reenactment of the crime with Jordan and Max as the killer and victim. Max now lives with a woman named Evelyn (Lois Nettleton), an old friend from high school who is a widow, and owns a bar called Cavanaugh's. His favorite dinner is vegetable lasagna and he believes Jordan is pigheaded and stubborn.

When Jordan was born, Max followed an old Irish Catholic tradition and gave her a rosary for Confirmation. Jordan spent a year in Italy and can speak perfect Italian. She doesn't like to be challenged in her work and gets extremely emotional when a murder baffles her. She assures the victim, "I'm gonna find out who did this to you." Jordan lives at 43 Victor Drive, Apartment 311, and thinks like a cop; she can take the simplest assignment and turn it into a murder investigation. Jordan graduated from Boston University—top five in her class—and often works with Detective Woody Hoyt (Jerry O'Connell) of the Boston P.D. Jordan's favorite color is purple and she has a chipped tooth from an accident she suffered in the second grade. Jordan later says the book *Catcher in the Rye*, which she read at the age of 15 changed her life and prompted her to become a medical examiner—not the game she played with her father.

Jordan's superior, Dr. Garrett Macy (Miguel Ferrer), is the Chief Medical Examiner. He runs the center and believes, "This place is going to hell and it's about to get crazier" due to budget cuts. Garrett keeps a bottle of Pepto Bismol in his desk drawer, has insomnia, high blood pressure and is allergic to strawberries. He has a hand puppet dog "that my shrink gave to me to say things to that I can't say to other people." Garrett collects old records—mostly jazz and blues from the 1920s and '30s—and is divorced from Maggie (Lindsay Frost). He is now struggling to raise his rebellious teenage daughter, Abby (Alex McKenna). Abby attends Loyola High School and she and Garrett have a yearly tradition of eating at Yang Chao's Restaurant. Garrett says, "I'm more than a medical examiner, I'm an interesting guy." He writes poetry and plays jazz drums. Garrett drives a car with the license plate 50F VBI and, as a kid, he was a big comic book collector. When Garrett substitutes for Max and plays Jordan's game, he says, "The last time I did this I had nightmares for a week."

Lily Lebowski (Kathryn Hahn) is the intake girl who coordinates matters. She has a crush on Garrett and goes out of her way to please him. As a kid, her favorite TV show was "The Uncle Ha Ha Show" about a clown. On her seventeenth birthday Lily says, "I wished for bigger breasts." Lily is later the grievance counselor at the center.

Nigel Townsend (Steve Valentine) and Grace Yukora (Tamlyn Tomita) also work with Garrett. Nigel is a ballistics expert with knowledge in many other fields, such as DNA, blood and figuring out where an insignificant piece of something came from. Grace believes there are no bad guys, only dead bodies. She is a coroner and promises her subjects closure. Wendy Melvin and Lisa Coleman composed the theme "Crossing Jordan."

Related Series

1. Quincy, M.E. (NBC, 1976–1983). See entry.

2. One West Waikiki (CBS, 1994). Dr. Dawn Holliday (Cheryl Ladd), called Holli, is the Chief Medical Examiner for the Hawaiian Police Department. She is based at the M.E. Building at One West Waikiki and assists Mack Wolfe (Richard Burgi), a maverick cop with the Hawaiian P.D. Holli, formerly the Deputy Chief Medical Examiner for the L.A.P.D., is dedicated to her job. She is determined to see that what happened to her does not happen to anyone else. When Holli was a child her mother died. Holli has never been able to obtain the cause of death (listed as unascertainable). She studied medicine, went into forensics and says, "I will never give up on a homicide." See also *C.S.I.: Crime Scene Investigation* and *Unsub*.

22. C.S.I.: Crime Scene Investigation (CBS, 2000)

The Criminalistics Division of the Metropolitan Las Vegas Police Department, located on North Trop Boulevard, is considered the number two crime lab in the country. It solves crimes most labs render unsolvable. At the University of Western Nevada, the lab works with the Anthropology Department to maintain The Body Farm, a morbid, desolate area where bodies donated to science are studied and tracked by a team of scientists. Although it appears disturbing to the viewer, Chief C.S.I. Investigator Gil Grissom (William Petersen) claims, "It's not creepy; it's a controlled study of situational decomposition in a very helpful place." The sign posted on the gate surrounding the farm reads "Private Property — Keep Out. All Persons in Violation Will Be Prosecuted Under Section 42.4.323.8470 of the Nevada Penal Code."

Gil is head of a level three C.S.I. team that includes Catherine Willows (Marg Helgenberger), Sara Sidle (Jorga Fox), Nick Stokes (George Eades) and Warrick Brown (Gary Dourdan). Gil and his associates call themselves Forensic Criminologists and handle each case they receive objectively with no regard to race, creed or bubble gum flavor. "Evidence is like a fine wine," Gil says. "You can't just drink it, you've got to let it breathe." While Gil's team uses the latest scientific equipment to solve crimes, they are not always assigned to investigate murders. "We handle cases involving alive people — from drunk drivers to a child who is a victim of molestation to robberies. When the pieces of a puzzle just don't fit, they call us in."

The team is trained to avoid verbal evidence and rely on what they find at the scene. "We are crime analysts," says Catherine. Weather can sometimes be a problem. If it should rain, as an example, the team has three minutes to bag the body and gather evidence. In a missing person's case, Gil says, "The first 24 hours are gold; after that it's quicksand and the worst it can get is a dead end." While Gil is reluctant to admit defeat, he does say of rain-soaked cases, "The killer got lucky tonight."

The program, which can be unsettling at times, focuses on the meticulous step-by-step process the investigators follow as they gather evidence to solve crimes. Stories are then presented in three ways: conventional, flashbacks to illustrate various versions of a crime and by computer animation to show how a weapon caused injury or death.

Gil was born in Santa Monica, California, on August 17, 1956. He attended UCLA and has a Bachelor of Science degree in biology. His special skill is entomology (the study of insects). Gil was originally supervisor of the graveyard shift. He was promoted to head of the crime lab when his superior, Captain Jim Brass (Paul Guilfoyle) was transferred to the police department's homicide division. Gil has a rather bizarre background. At the age of eight he would go to the beach at Marina Del Rey to collect dead birds to perform autopsies. As he grew older, he would find dead cats and dogs and do the same thing, teaching himself the ins and outs of death. Gil worked his way through college and at the age of 22 became the youngest coroner in the history of Los Angeles County. Eight years later he was recruited by the Las Vegas Police Department to run their field office. Gil mentioned that his mother ran an art gallery and that his father was in the import/export business.

Gil has a fascination with insects and gets a migraine headache about once a year. He doesn't like people in his house, gets frustrated if he can't solve a case and likes to be in command of his troops. He enjoys chocolate covered grasshoppers for a pick-me-up. Gil constantly experiments with the why and how of a killing — more with the how as why doesn't make sense. He also has a habit of leaving his experiments in the community refrigerator when the lab's refrigerator is full. Gil can speak in sign language taught to him by his mother, who was partially deaf and welcomes the assist of people outside the profession to help him with a case; for example, a deaf teacher helping him solve the murder of a hearing impaired student. Gil's greatest challenge is to find Paul Millander (Matt O'Toole), a brilliant serial killer he is unable to catch. When he was a child, Paul saw his father killed over a money dispute. He now kills on a specific day each year — the day of his father's murder, which is also Gil's birthday. Gil is also an expert at poker and often wins — "It's how I funded my first body farm at college." He also likes to think he is smarter than a criminal and find the evidence he may have left behind and overlooked. "I hate it when the criminal is smarter." As the series progressed, a deafness problem that plagued his mother, began to develop in Gil.

Catherine is Gil's senior investigator. She was born on a ranch in Bozeman, Montana, on March 26, 1963 and has a Bachelor of Science degree in medical technology from West Las Vegas University. Her specialty is blood splatter analysis. Catherine began her working career as a waitress in Seattle. She became bored and went to Las Vegas where she put herself through school, first by waiting tables then as an exotic dancer. Catherine is divorced from Eddie and the mother of Lindsay (Madison Reynolds). Catherine mentioned she married Eddie when she first became a stripper. She does not mention working or going to school when raising Lindsay. Catherine loves her job and says, "We're like a bunch of kids getting paid to work on puzzles. You feel like King Kong on cocaine when you solve a puzzle." Catherine scrutinizes every crime scene. She collects and sometimes photographs the evidence and recreates what happened by piecing together the evidence she has found. Catherine was recruited by Gil to work at the lab and believes human behavior plays a part in solving a case. Gil believes only the forensic evidence is necessary to find the means.

Sara, employee number 037-784, was born in Tamalas Bay, California, on September 16, 1971. She has a Bachelor of Science degree in physics from Harvard University and her specialty is material and element analysis. She also attended graduate school and has a degree in theoretical physics. Sara worked in the San Francisco Coroner's Office for five years before being transferred to its crime lab. She left the City by the Bay for a job with Gil and his team. Sara is an expert on arson fires, likes plants and maxes out each month on overtime. Her parents ran a bed and breakfast and she became interested in police work as a child. She listened to police scanners at home and studied forensic magazines in her spare time. Gil believes she becomes too involved in a case, especially when a victim survives and she has vowed to find the culprit responsible for the assault. Her car license plate reads 019 ATO. If an unknown substance is found at a crime scene, Sara delights in trying to figure out what it is.

Nick was born in Dallas, Texas, on August 18, 1971. He has a Bachelor of Science degree in criminal justice from Rice University and his specialty is hair and fiber analysis. Another episode mentions he is a graduate of Texas A&M University. Nick previously worked with the Dallas Police Department before being transferred to its crime lab, C.S.I. Level 1. He was then transferred to the Las Vegas Crime Lab. Nick likes being around people but is easily frustrated when he gets upset over a case. "Sometimes I hate this job," he says. He dislikes peanut butter and finds watching The Discovery Channel beneficial to his work.

Warrick was born in Las Vegas on October 10, 1970, and possesses a Bachelor of Science degree in chemistry from the University of Las Vegas. His specialty is audio-video analysis. He is also the team's crime scene photographer and is an expert at figuring out what item was used to do what. Warrick worked as a casino runner as a teenager and put himself through college working as a taxi driver, bell captain at the Sahara, helicopter tour guide over the Grand Canyon and grave digger before becoming a part of Gil's unit. He is a stickler for gathering evidence and brilliant at piecing together fragments of objects to make them whole or identifiable. Warrick can visually detect evidence others may have overlooked but suffers from a gambling problem which is not fully under control.

Jim Brass was born in Newark, New Jersey, on January 3, 1953. He has a B.A. in history from Seaton Hall University and has logged 22 years on the police force—first in New Jersey then with the Las Vegas P.D. He was mainly an administrator at C.S.I. before being transferred to homicide. He is most often assigned to the same cases as Gil's unit. Jim lives at 554 Applegate Way and believes that every police recruit should experience an autopsy on their first night to see if they have what it takes to be a C.S.I. investigator. Although he is a captain, Jim introduces himself to suspects as Detective Brass.

The theme "Who Are You" is written by Pete Townsend and performed by The Who.

Spinoff Series

C.S.I.: Miami (CBS, 2002). The gruelling, sometimes upsetting work of the Crime Scene Investigation team of the Miami Dade County Crime Lab. Horatio Caine (David Caruso) heads the team; he is assisted by Calleigh Duquesne (Emily Procter), Megan Donner (Kim Delaney), Tim Speedle (Rory Cochrane), Eric Delko (Adam Rodriquez) and Alexx Woods (Khandi Alexander). While information is plentiful on the original series, the same cannot be said for its spin off. Character information as of 12-31-02 is very limited.

Horatio was a homicide detective and member of the bomb squad where he learned his expertise in explosives. He is at his best when all the evidence does not point to the person he believes is the killer and he must dig deeper. There are occasions when probing further does not bring him the evidence he needs, and the killer walks. When such things happen—and they do—he vows to keep digging until he finds what he needs. Horatio is also an expert on engraving and jewelry and says, "We treat each suspect as an innocent—that's how we sleep at night." If there is any doubt about evidence, "Bag it and tag it," he says. While virtually every law enforcer would like to know the reason why a culprit does what he does, Horatio is satisfied with knowing he caught a killer. The motive doesn't appear to matter to him.

Calleigh is a ballistics expert. She is from the South and called The Bullet Girl. Megan is a DNA expert. While Horatio likes to go on hunches, Megan says, "Show me the evidence." Megan and Horatio have their slight disagreements but both like to re-enact the evidence to see how something may have happened. Megan says, "The problem with the obvious is that it can make you overlook the evidence." She is a widow and enjoys an unusual sport—shark fishing.

Tim is the team's chief investigator. He has street connections and believes in trusting his gut instinct. He calls Horatio "H." Eric is the team's underwater recovery expert. He also doubles as the crime scene photographer. He calls Horatio "Boss."

Alexx is the no-nonsense, know-it-all coroner. She talks to her subjects as she tries to figure out what happened to them. She is married and the mother of two children. The most disturbing aspect of her work is performing an autopsy that involves fetal recovery. It totally depresses her as well as the viewer who gets to witness bits and pieces of such proceedings.

The episode of November 25, 2002, "A Horrible Mind," was the final appearance of Kim Delaney, who was dropped after this tenth episode. Kim's Megan character received less air time each week with Calleigh becoming more versatile and knowledgeable in DNA matters. A previously minor character, that of Detective Adell Sevilla (Wanda DeJesus), became more prominent as the Miami Dade County police officer who works alongside Horatio and his team much in the same manner as Jim Brass works with Gil Grissom's team. It was later revealed that Megan resigned when she felt her work reminded her too much of her husband's death.

C.S.I.: Miami *See* C.S.I.: Crime Scene Investigation

23. Danger Theater (Fox, 1993)

Robert Vaughn hosts a series that dares to take a bite out of the butt of crime via three short parodies: *The Searcher, Tropical Punch* and *357 Marina Del Rey.*

1. The Searcher. Diedrich Bader plays the Searcher, a motorcycle riding, mysterious avenger who finds nothing but trouble in his effort to help people. "Someone needs help, so they call me. That's what I do. I help people. They call me the Searcher." He rides a hog ("That's my motorcycle") and dresses in black like his hero Marlon Brando from his favorite film *The Wild One* ("That's my favorite, not Brando's"). If you need to contact him, "You can call me toll free. Just dial 1-800 Search Me."

As a boy, called Little Searcher, Searcher (the only name given) had a pet rabbit named Snookie, whom he carried around as a good luck charm figuring a whole rabbit was luckier than just the foot, and had a favorite TV show called "Jimmy Jake's Barnyard Follies." Jimmy Jake's dummy, Farmer Joe, was Little Searcher's childhood hero.

2. *Tropical Punch.* A spoof of *Hawaii Five-O* with Mike Morgan (Adam West), Captain of the Tropical Punch Unit of the Hawaiian Police Department. He is assisted by Tom McCormick (Billy Morisette) and Al Hamoki (Peter Navy Turasosupo). Mike is the rough and tough older cop who acts tough but is actually all talk and no action. He convinces his sidekicks to do all the dirty work. Mike loves to paint in his spare time; Al lives to eat.

3. *357 Marina Del Rey.* Clay Gentry (Ricky Harris) and Rake Rowe (Todd Field) are inept yuppie detectives just out of college who set up operations in a coffee shop at 357 Marina Del Rey. They wanted to make a difference and became private investigators to solve crimes. Their cases involve the nastiest and meanest people in town but Clay and Rake appear to be more concerned with fashion and frequenting the cappuccino bar than solving crimes.

24. Decoy (Syndicated, 1957–1958)

Patricia Jones (Beverly Garland) is a police woman with the 16th Precinct of the Police Department of New York City. The term N.Y.P.D. had not yet come into use. Patricia, called Casey, wears badge number 300 and earns $75 a week. She lives in an apartment at 110 Hope Street and Murray Hill 3-4643 is her phone number. Hoods call Casey "A Dame Copper." Like the series *Naked City*, Decoy was filmed on the streets of New York and is quite realistic in its presentation; storylines capture the feel of the city at the time. Casey is attractive and alluring but she is somewhat of a loner. She is totally dedicated to her job and she does suffer for it not only in long hours and dangerous cases, but she is shot at and she does take beatings from thugs; seeing her with a bruise or disheveled clothing and hair is not unusual. The series is "Presented as a tribute to the Bureau of Police Women,

Police Department, City of New York" as seen in the opening theme. See also *Police Woman*.

25. Dellaventura (CBS, 1997)

Anthony Dellaventura (Danny Aiello) is a former New York City police officer turned private investigator who says, "If you need me, I'll be around." His clients are people who have no where else to turn and his fee is $100 per hour per associate. He works with Jonas Deeds (Byron Keith Minns), Ted Naples (Rick Aiello) and Geri Zarius (Ann Ramsay).

Anthony's philosophy is "Expect the unexpected." He was a detective with the 27th Precinct of the N.Y.P.D. for 15 years and liked to do things his way. The department didn't want that "so it was time we parted." Anthony carries a gun but would rather shoot off his mouth. He drives a car with the license plate S38 ICX and hangs out at the Knickerbocker Bar and Grill; root beer is his favorite drink. He likes each case to end on a happy note — "I like happy endings."

Geri is a sweet-looking girl "but don't let that fool you," says Anthony. She is tough, an expert on weapons and explosives and proficient at breaking and entering. Ted is an ex-fighter who uses his fists as weapons. Joe, a Catholic, is an electronics surveillance expert Anthony uses when people or places need to be monitored. "He can infiltrate any organization at any time," says Anthony. Joe Delia composed the theme.

26. Department S (Syndicated, 1971–1972)

Department S is a special branch of Interpol, the International Police Force, that attempts to solve complex crimes that are considered unsolvable by any police organization in the world. Sir Curtis Sereste (Dennis Alaba Peters) is the Director of Department S, which is housed in the Interpol Building at 1703 DeMarne Street in Paris, France. Jason King (Peter Wyngarde), Annabelle Hurst (Rosemary Nicols) and Stewart Sullivan (Joel Fabiani) are its top operatives.

Jason, the successful writer of Mark Cain mystery novels, attempts to solve each case as if it were a plot for one of his books. *Two Plus One Equals Murder* and *High Fashion Murder* were two of his book titles that were given. Jason is an incurable romantic ("I thrive on excitement") and enjoys relaxing in the sun of Jamaica "to unravel my thoughts." He enjoys skiing, romancing the ladies and an occasional drink, if not at a bar or fancy supper club, from the flask that he carries with him. Jason lives at 43 Puchard

Street and drives a car with the license plate BE2083E. He has an excellent memory for details and can sketch the likeness of a suspect he has seen. Despite his crime-solving abilities, Annabelle and Stewart believe Jason is accident prone as it is usually he who gets shot or takes a beating.

Annabelle, a pretty, scientific minded young woman, provides the team's research — "Digging up the facts we need," says Jason. She is an art expert and can decipher the most complex codes. She can spot counterfeit money simply by touching it. "Who needs micro chemical analysis when we have Annabelle," says Stewart. She is capable of picking locks and opening safes. Annabelle and Stewart often go undercover as husband and wife. When a beautiful girl is needed to infiltrate a crime ring, Annabelle dons a long blond wig to cover her short brunette hair and sexy clothes as opposed to her conservative business outfits. She lives at 86 LeParses Avenue and drives a white sedan with the license plate 874 Y3L, later LBY 143.

Stewart, the American member of the British team, reports directly to Sir Curtis for their assignments and oversees each case. He believes that, although they have computers, Jason's mind is faster at deciphering information. He expects progress reports from Jason and Annabelle as cases unfold and he is usually the one who coordinates travel plans when a case requires the team be in different places at the same time. He is an expert in explosives and provides the muscle when needed. Stewart resides in an apartment on Madeleine Drive and drives a car with the license plate YYM 297. Edwin Astley composed the theme.

Spinoff Series

Jason King (Syndicated, 1972). Rosemary Nicols and Joel Fabiani were dropped to focus on Peter Wyngarde as Jason King, a mystery novelist who solves crimes to acquire story material.

27. Diagnosis Murder (CBS, 1993–2001)

Community General is a state-of-the-art hospital in Los Angeles. While it is supposedly haunted by the ghost of Blair Lawson, a nurse who mysteriously disappeared in the basement in 1975, its staff and doctors are dedicated to saving human lives. The cost-efficient Norman Briggs (Michael Tucci) runs the hospital. Dr. Mark Sloan (Dick Van Dyke) is the administrator (later head of internal medicine) and doctors Jack Stewart (Scott Baio), Amanda Bentley (Victoria Rowell) and Jesse Travis (Charlie Schlatter) assist Mark. Scott Baio's character is also known as Dr. Jack Vincent. Jesse replaced Jack when Jack left to start a private practice in 1995. In the pilot, Dr. Amanda Bentley was white, played by Cynthia Gibb. The Jack Stewart character was originally Dr. Jack Parker and played by Stephen Caffrey. The pilot also saw Mariette Hartley as the hospital administrator, Kate Hamilton.

Mark treats his patients as individuals, referring them to specialists if necessary. He performs 17 percent more cat scans and MRIs than any other doctor at Community General. Mark, a widower in his 60s, tries to keep in shape by walking five miles a day although at times he just paces back and forth in his office to make up for walking when something troubles him. Mark is an amateur magician and performs tricks for the children at the hospital. His office is cluttered, but one can see posters of magicians Harry Blackstone and Thurston on the walls. Mark roller skates to work when his car breaks down, constantly forgets to activate his beeper and moonlights as a detective, serving as the Special Medical Consultant to the L.A.P.D. Norman objects to Mark playing detective and constantly reprimands him for doing so. Mark says, "I'm a homicide consultant for the police department although I give them more problems than solutions." Mark assists his son, Detective Steve Sloan (Barry Van Dyke) and often finds evidence overlooked by investigators to warrant further investigation into a case. It was mentioned in one episode that Mark helped solve over 150 murders; in another episode, Mark was said to have the honorary title of police consultant; regardless, once he gets involved in a case "and I get something in my head, I have to go with it" until he solves the crime.

Mark appeared as a contestant on the TV game show *Through the Roof*, where he won $150,000 answering questions. He donated one half of the money to the Children's Aid Relief and the other half to breast cancer research. Mark frequents a bar called JAX and drives a Jaguar with the license plate 55 JAB (also seen as YEB 257, 55 18G, 200 PCQ and OSRQ 590). Mark's father, James Sloan, was a homicide detective (Badge 618) who abandoned his family when Mark was 10 years old. As an intern, Mark worked in a free clinic at the docks and takes cream and three sugars in his coffee. His late wife was named Catherine. Producer Stephen J. Cannell proposed a TV series based on Mark called "Dr. Danger" that never made it past the pilot stage. In one episode, Dick Van Dyke also played his four cousins: Julian Nash, Jonathan Nash, Judith Nash and J. Edison Nash. The Tanner Foundation holds the principle interest in Community General Hospital.

While Mark does involve himself in Steve's work life, he distances himself from Steve's personal life. In some episodes, Steve lives with Mark at his beach house; in others, Steve has his own apartment. Steve is with the 15th Precinct of the Metropolitan Division of the L.A.P.D. and is later promoted to lieutenant. He appeared on the game show *Make a Date* and pooled resources with Jesse to open Bar-B-Q Bob's (also seen as BBQ Bob's), a restaurant in the Fontaine Mall. Steve, an excellent cook, won the police department's chili contest in 2001. Steve's license plate reads YHVS 668.

Amanda was adopted when she was 10 years old. She studied dance at the Ballet School in New York City and her adoptive parents saw Amanda becoming a doctor and steered her in that direction. Amanda wears a size seven surgical glove and is a technical advisor on the television series *Med Squad*. Amanda later quits her job at the hospital for a position with the L.A. Medical Examiner's Office. She married Colin Livingston, a Navy man, at the Chapel of Singing Nuns in Las Vegas, has a dog named Yoda and drives a car with the license plate TAS 372 (later 9CFE 850). Jack and Jesse are residents in internal medicine under Mark's supervision. Jesse claims Mark is the Will Rogers of the medical profession — "He hasn't met a man he didn't like."

In the opening theme, the book *The Greatest Cases of Sherlock Holmes* is seen. Dick DeBennedictis composed the theme "Diagnosis Murder."

Note: While not technically a spin off from *Jake and the Fatman* (see entry), the character of Dr. Mark Sloan (Dick Van Dyke) was introduced in the episode of March 20, 1991 ("It Never Entered My Mind"). Three television movies followed before the actual series: *Diagnosis Murder* (January 5, 1992), *The House on Sycamore Street* (May 1, 1992) and *Twist of the Knife* (February 13, 1993). The series was originally titled *Diagnosis Murder: Starring Dick Van Dyke*. On February 6, 2002, CBS aired a follow-up television movie called *Diagnosis Murder: Town without Pity* that reunited Dick Van Dyke, Barry Van Dyke and Charlie Schlatter in a story that finds Mark attempting to solve the murder of his daughter, Carol (Stacey Van Dyke), a carefree woman who was kidnapped then killed.

28. Dick Tracy (ABC, 1950–1951)

When people hear the name Dick Tracy they say, "He's not just from police headquarters, he's from Homicide." Dick Tracy (Ralph Byrd) is a master police detective in a large, unidentified metropolis. He is with the 12th Precinct, also called Headquarters, and rides in a car with the code 15. He is fair and honest and will never waste a bullet. "I always hit what I aim at." He is a thorough investigator and often relies on tips from his many snitches to solve a crime. He has to think like a criminal in order to outwit criminals and bring them to justice. Dick is married to Tess Trueheart (Angela Greene) and they live in an unidentified home that appears to be in a suburban neighborhood. While Dick enjoys the homemade meals Tess prepares, he often snacks on hot dogs and hamburgers when on the job. Dick's job often leaves him little time to spend with Tess. As they are about to do something, like go to a movie, Dick gets a call from headquarters to report for duty. "Sometimes I wish I were born a super criminal," says Tess, "because then I might get to see something of Mr. Dick Tracy."

Dick works with Sam Catchem (Joe Devlin); Pat Patton (Pierre Watkin) is the police chief; J. Blackstone Springem (John Harmon) is the crooked criminal attorney; and Officer Murphy (Dick Elliott) is the overweight, jovial stationhouse cop. Dick and Sam communicate with each other via two-way wrist radios that allow voice communication when on assignment. The series is based on the comic strip by Chester Gould.

The Dick Tracy character next appeared on television in a 1961 animated series called *The Dick Tracy Show*. Dick (voice of Everett Sloane) rarely participated in crime solving. He served as the chief and dispatched various cops, such as Heap O'Calorie, Hemlock Holmes, Joe Jitsu, and Speedy Gonzalez, to apprehend the criminals; for example, The Brow and Oodles, Flattop and Bee Bee Eyes, Stooge Villa and Mumbles, and Prune Face and Itchy. Mel Blanc, Benny Rubin and Paul Frees provided other voices.

Ray MacDonnell became the next Dick Tracy in an unaired pilot that was produced in 1967 and called simply *Dick Tracy*. Davey Davison played Tess Trueheart Tracy; Eve Plumb, their adopted daughter, Bonny Braids; and Jay Blood, their son, Junior Tracy. Monroe Arnole was Dick's partner, Sam Catchem; Ken Mayer played Police Chief Pat Patton; and Liz Shutan was Detective Liz. Tracy's address was given as 3904 Orchid Drive and his phone number was 555-7268. Tracy had a secret lab in his home located behind a firing range target figure and a two-way wrist TV. The pilot story finds Tracy trying to stop the evil Mr. Memory (Victor Buono) from destroying a NATO peace conference. The group, the Ventures, perform the theme "Dick Tracy."

29. **The District** (CBS, 2000)

The *New York Times* calls Jack Mannion (Craig T. Nelson) the most innovative crime fighter. He served in the Vietnam War, was a New York City Transit Cop (Badge 203), Police Commissioner of Newark, New Jersey, then Police Chief of Boston. He is now the Police Chief of Washington, D.C., hired by Deputy Mayor Mary Ann Mitchell (Jayne Brook) to clean up the District, which has the worst crime rate in the nation.

Jack is, as he calls himself, a numbers guy. He believes in gathering crime statistics on a daily basis and crunching them relentlessly to see what is happening in his city and to know who is responsible for what. He begins by establishing Comp Stat, a state-of-the-art computer room where he appoints

Ella Mae Farmer (Lynne Thigpen) as Director of Analysis. Ella introduced computers to the department 15 years ago and is most knowledgeable in the field of crime analysis. All cases that are in progress or labeled as unsolved are programmed into the computer and acted upon. The abandoned firing range room serves as the headquarters for Comp Stat.

Jack is caring and compassionate. He wants to make D.C. liveable again and make its police force the best in the country. Jack is also arrogant, pushy, tasteless and smug. The word "no" is not in his vocabulary. When he declares war on crime, he uses military lingo and says he loves movies — "I'm a cross between *Forrest Gump* and the *Rain Man*. Call me Rain Forrest." Jack doesn't always have the answers to questions asked of him. When this happens, he tells stories and talks about a particular movie to help find an answer.

Jack holds a general meeting with the individual police department chiefs each morning. The prior day's crime reports from each district are fed into the computer and analyzed by Ella. Based on the results, Jack instructs his chiefs as to what they must do to improve their district. Jack believes "To win the war on crime first you believe you can." Jack enjoys drinks at a bar called Teddy R's and has two children — Jack, Jr., who is attending Michigan State College, and Beth, who ran off to become a groupie with a rock band. As a kid, she had a pet cat named Cleopatra. Jack has been married three times, loves to play the accordion — Ella calls it noise, not music — and keeps a jar of jellybeans in his desk drawer. He is also crazy about a milk chocolate covered candy called Jiffy Bar. Jack relaxes when he can on his boat, the *Betty-O*, docked at Slip 38 at the Washington Channel and Marina. He has a dog named Cujo and also likes opera, chess and white asparagus.

Joe Noland (Roger Aaron Brown) is the black Deputy Police Chief. He says, about Jack, "You love him or you hate him. He is called The Great White Hope, the Champion of the Underdog." Joe resented Jack during first-season episodes as he wanted the job of police chief, but learned to like him when he got to know and understand him ("He changed the way the police police the city"). Chunky monkey is his favorite flavor of ice cream; he is also in charge of the precinct's choir.

Temple Paige (Sean Patrick Thomas) is a tough black cop with a drug problem. He lives in the projects on Basin Street and served in the Gulf War but has seen more gunfire on the streets than he did in the war. His mobile car code is 6047.

Nick Pierce (Justin Theroux) is the director of public affairs. Jack calls him director of smokes and beers. Nick was replaced in third season episodes by Kendall Truman (Kristen Wilson) as the new press secretary. Officer Nancy Parras (Elizabeth Marvel) is an officer in Jack's division. She is handy with tools and knows how to fix things. She had to as she had brothers who couldn't screw in a light bulb. Nancy has been diagnosed with Hodgkins disease.

Michael Hoenig composed the theme "The District."

30. Dog and Cat (ABC, 1977)

In an attempt to start a program that teams male and female police officers called Dog and Cat units, the 42nd Division of the Los Angeles Police Department teams Sergeant Jack Ramsey (Lou Antonio) with Officer J.Z. Kane (Kim Basinger) in an experimental Dog and Cat team. Their superior is Lieutenant Art Kipling (Matt Clark).

Jack is a hothead as Art calls him and has been on the force for 14 years. Prior to his current assignment, Jack was partners with Earl Seagram, a cop who was killed during a stakeout at the Welcome House Cafe in Venice, California. Jack drives a somewhat run down sedan, license plate 751 FTR, with a number of problems — from stuck doors to a bad starter to a smoking muffler. Jack's apartment at 36 Rosewood Avenue is a reflection of his disorganized life. He was born in Los Angeles and has a difficult time working with J.Z., a country-born girl. He believes a Dog and Cat team will not work but sticks with it "because it's my job. Who knows, maybe after a while we can work together."

J.Z. is a beautiful blonde from Georgia. She now lives at 2317 Englewood Road, loves country and western music and TV dinners ("I hate cooking"). J.Z. — no other first name given — drives a Volkswagen with a Porsche 912 engine that she installed herself. The car is now capable of high speeds. J.Z. claims she does things by her feminine intuition and held a job as a cashier at the Greenwich Theater, a porno movie house, while "working my way through the police academy." Prior to being teamed with Jack, J.Z. worked as an undercover cop amid the hookers, sleazy producers and pornographic filmmakers of Venice. J.Z., an excellent shot, attributes her various skills to "my uncle back in Georgia," who apparently taught her everything she knows, including how to be street smart.

Jack and J.Z. have little in common and constantly argue about everything; for example, J.Z. likes animals, Jack doesn't — "I go to the zoo once a year, that's as close to Nature as I want to get." Jack also calls J.Z. "Farm Girl"— "You're from the sticks. I'm from the pavement." Barry DeVorzon composed the theme "Dog and Cat.

31. Downtown (CBS, 1986)

John Forney (Michael Nouri) is a veteran undercover detective with the

Metro Division of the L.A.P.D., Unit 6; Alpha is his car code. ILNN 506 is his car license plate, and he has a dog named Bob. After 14 years on the job, Forney is promoted to Special Parole Officer and assigned to the Los Angeles Special Projects Field Office at 339½ East Front Street. There he is assigned to watch over four felons: Jesse Smith (Mariska Hargitay), Harriet Conover (Millicent Martin), Terry Corsaro (Blair Underwood) and Dennis Shothoffer (Robert Englund).

Jesse, file number 372-237A, is a beautiful and rebellious girl who grew up in Oakland, California, with six brothers. "They were Hell's Angels," she says, "and three joined the Marines." John believes her background affected her personality. Jesse is a karate expert, but has been arrested on numerous occasions for assault and battery. Harriet, file number 238-718A, is a genteel British socialite and expert con artist. She was initially arrested for selling beachfront property that was actually under water. Terry, file number 504–632A, is a street-wise black youth with an arrest record for car theft. Dennis, file number 845–231A, believes he is a nobody. To overcome his feelings of inadequacy, he pretends to be someone else to feel important. He was arrested for impersonating a doctor and performing three operations.

John calls his charges "Losers—all eight balls who are like children. Once the nursery door is opened, they run loose and get busted for the same thing they were put away for in the first place." John is very good at putting criminals away and has an impressive record—two life-saving medals, a citation for rescuing hostages, and a heroism award for saving a man from a burning car. He now has to keep four criminals out of trouble as an arrest will mean their immediate incarceration. Harriet's large home at 145 Mara Linda Lane provides John with a base of operations. The four live together with Harriet acting as a den mother to the other three. John finds that by incorporating his charges unique skills in his undercover work, he can put their bad habits to good use.

Delia Bonner (Virginia Capers) is the head of the Special Parole Program and believes John is the right man for the job. The jails are overcrowded and releasing less dangerous criminals is one way of easing the burden. John believes that if the jails are overcrowded, just build more jails.

Johnny Harris and Barry Goldberg composed the theme "That's What I Want."

32. Dragnet (NBC, 1951–1959; 1967–1970; Syndicated, 1989–1990; ABC, 2003)

As the theme music plays, an announcer's voice tells us "The story you are about to see is real; the names have been changed to protect the innocent. Fatima cigarettes, best of all king size cigarettes, brings you *Dragnet*." Following an introduction to the evening's story, the voice of Sergeant Joe Friday (Jack Webb) is heard: "This is the city, Los Angeles, California. I work here. I carry a badge." Sergeant Friday, Badge 714, is with the Homicide Division of the L.A.P.D., although he is also seen solving cases associated with robbery, car theft and missing persons. Joe lives at 4646 Cooper Street, Apartment 12, and has been working on the force for 11 years. He was a rookie in 1940. Friday is a no nonsense detective with virtually no sense of humor. He is all work and totally dedicated to solving crimes. He likes to take his time at crime scenes and study the evidence; "I sometimes get a notebook full of notes and a crime lab full of evidence but nothing to tie them together. I've got the pieces; I've just got to put them together." Joe drives a car with the license plate 58 0216 and his car code is Eighty-K, although it also sounds like A-D-K.

The series was first broadcast on radio (1949) then concurrently on radio (1951–1957) and TV (1951–1959). Jack Webb played the same role with Barton Yarborough also doing double duty as his first partner, Officer Ben Romero. *Dragnet*'s actual TV pilot aired on December 16, 1951, as a segment of *Chesterfield Sound Off Time*. On December 19, 1951, Barton Yarborough died of a heart attack. In subsequent weeks, the three episodes filmed with Yarborough aired. In the fourth episode, titled "The Big Sorrow," it was mentioned that Officer Romero had died of a heart attack. It is also in this episode that Joe shows compassion.

Joe was next teamed with Sergeant Ed Jacobs (Barney Phillips) then with Officer Frank Smith (Herb Ellis, Ben Alexander); these actors also played the same roles on the radio version. Joe mentioned that he was a rookie when he first met Ben. Early episodes feature Dorothy Abbott as Joe's fiancee, Ann Baker.

Joe's case investigations are realistically portrayed and are followed from the crime to the conviction (the sentence the felon received). The program introduced two terms into the general language: M.O. (Method of Operation) and R.I. (Records and Identification). "My name is Friday—I'm a cop" and "Just the facts, ma'am" became Joe's catchphrases. While Joe did not have a steady superior—different captains appear in various episodes—headquarters was said to be at 1335 Georgia Street. Hal Gibney and George Fenneman were the announcers; Walter Schumann composed the theme "Dragnet"—also known as "The Dragnet March" and "Danger Ahead." The series is also known as *Badge 714*, the title used when first syndicated.

The same format, theme song and tough, emotionless but dedicated

Sergeant Joe Friday (Jack Webb) returned for a color series (1967–70) now syndicated as *Dragnet*. It was originally broadcast as *Dragnet '67*, *Dragnet '68*, *Dragnet '69* and *Dragnet '70*. Joe was now partners with Officer Bill Gannon (Harry Morgan). In 1989 (to 1990), a new syndicated version appeared called *The New Dragnet* that realistically depicted the gruelling case investigations of detectives Vic Daniels (Jeff Osterhage) and Carl Melina (Bernard White). Vic and Carl are with the West L.A. Police Department and had two superiors: Captain Lussen (Don Stroud) and Captain Bolz (Thalmus Rasalala). Bill Fulton composed "The New Dragnet Theme" and the program closed with this statement: "The characters and events depicted in this photoplay are based on facts; however, names have been changed to protect the privacy of the individuals."

In February of 2003, ABC premiered a 13 episode update of the original series called *Dragnet*. Ed O'Neill portrayed the tough, virtually emotionless Detective Joe Friday with Ethan Embry as his much younger, somewhat wet-behind-the-ears partner, Detective Frank Smith. Joe (badge number 714) and Frank are with the Robbery and Homicide Division of the L.A.P.D. The series also follows the format of the original as it is totally dedicated to Joe and Frank's case investigations with virtually no factual information about the characters. Episodes open with the words of an unidentified announcer ("The story you are about to see has been inspired by actual incidents; the names have been changed to protect the innocent") and close with the punishment handed down to a felon. Mike Post composed the updated version of the original "Dragnet" theme.

33. The Eddie Capra Mysteries (NBC, 1978–1979)

Eddie Capra (Vincent Baggetta) is an attorney with the mind of a detective. He was born in Brooklyn, New York, and attended Brooklyn Polytech High School. After graduating from the New York University School of Law, he acquired a job in Los Angeles with the prestigious law firm of Devlin, Linkman and O'Brien. Unlike the three-piece suit attorney, Eddie is unconventional; he dresses casually, takes a real interest in his clients' problems, and will go to any lengths to prove them innocent — even if it means breaking all the rules, which causes friction between Eddie and his employer, J.J. Devlin (Ken Swofford), the only one of the three partners who is seen.

Eddie lives at 64 Holland Drive in Los Angeles. His car license plate reads 836 PCE and 656-1656 is his phone number. Eddie's romantic interest is Lacey Brown (Wendy Phillips), the receptionist at the law firm. Lacey is the mother of Jennie (Seven Ann McDonald), a pretty 11-year-old girl who attends Franklin Elementary School. She longs to be a professional singer. Lacey lives at 10360 La Paloma and drives a station wagon with the license plate number XJQ 492.

In the busy opening theme, the following actions occur: 1. Eddie breaks into Apartment number 4; 2. A stopwatch reads 13 seconds; 3. A broken clock is stopped at 11:25; 4. Fingerprints of the right thumb, index finger and middle finger are seen; 5. A bullet hole is seen in the left lens of a pair of eyeglasses; 6. Eddie hands Lacey a gun and the stopwatch; 7. The right rear hubcap of a car flies off as it makes a sharp turn; 8. An H-O scale Southern Pacific 0-4-0 tank locomotive, engine number 14, derails (the tower signal seen just before the model engine derails has the number 122 on its mast).

John Addison composed the "Theme from the Eddie Capra Mysteries."

34. Ellery Queen (DuMont, 1950–1953; Syndicated, 1954–1955; NBC, 1958–1959; 1975–1976)

Ellery Queen, the fictional detective created by Frederic Dannay and Manfred B. Lee, first appeared in the 1928 novel *The Roman Hat Mystery*. In 1933, the first Ellery Queen feature film appeared, *The Spanish Cape Mystery*, with Donald Cook in the title role. Eight additional Ellery Queen films followed featuring as Ellery, Eddie Quillan, Ralph Bellamy and William Gargan. In 1939 through 1948 a radio series appeared with Hugh Marlowe, Carleton Young, Sydney Smith and Larry Dobkin portraying Ellery Queen. Television joined the bandwagon in 1950 and six versions were produced.

1. *Ellery Queen* (DuMont, 1950–1953). Richard Hart then Lee Bowman (Ellery Queen), Florenz Ames (Inspector Richard Queen), Charlotte Keane (Nikki Porter).

2. *The New Adventures of Ellery Queen* (Syndicated, 1954–1955). Hugh Marlowe (Ellery Queen), Florenz Ames (Inspector Richard Queen).

3. *The Further Adventures of Ellery Queen* (NBC, 1958–1959). George Nader then Lee Phillips (Ellery Queen), Les Tremayne (Inspector Richard Queen).

4. *Ellery Queen: Don't Look Behind You* (Unsold Pilot, NBC, November 14, 1971). Proposed series title: "The Further Adventures of Ellery Queen." Peter Lawford (Ellery Queen), Harry Morgan (Inspector Richard Queen). Based on the 1949 novel *Cat of Many Tails*, the story finds Ellery seeking a fiend who kills males with blue cords and females with pink ones.

5. *Ellery Queen: Too Many Suspects* (Pilot for the 1975–1976 series; NBC, March 23, 1975). Jim Hutton (Ellery Queen), David Wayne (Inspector

Richard Queen). The story finds Ellery attempting to solve the murder of a fashion designer.

6. *Ellery Queen* (NBC, 1975–1976). Jim Hutton (Ellery Queen), David Wayne (Inspector Richard Queen).

Ellery Queen is a gentleman detective and writer who intervenes in baffling police matters to solve the case and get story material. He lives with his father, Richard Queen, an inspector with the Third Division of the N.Y.P.D.'s Center Precinct. Ellery will not accept a fee for his services as he considers investigative work research material. In the 1975 version, 212–A West 87th Street is mentioned as Ellery's address.

The first series added the character of Nikki Porter, Ellery's ever-faithful secretary and the girl who looks out for him because he won't look out for himself. *The Further Adventures of Ellery Queen* became simply *Ellery Queen* one month after it premiered. When the show moved production from New York to Los Angeles, Lee Phillips replaced George Nader as Ellery Queen and the character of Inspector Richard Queen was dropped. The stories also became original mysteries as opposed to adapting the novels to TV.

The 1975 series was set in 1947 and added the characters of Simon Brimmer (John Hillerman), a criminologist who tried to solve crimes before Ellery for his radio series, "The Case Book of Simon Brimmer"; and Frank Flannigan (Ken Swofford), an investigative reporter for the New York *Gazette*. Sergeant Velie, Richard's assistant, was played by Tom Reese. The radio series allowed listeners to play detective and try to guess "Who done it" before Ellery. All clues were given. The TV series tried to do the same thing. Viewers were given all the clues and nothing extra was given to Ellery. Keeping an eye out for the small, seemingly unimportant things was the key to solving the crime.

35. Eye to Eye (ABC, 1985)

Doyle and Poole — Private Investigators is a detective agency owned by Oscar Poole (Charles Durning) and Tracy Doyle (Stephanie Faracy), the slightly offbeat daughter of Oscar's original, late partner, Howard Doyle. When she was five years old Howard walked out on Tracy and her mother. Tracy and her mother survived as best as they could and Tracy became a Jill of all trades. Twenty years later, Howard attempts to re-establish ties with Tracy, but is killed during a case investigation before he can do so. Feeling that her father deserved better, Tracy teams with Oscar to find the killer. Oscar finds the case routine and boring; Tracy feels needed and wanted and convinces Oscar to let her remain his partner.

Doyle and Poole is located on Ventura Boulevard in Los Angeles. Tracy lives in a loft over a factory at 120 Waverly Boulevard; 555-0980 is her phone number and IGH 0568 is her car license plate number. In addition to solving crimes, Tracy does interior decorating, sells real estate and star maps, caters parties, is a Smoke Enders counselor and the personal manager of a famous singer. She has a dog named Pal, and her telephone answering machine message says, "Hi, this is Tracy. I'm not in right now. Wait a second, I think I hear myself coming up the elevator. No, it wasn't me, better leave a message."

Oscar is the aging private detective who calls Tracy "Doll" and "Pussycat." When rough characters are encountered, it is Oscar who takes the beating—"I didn't think he'd beat us up," says Tracy. Oscar clarifies it—"He didn't beat us up. He beat me up." Oscar and Tracy eat lunch at a fast food place called Tail of the Pup and dine at Sardi's. Oscar's lady love is Diane (Rita Taggert), a waitress at Sardi's. Oscar's favorite pastime appears to be buying Diane lingerie at Frederick's of Hollywood.

Jimmie Haskell composed the theme "Eye to Eye."

36. **Fastlane** (Fox, 2002)

The Candy Store is a secret L.A.P.D. warehouse that stores seized cars and weapons. It is also the headquarters for a team of undercover cops who use the contents of the warehouse to help bring criminals to justice. Wilhelmina Chambers (Tiffani Thiessen), called Billie, is a lieutenant who heads the unit. Detectives Van Ray (Peter Facinelli) and Deaquon Hayes (Bill Bellamy) are the young, ambitious and reckless agents she commands.

At first glance, Billie appears to be a beautiful and sensual woman. While she doesn't hesitate to use these assets in her undercover work, she is also tough and strictly business. She adheres to the rules she makes and expects Ray and Deaquon to follow them. Billie has been assigned by the department to apprehend criminals who appear too dangerous for ordinary law enforcers to handle. She has one commandment, that if broken, means immediate expulsion from the unit: "You never drop cover, you never flash a badge." Van and Deaquon's assignments require them to get the facts and report to Billie before busting a criminal. It is usually at this point that Billie actually enters a case—and often finds herself breaking her own rules big time if it means bringing a case to a satisfactory conclusion. Although Billie says, "We seize it, we keep it," she becomes upset when Ray and Deaquon wreck the equipment they are using. Steve McQueen is Billie's favorite actor and his movie *Bullet* gave her the inspiration to become a cop; "I identify with Steve McQueen," she says. Her beeper code is "Billie Club"; 2QCE 265 is her car license plate number.

Prior to becoming head of the Candy Store, Billie worked undercover as a narcotics cop. Her work for the unit earned her a gold shield, but it almost cost her her life. During one case, she passed herself off as a crooked cop. It worked, but in order to prove herself and break up a heroine ring, she shot heroine and became addicted. Her superior pulled her off the case and saved her life, but it cost Billie an important collar. The incident constantly frustrates Billie and she has taken up a bad, unflattering habit of smoking cigarettes which appears to disgust Van and Deaquon as they are trying to get her to quit.

Van dislikes his real first name of Donovan and uses an abbreviated version of it. He is the son of Raymond Ray, an expert counterfeiter known as "Ray Ray," who is serving time in prison. Van possesses a great deal of knowledge about counterfeiting and it sometimes helps him in his undercover work wherein he usually uses the alias Van Strummer. Van has a weakness for beautiful women and "becomes dumb around them," says Deaquon. Billie says, "Van gets too emotionally involved with his assignments and ruins his perspective." Van trusts people, takes unnecessary chances and takes things personally. He is always out to even up the score. He enjoys racing cars and being frisked by beautiful women when he goes undercover. Van's beeper code is "Vantogo" and EHO 537 is his car license plate.

Deaquon uses his streets smarts to deal with crime. He grew up in Torrence, California, but eventually drifted to New York where he ran with a gang before he turned his life around. He became a cop for the N.Y.P.D. and soon worked for its undercover narcotics unit. Deaquon's brother, Andre Hayes, is also a cop, for the L.A.P.D., and Van's partner. When Andre is killed during a case investigation, Deaquon travels to California to avenge Andre's death. He eventually meets Van and together manage to get arrested for fighting. They are bailed out by Billie, who has just been given permission to initiate her undercover team. With Billie's help, Deaquon and Ray find Andre's killers (drug dealers). Billie proposes her idea to Van and Deaquon and they accept. Deaquon's favorite movie is *The Towering Inferno*— by coincidence, a Steve McQueen movie. His middle name is Lavelle and "PRPL Hayes" is his beeper code. He enjoys Cocoa Puffs cereal for breakfast.

Bigg Snoop Dog and Charlie Clouser perform "The Theme from Fastlane."

37. Father Dowling Mysteries (NBC, 1989; ABC, 1990–1991)

Father Frank Dowling (Tom Bosley) is pastor of Saint Michael's Roman Catholic Church in Chicago. He is, as he says, "in the business of helping people." While he does so by comforting parishioners, he is also an avid mystery reader and fancies himself as an amateur sleuth. Sister Steve (Tracy Nelson), a nun at Saint Michael's Convent, works closely with Father Dowling, whom she calls Frank, helping him with his religious duties and assisting him as they turn detective to help people in trouble and solve crimes.

Frank has been a priest since 1958 and pastor of Saint Michael's for nine years. Prior to entering the seminary, Frank worked as a counselor for a parish youth group. It was here that Frank fell in love with a girl named Mary Ellen Connell. Thoughts about marriage forced Frank to change his plans about becoming a priest when he asked Mary Ellen to marry him. She accepted, but after a brief romance Mary Ellen felt that Frank was destined to become a priest and convinced him to return to the seminary. "I knew she was right," Frank says of the incident when he related the story to Sister Steve. Tom Bosley also played his twin brother Blaine, a con artist who sometimes complicates Frank's life.

Frank is a Cubs baseball fan; the literary character Sherlock Holmes is his mentor and he reads *Amateur Sleuth* magazine. Frank's exploits became the basis of an unsold television series called "Father Flaherty Investigates." Frank most often assists Sergeant Clancy (Regina Krueger) of the Homicide Bureau of the Chicago Police Department.

Sister Stephanie, affectionately called Sister Steve by her students at Saint Michael's Elementary School, is really Stephanie Oskowski, a streetwise juvenile delinquent Frank first met at F.W. Woolworth when he caught her stealing. Frank took the troubled girl under his wing and they became friends. His guidance helped her to make the right decision about becoming a nun. She was assigned to the Holy Mother Convent before coming to Saint Michael's. Stephanie's middle name taken at Confirmation is Sivle — Elvis spelled backward after her favorite singer, Elvis Presley. Steve can hot wire a car and has quick reflexes ("It's what you get from playing stickball in a rough neighborhood"). She also has street knowledge and the ability to pick locks. Her favorite part about helping Frank is going undercover in various disguises. Steve's favorite Chicago Zoo animal is Diogenes, a monkey she has known since she was a child. Steve can also cook and sometimes prepares the meals for Frank when Marie (Mary Wickes), the rectory cook and housekeeper, is out of town.

Marie first began working at Saint Michael's in 1967 when a Father Hunnicker was pastor. She feels that no matter what priest is in charge, all the hard work falls on her — cooking, cleaning and shopping. While Frank and Steve enjoy everything Marie cooks, their favorite dessert is her strawberry and rhubarb strudel. Marie drives a car with the license plate CGR

438 and was given two last names — first Brody then Gillespie. She did mention having two sisters — Mildred, who lives in Cleveland, and Rose, who lives in Florida.

While a normal rectory has several priests living there to accommodate those serving the parish, it appears that only Father Dowling is a resident at Saint Michael's Rectory. An occasional visitor is Father Philip Prestwick (James Stephens), the harassed Archdiocese liaison who finds Marie's cooking the best part of his stay. He has a fear of traveling; when he was eight years old, his parents lost him at O'Hare Airport. He also has a fear of elephants; when he was seven years old, an elephant at the zoo stole his sno-cone.

The church funds are kept at the First National Bank of Chicago. The parish station wagon has the license plate R3H 698 and is used by Frank and Steve for their investigative work. Frank doesn't drive and relies on Steve for all his transportation. In the pilot episode, the church car is a sedan (plate AA 101), and Frank helps his nephew, Phil Keegan (Robert Prescott) who is a police detective with the Metro Police Squad.

Dick DeBenedictis composed the theme.

Related Series (priests or rabbis as the central character)

1. *Sarge* (NBC, 1971–1972). Father Samuel Patrick Cavanaugh (George Kennedy) is a Catholic priest assigned to the St. Aloysius Parish in San Diego, California. Father Cavanaugh was a former police sergeant — worked under the name Sarge Swanson — who entered the priesthood after an assassin's bullet meant for him killed his wife instead. Although still emotionally shattered by the incident, Sarge, as Father Cavanaugh is called, uses his experiences as a police officer to solve the problems of his urban community.

2. *Lanigan's Rabbi* (NBC, 1977). David Small (Bruce Solomon) is a rabbi with the mind of a detective. He oversees the Temple Beth Hallel Synagogue in Cameron, California, and is friends with and assists Paul Lanigan (Art Carney), the community's Irish police chief.

Paul has been a cop for 22 years and lives with his wife, Kate (Janis Paige) at 3601 Sycamore Lane. He has an office in Room 121 of the Cameron P.D. and WQW 898 is his license plate number. Paul drinks a special blend of coffee he calls Turkish Coffee.

David and his wife, Mirian (Janet Margolin) live at 171 Circle Drive. His license plate reads 886 LYN and 555-1211 is his phone number. Stuart Margolin played Rabbi David Small in the TV movie pilot *The Rabbi Slept Late* (NBC, June 17, 1976).

3. *Helltown* (NBC, 1985–1986). Father Noah Rivers (Robert Blake) is pastor of St. Dominic's Parish and Orphanage in Helltown, a tough East Los Angeles neighborhood. Noah is actually an ex-con who turned his life around and became a Catholic priest. He now believes in protecting people from criminals and uses his street smarts as well as his forceful, and sometimes violent, nature to bring criminals to justice which has earned him the nickname "Guardian Angel of the Street"; in prison, he was called "Hardstep."

Mother Mary Margaret (Natalie Core), called "Maggie Jiggs," runs the orphanage. One Ball Tremayne (Whitman Mayo) is the pool hustler who helps Father Noah; and Brandy Wine (Tracy Morgan) is Noah's friend, hostess at the local bar, Roy Bean's.

Related Projects (unsold pilots with a priest or nun as the central character)

1. *Sanctuary of Fear* (NBC, April 23, 1979). The pilot film for a proposed "Father Brown, Detective" series. Father John Brown (Barnard Hughes) is an eccentric Catholic priest who is also pastor of the St. Eustacious parish in Manhattan. Father Brown is fascinated by murder and mayhem and considers himself to be an amateur sleuth. The series was to relate Father Brown's efforts to help the police, especially Lieutenant Bellamy (Michael McGuire) solve crimes. The pilot story finds Father Brown helping Carol Bain (Kay Lenz), a girl who witnessed a shooting but can't convince anyone that it actually happened. Based on the character created by G.K. Chesterton.

2. *Sister Michael Wants You* (CBS, May 13, 1994). Sister Michael (Delta Burke) is a Catholic nun and teacher assigned to the St. Claire Convent at 2810 Marlboro Road in Los Angeles. Her real name is Margaret Donovan and she is the daughter of Charlie Donovan, a famous mystery writer. Margaret grew up as a tomboy and was influenced by her father's writings; so much so that she possesses an uncanny knowledge of crime and believes she is an amateur sleuth. Sister Michael is also a Mother Superior, making her the youngest such Mother Superior in the Catholic church's history. The pilot story finds Sister Michael attempting to solve the murder of one of her former students. Aired on *Diagnosis Murder*.

38. The Gallery of Mme. Liu Tsong (DuMont, 1951)

Liu Tsong (Anna May Wong) is a beautiful Chinese woman who operates a chain of art galleries. Liu Tsong, whose name means Frosted Willow, was originally depicted as a tolerant, well-meaning business woman who not only had to face the problems of running her own empire—The Gallery of

Mme. Liu Tsong — but become her own detective to solve crimes associated with the art world (basically forgers and thieves who crave great works of art). She was not a fighter and did not use martial arts skills. She was clever and used her wits to bring criminals to justice.

Liu Tsong was born in Los Angeles and is the daughter of parents who operated a Chinese laundry. She worked after school and on Saturdays in the laundry ironing clothes and at an early age developed an interest in art. She carried this fascination with her into adult life, at which time she began her business. Six episodes later, the series became *Mme. Liu Tsong* and Anna May Wong was depicted as the owner of an import company that dealt with various art objects. While acquiring precious paintings was still her goal, she now had a large inventory and more corruption to fight. "I was now a good girl against bad men. A combination of the daughter of Fu Manchu and the daughter of the Dragon." Her new venture lasted for only five episodes. Liu Tsong, who speaks fluent Chinese but with an American accent, mentioned that Groucho Marx was her favorite comedian. With this series, Anna May Wong became the first Oriental personality to star in an American television program.

Related Project (Unsold Pilot)

Josephine Little (NBC). Three pilots were made about Josephine Little (Barbara Stanwyck), the owner of an import-export business in Hong Kong who risks her life to help people in trouble. The episodes, broadcast on *The Barbara Stanwyck Theater*, are: "The Miraculous Journey of Tadpole Chan" (November 14, 1960), "Dragon By the Tail" (January 30, 1961, with guest Anna May Wong as Ahsing) and "Adventure in Happiness" (March 20, 1961).

39. Get Christie Love (ABC, 1974–1975)

Christie Love (Teresa Graves) is a stunning undercover police woman with the Homicide Division, Metro Bureau of the L.A.P.D. Christie considers her beauty, charm, wit and understanding of human nature as her weapons. She wears badge number 7332 and lives at 3600 La Paloma Drive. Her phone number is 462-4699 and her car license plate reads 343 MCI, later 089 LIR. Christie's favorite eatery is Papa Caruso's Restaurant. She keeps her shooting skills sharp by practicing at a range called Hogan's Alley. Christie never shoots to kill — "Just enough to stop 'em." Christie uses the word "Sugah" often and "You're under arrest, Sugah" became her catchphrase.

Lieutenant Joe Caruso (Andy Romano) is Christie's partner; their car code is 5-Baker-5. Although Joe says, "My partner is a mean lady," Christie tends to panic and scream when she gets into a tight situation.

Arthur P. Ryan (Jack Kelly) is Christie's superior; his car code is 10-William-10. In the pilot episode (ABC, January 22, 1974), Andy Romano played Sergeant Seymour Greenberg, and Harry Guardino was the captain, Casey Reardon. Titos Vandis played Joe's father, "Papa" Luigi Caruso, the restaurant owner. See also *Police Woman*. Luchi DeJesus composed the theme "Get Christie Love."

40. The Great Defender (Fox, 1995)

"Do you need a lawyer? Call me, Lou Frischetti. Divorce, Accident, Criminal. Call me at 1-800-55-Legal" is one of a series of TV commercials called "The Great Defender" that are run by Lou Frischetti (Michael Rispoli), a fast-talking Boston attorney who represents the clients nobody else wants— from hookers to bookies.

Lou believes in justice for all and will use every trick in the book to defend his clients whether they are accused of petty theft or murder. Lou has a night school degree from the East Podoc School of Law. He is a bit unethical and knows what is going on—in the courtroom, the police precincts and on the streets. He sometimes invents his own theories about the law and promises his clients that "if there's trouble, I'll be there on the double." These are the qualities that attract Jason DeWitt (Richard Kiley), senior partner in the prestigious Beacon Hill law firm of Osborne, Merritt and DeWitt. Jason feels Lou is the man they need to bring life to the firm and get it out of a rut. Lou agrees, provided he can also hire his staff: his gorgeous investigator, Frankie Colletti (Kelly Rutherford) and his receptionist, his mother, Pearl Frischetti (Rhoda Gemignani).

Jason, a graduate of Harvard Law School, takes the heat for allowing Lou to use his street tactics to get results. The other partners feel Lou and his staff will bring the law firm down, not improve it. Frankie is Catholic and comes from an Italian background as does Lou. She respects her parents but prefers not to be called by her Christian name of Francesca—"I'm a Frankie, not a Francesca." Frankie grew up as a tomboy in Boston and is a graduate of Boston University. She has a degree in business management but became disenchanted with following that career choice and found a job as a secretary to then budding lawyer Lou Frischetti. Lou needed an investigator and quickly recruited Frankie for the job. Frankie is single and lives at 01342 Arlington Drive, Apartment 703. Lou lives with his mother at 462 Marlon Road. Jay Gruska composed the theme "The Great Defender."

41. Griff (ABC, 1973–1974)

Wade Griffin (Lorne Greene) is a former police captain with the Parker Center Division of the L.A.P.D. He is now a private detective who operates Wade Griffin Investigations at 19734 Mays Street in Westwood, California. Wade, called Griff, occupies office 1103½ and shares the floor with the following businesses: J.M. Bachman, D.D.S. (office 1103), and D.E. Mitner, Real Estate (office 1105). One other business is also listed on the building directory (1105½), but camera angles prevent the viewer from reading it. Griff's office phone number is 555-6696, and he drives a sedan with the license plate number 795 DCH. In another episode, his license plate reads A1121. His favorite restaurant is Farino's and he also does volunteer work for the Boys' Club. He carried badge number 26 when he was a police officer.

Mike Murdock (Ben Murphy) is Griff's legman and drives a car with the license plate 634 QTV. Grace Newcombe (Patricia Stich) is Griff's secretary. She lives at 43 Ridgedale Lane, Apartment 5C; 555-5515 is her phone number. Barney Martin (Vic Tayback) replaced Wade as the new police captain; his favorite lunch is pastrami on rye with mustard. The Parker Center Building, number 150, is dedicated to William H. Parker, 1950–1966, as stated on the plaque in front of the building.

Mike Post and Pete Carpenter composed the theme "Griff."

42. Hack (CBS, 2002)

The last line in the closing of each episode of *Naked City* was "There are eight million stories in the Naked City. This has been one of them." According to Mike Olshansky (David Morse), "There must be eight million and one because you sure don't know mine."

Mike is the subject of a police scandal. He had a record of 159 drug busts and was shot once in the shoulder. He also believes that being shot at and risking his life day after day entitles him to hazard pay. Since the Philadelphia Police Department does not see things Mike's way, Mike created his own fund. During a drug bust, 40 grand was left on a table. Mike and his partner, Marcellus Washington (Andre Braugher) turned in $32,000, keeping four thousand each for themselves as hazard pay. Mike was caught and discharged ("No modified duty, no pension. Goodbye"). Marcellus was not caught and Mike did not turn him in. They are still good friends.

Mike is bitter although he says classical music calms him. The scandal cost him his marriage and his close relationship with his son. To make ends meet, Mike acquired a job as a cab driver for the Victory Cab Company although South Side Taxi Exchange is seen on the door of his hack. Although not a cop, Mike can't stop thinking about crime. His police upbringing (six uncles in law enforcement) can't let crime fighting go unnoticed. "I'm just a cabdriver, but deep down I'm still a cop." It is when Mike has a consultation with his friend, Father Tom Gizelak (George Dzundza), that Mike is made to see his pain. "It's called change," Father Tom tells him, and he must atone for his disgrace.

Mike works the night shift. After dropping off a fare, Mike sees a mugging about to take place and steps in. He saves a man and believes he has found a purpose — to help those who are unable to help themselves. "You got a problem? I can look into that for you," he tells potential clients.

Although not an official private detective, Mike takes on the responsibilities of one. He tells his clients after solving the case, "You will testify against these monsters and send them to jail. You will tell the police everything but you will leave out one detail — me. I was never here."

Mike is under a felony indictment and is not permitted to carry a gun. He uses tools or whatever is handy as a weapon. Mike's cab number reads P-2626; 555-0100 is the cab company phone number; and H-18840 is his cab certificate number which expires 11-30-03. TX 2300 is his cab license plate number and Mike's favorite hangout is a bar called Bernie's Tap. Father Tom, nicknamed "Grizz," is pastor of Saint Victor's Church. Heather (Donna Murphy) is Mike's estranged wife, a nurse; Michael, Jr. (Matthew Borish) is Mike's son, with whom he is trying to become a father again. In early episodes, Mike, Jr. is bitter and used his middle name of David as his first name. As the series progressed, Mike, Jr. went back to using his original first name; however, Heather filed for divorce.

Stephen Phillips composed the theme.

43. **Hardball** (NBC, 1989–1990)

Charlie Battles (John Ashton) is a veteran police officer with the Metro Division of the Los Angeles Police Department. Joe Kaczierowski (Richard Tyson) is his young, street-wise partner. Together, they incorporate experience with youthful enthusiasm to apprehend criminals. They are members of the Slammers baseball team and 1-K-9 is their car code.

Charlie, badge number 6483, fought in the Korean War (52nd Unit of the U.S. Army Air Corps). He is forceful and sometimes incorporates his battle experiences to deal with criminals. Charlie weighs 205 pounds, eats Oaties breakfast cereal and drives a car with the license plate 2LYN 596. While not a gourmet cook, Charlie claims he can make the best chili in town.

Joe, called "Kaz" by Charlie, was formerly a vice squad detective with the San Diego Police Department. He weighs 192 pounds and rides a motorcycle with the license plate 25862L. Kaz prefers undercover work and uses various disguises to accomplish his goal. He wears badge number 696 and listens to radio station KRTW. Lydia Cornell plays his favorite D.J., the sexy-voiced Jamie Steele. Eddie Money sings the theme "Roll It Over."

44. Hardcastle and McCormick (ABC, 1983–1986)

Milton C. Hardcastle (Brian Keith) is a Los Angeles Criminal Courts judge who has been nicknamed "Hardcase" for his harsh courtroom sentences and outrageous procedures. Milton was born in Clarence, Arkansas, and was a police officer before becoming a judge. He now faces retirement. Rather than give up his crusade against injustice, Milton decides to continue his battle against crime. During his time as a judge, the cases of 200 criminals were dismissed due to technicalities. Now, with time on his hands, he has set his goal to bring to justice those who escaped doing time.

Mark McCormick (Daniel Hugh Kelly), a race car driver up for his third offense for grand theft auto, is brought before Judge Hardcastle days before his retirement. Feeling that Mark possesses the abilities he needs to help him in his crusade, Milton offers him a choice: serve time in jail "or work with me." Mark, nicknamed "Skid" because of his reckless driving, chooses to work with the judge who becomes his parole officer.

Mark and the judge set up headquarters—Hardcastle and McCormick, Inc.—at 101 Pacific Coast Highway in Malibu Beach, California, on an estate owned by Milton called Gull's Way. Although strangers when they first met, Mark and the judge become close. They constantly bicker over the legalities of a case; Mark wants to do it his way, the judge by the book. As the series progressed, it became evident that Milton saw Mark as the son he and his late wife never had; and Mark saw the judge as the father who had been absent from his life (ran off when he was a child).

Gull's Way overlooks a portion of the beach called Seagull Beach. Milton proposed to his wife here and he considers it his own private beach. He drives a black and gray pickup with the license plate 2P34 525. Milton also served as the substitute judge on the television show "You Be the Judge."

Mark, who turned to a life of crime to supplement his racing income, drives a red Manta sports car called the *Coyote*—also its license plate—and became so impressed by Milton that he began attending law school. In the last episode he was offered a paralegal job and worked part time at the law firm of Malcolm, Hughes and Dewitt doing investigative work. It was also at this time that Mark's parole was up. Though no longer bound to the judge, he decided to remain with him to help him complete his goal.

David Morgan sings the first season theme "Drive"; Joey Scarbury performs the subsequent theme "Back to Back."

Proposed Series Spinoff (Unsold Pilot)

Hardcastle, Hardcastle, Hardcastle and McCormick (February 4, 1985). A series that was to revolve around May and Zora Hardcastle (Mildred Natwick, Mary Martin), the elderly, spinster sisters of Judge Milton C. Hardcastle. The sisters are avid mystery fans and consider themselves amateur sleuths. Stories would have focused on their efforts to solve the various crimes they encounter. In the pilot episode, May and Zora seek the help of Milton and Mark to solve the murder of a famous mystery writer.

45. The Hardy Boys (ABC, 1957; 1969; 1977; NBC, 1967; Syndicated, 1995)

The adventures of Frank and Joe Hardy, the sons of famed private detective Fenton Hardy, were created in 1926 by Edward Stratemeyer. As owner of the Stratemeyer Syndicate, he created story plots but used ghost writers to compile the stories under the pseudonym Franklin W. Dixon. The first Hardy Boys book, *The Tower Treasure*, appeared in 1927, and to December 31, 2002 over 400 stories have been published in several different book series. Surprisingly, a feature film or movie serial was never produced. Television, however, jumped on the bandwagon in 1957, and to December 31, 2002, four live action series, an unsold pilot and an animated series have been produced.

The overall setting for each of the series is the town of Bayport on Barmet Bay, an inlet three miles inland from the Atlantic Ocean. The town has a population of about 50,000 and the Hardys live in a large home at the corner of Elm and High Streets. The principal characters in each of the stories are amateur sleuths Frank and Joe Hardy, the sons of master detective Fenton Hardy. Fenton was a former detective with the N.Y.P.D. who now works as a private investigator in Bayport; he quit the force so he could solve crimes on his own. His knack for solving complex mysteries have made him a much sought after detective. While Fenton is married to Laura in books, he is a widower on television and he, the house and his sons are cared for by Fenton's spinster sister, Gertrude Hardy, affectionately called Aunt Gertrude. She lives with Fenton on the TV versions, but only visits in the books.

Frank and Joe attend Bayport High School. Frank is the older, more serious brother. He tends to think about something before acting upon it. He is astute at figuring out, then analyzing, clues. Joe is a year younger than Frank and too impatient. He often plunges into a situation without thinking first and worries about the consequences after the fact. While both boys are scientifically inclined, it is Frank who sets the investigative pace of a case, usually connected to one involving Fenton.

The Television Versions

1. ***The Hardy Boys and the Mystery of the Applegate Treasure*** (ABC Serial, January 7 to February 1, 1957, as a segment of *The Mickey Mouse Club*). An adaptation of the first book, *The Tower Treasure*. Iola Morton, a character from the books, appears in this and the next version only. Iola is Joe's age and his classmate at Bayport High School. She is very pretty and very prone to danger. She is constantly being saved by Frank and Joe. In books, Joe dated Iola. On television, Joe liked Iola but didn't date her. He spent more time avoiding her innocent romantic advances than accepting them.

The Hardys address is given as 8966 Elm Street; 16–943 is Fenton's license plate number. *The Cast:* Russ Conway (Fenton Hardy), Tim Considine (Frank Hardy), Tommy Kirk (Joe Hardy), Carole Ann Campbell (Iola Morton), Sarah Selby (Aunt Gertrude). The story finds Frank, Joe and Iola, who wants to be a Hardy Boy for the excitement it offers, attempting to find a pirate's treasure that was stolen from the estate of Silas Applegate (Florenz Ames), the owner of the rundown mansion where most of the action takes place.

2. ***The Hardy Boys and the Mystery of Ghost Farm*** (ABC Serial, September 30 to October 15, 1957, as a segment of *The Mickey Mouse Club*. An original story — not adapted from the books — that uses the same cast as the prior serial. Here, Frank, Joe and Iola attempt to solve the mystery of a supposedly haunted farm. The farm is deserted but Joe believes a ghost is feeding and caring for the animals. In reality, it is the farm's owner, who faked his death to collect the insurance money and care for the animals.

3. ***The Hardy Boys*** (Unsold Pilot, NBC, September 8, 1967). Richard Anderson as Fenton Hardy; Tim Matthieson (now Tim Matheson) as Joe Hardy; Rick Gates as Frank Hardy; and Portia Nelson as Aunt Gertrude. The story, titled "The Mystery of the Chinese Junk," finds Frank and Joe attempting to find a stolen Jade collection.

4. ***The Hardy Boys*** (Animated Series, ABC, 1969–1971). *Voices:* Byron Kane (Frank Hardy, Fenton Hardy), Dallas McKennon (Joe Hardy), Jane

Webb (Aunt Gertrude). Frank and Joe have established a band called The Hardys, wherein they each sing and play guitar, with their friends: guitarist Pete Jones (Byron Kane), singer Wanda Kay Breckenridge (Jane Webb) and drummer Chubby Morton (Dallas McKennon). Stories find them investigating mysteries in the various cities they visit. A real life rock band called The Hardys was formed to perform the music heard on the show and match the animated characters. Reed Karling was Frank Hardy; Jeff Taylor, Joe Hardy; Deven English, Wanda Kay Breckenridge; Bob Crowder, Pete Jones; and Nibs Soltysiak, Chubby Morton.

5. *The Hardy Boys Mysteries* (ABC, 1977–1979). Also known as *The Hardy Boys–Nancy Drew Mysteries*. The series continues the crime-solving exploits of Frank and Joe Hardy (Parker Stevenson, Shaun Cassidy), the amateur sleuths of world famous private detective Fenton Hardy (Edmund Gilbert). Edith Atwater played Aunt Gertrude and Lisa Eilbacher was Callie Shaw, Fenton's secretary. As originally written, Callie and Frank attended Bayport High School together. He often dated her, but on TV they were just good friends. Frank and Joe also worked with Nancy Drew (see *Nancy Drew*) and government agents Harry Gibbon (Philip R. Allen) and Harry Hammond (Jack Kelly).

6. *The Hardy Boys* (Syndicated, 1995–1996). The series is set in Bayport and the Hardy Boys have graduated from high school. Frank (Colin Gray) is now 22 years old and a reporter for the *Bayport Eagle*. Joe (Paul Popowich), two years younger, is a student at Bayport College and a computer enthusiast. Frank's license plate reads H3B IF2. Fiona Highet plays Kate Craigen, the paper's city editor (Frank's boss) and Ken Samuels appears as Fenton Hardy. Frank and Joe team to solve crimes in conjunction with the Bayport Metro Police Department. Frank is still depicted as the more responsible brother while Joe maintains the trouble attracting traits of the first serial and books.

Related Project (Unsold Pilot)

The Tom Swift and Linda Craig Mystery Hour (ABC, July 3, 1983). An adaptation of the Tom Swift detective stories created by Edward Stratemeyer. Tom Swift (Willie Aames) is a scientific genius who teams with his cousin, Linda Craig (Lori Loughlin) to solve crimes. In the pilot episode, "The Treasure of Rancho del Sol," Tom and Linda attempt to rescue their grandfather, Bronco (William Windom) from fortune hunters seeking a legendary treasure. *Other regulars:* Kathy Hamilton (Amanda Wyss), Linda's cousin; Rad Gorman (Christopher Blande), Tom's friend; and Grandma Malloy (Carmen Zapata), Bronco's wife.

46. Harry O (ABC, 1974–1976)

On Friday, January 18, 1969, police detective Harry Orwell and his partner responded to a burglary-in-progress at a drugstore. It is 1:20 A.M. when a shootout occurs between the cops and the suspect. Harry is shot in the back and his partner is killed.

When the series begins, Harry Orwell (David Janssen) has retired from the police department. He is living on his disability pension and supplementing his income by moonlighting as a private detective. He has a bullet lodged near his spine and vigorous activity like running after a suspect causes pain. Harry lives in a beach front house in San Diego and is working on a boat he calls *The Answer* ("which I'll have as soon as I put it back together. I'm going out on the ocean where they have no telephones; telephones bug me").

Harry has a gun but rarely uses it. He has a car but does a lot of walking. The car, an ancient Austin-Healey MG, needs numerous repairs — all of which Harry is unable to afford. He will ride the bus or spring for a cab when he needs transportation ("It's tax deductible"). Harry shops for groceries at the nearby Agryz Market.

Harry never discusses politics or the shooting that disabled him. He isn't particularly friendly, but a good friend to those who know him. He is a bit grouchy, more stubborn than he was before, and he is just now realizing that his chances for a true romance are becoming increasingly slimmer as he grows older. He wishes he were 17 again "because when I was 17 I once said, 'A woman is like a bus. There'll be another one along in a few minutes.' Now that was a long time ago."

When a case investigation takes Harry to Los Angeles, he rents an apartment. Shortly after, he learns that his home in San Diego is being torn down to make room for a high rise building. With the help of his neighbor, an airline stewardess named Betsy (Katherine Baumann), Harry finds a beach front home at 1101 Coast Road in Santa Monica; 555-4617 is his phone number. Linzy (a brunette Loni Anderson), Gina (Barbara Leigh) and Sue Ingham (Farrah Fawcett) become Harry's often bikini-clad neighbors. Sue, an airline stewardess, and Harry become romantically involved although Harry has a difficult time adjusting to Sue's Great Dane, Grover, a dog who just doesn't seem to like Harry.

First season episodes feature Henry Darrow as Manuel Quinlan, a lieutenant with the San Diego Police Department. Manuel, called Manny, was a by-the-books, uptight cop who trusted Harry and worked with him to bring criminals to justice. When the series locale switched to Los Angeles,

Lieutenant K.C. Trench (Anthony Zerbe) was brought on to replace Manny who was killed off in the episode "Elegy for a Cop." Trench had mixed feelings about Harry and disliked Harry's casual mannerisms and ability to rely on intuition rather than hard evidence. "I don't trust hunches," says Trench.

Billy Goldenberg composed the theme "Harry O."

Note: Two pilots were produced for the series.

1. ***Such Dust As Dreams Are Made Of*** (ABC, March 11, 1973). The pilot establishes that Harry was a detective with the Los Angeles Police Department and he was shot in the back by Harlan Garrison (Martin Sheen) while responding to a robbery-in-progress at a drugstore. Harry's police department contact is Lieutenant Arvin Grainger (Mel Stewart). The pilot story finds Harry as a private detective and being hired by the now free Harlan Garrison to protect him from a man who has put a contract out on his life. Richard Hazard composed the original theme.

2. ***Smile Jenny, You're Dead*** (ABC, February 3, 1974). Harry is established as a private detective working out of San Diego. In the pilot story, Harry investigates the death of a friend's son-in-law. Billy Goldenberg composed the theme.

Proposed Spinoffs (Unsold Pilots)

1. ***Lester*** (January 8, 1976). Second season episodes of *Harry O* feature Les Lannon in the recurring role of Lester Hodges. Les is a student criminologist who stumbles upon and solves crimes quite by accident. Two attempts were made to spin the character off into a series of his own. In the first pilot, titled "Mr. Five and Dime," Lester teams with Harry to crack a counterfeiting case.

2. ***Lester and Dr. Fong*** (March 18, 1976). The second pilot teams Lester (Les Lannon) with his college mentor, Dr. Creighton Fong (Keye Luke) for a proposed series dealing with their criminal case investigations. The story finds the duo seeking a killer who is systematically disposing of Lester's family.

47. Hart to Hart (ABC, 1979–1984).

Jonathan and Jennifer Hart (Robert Wagner, Stefanie Powers) are a husband and wife fascinated by crime. While not officially private detectives, they use their expertise as amateur crime sleuths to help people in trouble. Jonathan and Jennifer live at 3100 Willow Pond Road in Bel Air; 555-1654 (later 555-3223) is their phone number. They have a dog named Freeway, whom they found stranded on the freeway, and a man Friday, Max (Lionel Stander).

Jonathan is the wealthy head of Hart Industries, located at 112 North Las Palmas in Los Angeles. He started the company in March of 1969 when he issued its first shares of stock. The Hart Shipping Lines and Chem-O-Cal are two of the many divisions of Hart Industries, the phone number of which is 555-1271.

Jennifer, maiden name Edwards, was born in Hillhaven, Maryland. She had a horse named Sweet Sue, attended Gresham Hall Prep School, and majored in journalism at an unnamed college. After graduation, Jennifer moved to New York City to become a freelance journalist. While on assignment in England for the London *Herald*, Jennifer learns that Jonathan has come to the city to close a big deal (prevent Kingsford Motors from going bankrupt). Her efforts to get an interview with the press-shy Jonathan fail until they meet by chance at the bar of the Hotel Ritz and find an instant attraction to each other. After a brief courtship, they marry and honeymoon at the O'Berge Inn, Room 7, in San Francisco's Napa Valley.

Jennifer gets a little tipsy from champagne, lunches at La Scala's and has her hair done at Salvatore's on Wilshire Boulevard. Jennifer also appeared in a bit part (a party hostess) on her favorite daytime television soap opera, "Doctors' Hospital." Stefanie Powers also played her double, Dominique Bitten, a mobster's wife. Nikki Stefunos (Christina Belford) was Jonathan's romantic interest before Jennifer. Jonathan has pancakes for breakfast on Monday mornings.

Max does the cooking, cleaning, driving and whatever else needs to be done at home. He enjoys a good cigar and is addicted to gambling. He and Freeway did a commercial for Dog Gone It dog food. The Harts license plates read HART I, HART II (also seen as 2 HARTS) and HART III. Roger Nichols composed the theme "Hart to Hart."

Note: Robert Wagner, Stefanie Powers and Lionel Stander reunited for a series of TV movies that aired after the original series ended (Lionel appears in all but the last one in 1996): *Hart to Hart Returns* (1993), *Hart to Hart: Crimes of the Hart* (1994), *Hart to Hart: Hart Throb* (1994), *Hart to Hart: Home Is Where the Hart Is* (1994), *Hart to Hart: Old Friends Never Die* (1994), *Hart to Hart: Secrets of the Hart* (1995) and *Hart to Hart: Harts in High Season* (1996).

48. The Hat Squad (CBS, 1992–1993)

In Los Angeles in the 1940s, a special unit of police officers called the Hat Squad fought criminals. They were identified by their black fedoras and dusters and had no respect for the law; they did whatever it took to ensure justice. The squad was eventually retired when it was determined that the police officers were above the limits of the law.

Mike Ragland (James Tolkan) is a present-day captain with the 77th Precinct of the L.A.P.D. In an attempt to fight back at the new breed of criminal, Mike organizes a four man unit he calls the Hat Squad. Like the original unit, the new squad, nicknamed "The Hats," has little respect for the law. They wear black fedoras and dusters and specialize in solving violent crimes — "by whatever means we can within or just above the law." The new Hat Squad is made up of Mike and his three sons: Buddy Capatosa (Don Michael Paul), Raphael Martinez (Nestor Serrano) and Matt Matheson (Billy Warlock), three orphans of crime who were adopted by Mike and his wife, Kitty (Shirley Douglas, Janet Carroll) and raised to be police officers.

Buddy, the eldest son, drives a 1965 Mustang with the license plate THE BEAST; BH-2 is his car code. He believes the Fortunata crime family is responsible for his parents' deaths and has sworn to prove it and bring them to justice. Raphael, called Raffi, is a ladies' man; he calls himself "The Prince of Puerto Rico." He has the car code BH-1 and BVN 891 is his license plate number. He is a graduate of Jefferson High School and carries a special Jack of Spades playing card that is a certified weapon. It has razor sharp edges and he says, "It's my calling card." Raphael saw his parents gunned down and refuses to carry a firearm. Matt, the youngest, attended Hoover High School. He is taking night classes in pre-law and BH-3 is his car code. He is obsessed with apprehending criminals who prey on children. Mike and Kitty also have a younger, adopted 12-year-old son named Darnell Johnson (Bruce Robbins), who is being groomed as a future Hat Squad member.

The squad wears Second Chance bullet proof vests. Mike's car code is 1-Zero-30 (later X-Ray-6) and MXN 701 is his car license plate number. When a female decoy is needed, the Hats use the station's CPR doll (Officer Jill) because they fear using a real woman is too dangerous.

Mike Post composed the theme.

49. **Haunted** (UPN, 2002)

Frank Taylor (Matthew Fox) is an ex-cop turned private detective who says "I'm haunted." He can communicate with the dead and uses their help to solve crimes. For Frank it began during his investigation of a missing child. Frank found the child but was stabbed by the culprit. Frank was rushed to the hospital but flatlined during an operation to save his life. During the time he spent between the worlds of life and death, Frank experienced a brief encounter with the world beyond. He was resuscitated seconds later and brought back from the brink of death. But he retained a link with departed souls who now haunt him.

Frank's business, Frank Taylor Investigations, is located in an office above the Black Hawk Bar (street number 395) in Los Angeles. He was a cop for eight years before becoming dissatisfied with his job and starting his own service. The onset of a splitting headache is usually an indication that spirits are trying to contact him. Not all his unearthly encounters are nice; some are pure evil who seek to kill him, especially the pasty-white ghost of murderer Simon Dunn (John Mann) who literally haunts Frank and "scares the hell out of me." Frank was with the 10th Precinct, has a dog named Gus who can sense when spirits are trying to contact Frank, and drives a car with the license plate 23B 617.

Frank believes ghosts contact him because they are in limbo with unfinished business and cannot move on until they complete a mission. "That's where I come in," he says. Frank is divorced from Jessica Manning (Lynn Collins) and is the father of Kevin, a boy who mysteriously disappeared several years ago. Lynn is an assistant D.A. and helps Frank collar criminals "because I'm sick of seeing bad guys getting breaks." Frank often works with his former police partner, Marcus Bradshaw (Russell Hornsby), who calls Frank's lone pursuit of criminals Lone Ranger tactics. Marcus was previously a cop with the New Orleans Police Department.

Frank can also receive visions of people in danger. And sometimes Frank is too late to help. Mark Snow composed the theme "Haunted."

Press information states that *Haunted* "is the first series about a sleuth sought by poltergeists." This is simply not true. The following pilots and series used the premise long before *Haunted*.

Related Projects (Unsold Pilots)

1. ***The World of Darkness*** (CBS, April 17, 1977). Paul Taylor (Granville Van Dusen) is a sportswriter who helps the living through messages he receives from spirits. For Paul it began after a serious motorcycle accident. During an operation to save his life, Paul apparently dies. After two-and-a-half minutes of clinical death, Paul is resuscitated. Paul, however, retains a thread tying him to a world through which the dead compel him to help people threatened by the occult. The story finds Paul helping Clara Sanford (Tovah Feldshuh) battle an evil presence.

A second pilot, titled *The World Beyond*, aired on CBS on January 27, 1978. Here Paul Taylor (Granville Van Dusen) receives a message from the dead to help Marian Faber (JoBeth Williams) battle an evil creature of mud called a Golem.

2. *Landon, Landon & Landon* (CBS, June 14, 1980). Ben Landon (William Windom) is the owner of the Hollywood-based Landon Private Detective Agency. When Ben is killed during a case, he returns as a ghost to help his children, Holly and Nick Landon (Nancy Dolman, Daren Kelly) run the agency.

3. *Quick and Quiet* (CBS, August 18, 1981). T.C. Cooper (William Windom) is a disreputable private eye who owns the Los Angeles-based Quick and Quiet Detective Agency. When T.C. is killed during a case, his son, Elliott Cooper (Rick Lohman) inherits the agency as well as T.C.'s ghost, who has returned to make his ne'er-do-well son become a productive citizen.

4. *Justin Case* (ABC, May 15, 1988). Jennifer Spaulding (Molly Hagan) is an apprentice private detective who solves cases with a most unusual partner: the ghost of her boss, Justin Case (George Carlin) who was killed while investigating a case and has returned to guide Jennifer's life.

Related Series

1. *My Partner the Ghost* (Syndicated, 1973). Randall and Hopkirk — Private Investigators is a London-based detective agency. Jeff Randall (Mike Pratt) operates the agency with the help of the ghost of his late partner, Marty Hopkirk (Kenneth Cope). Marty was killed while investigating a case. He returned as a ghost to solve his murder, but in doing so, he violated an ancient rhyme — "Before the sun shall rise on you, each ghost unto his grave must go" — and is cursed to remain on Earth for 100 years. Marty resumes his former life to spiritually assist Jeff and watch over his wife, Jean (Annette Andre).

Jean, who cannot see or hear Marty, lives at 36 Paddington Square, Apartment E; Vincent 6-3840 is her phone number. Jeff resides at 112 Stable Mews, Apartment 7; 067-3864 is his phone number, and his license plate reads RXD 996F. The series is also known as *Randall and Hopkirk (Deceased)*.

2. *Shades of L.A.* (Syndicated, 1990). A shade is a ghost with unfinished business that has to be completed in order for it to find closure. Michael Burton (John DiAquino) is a detective with the Westside Division of the L.A. Metro Police Department. During a stakeout Burton is shot. While recuperating in a hospital, he has a mystical, near-death experience that places him in contact with the world beyond. He is now haunted by these spirits as they seek his help in completing their earthly missions so they can move on to their destinies.

Michael attended Radford High School (class of '75) and had the nickname "Bare Butt Burton" for mooning teachers. His car code is 2-Baker-3 and his license plate reads BLAST OFF. His badge number is seen as 2147 in the opening theme but is mentioned as being 508. Years ago Michael was shot in the head and carries a small fragment of the bullet in his brain. He believes that metal fragment provides contact with the shades.

3. *Dead Last* (WB, 2001). Jane Cahill (Sara Downing), Scott Sallback (Tyler Labine) and Vaughn Parrish (Kett Turton) are members of the rock band Problem. Their first CD sold 14 copies. Jane and Vaughn play guitar; Scott, the drums. They drive a van, plate 860 YAA, and take whatever gigs they can find. They also possess the Amulet of Sauryn, a magical jewel that compels them to right wrongs by helping ghosts find closure.

It began during a band rehearsal in a nightclub when a fuse blew. While checking the fuse box, Scott received an electric shock. He was thrown against a wall and onto the floor. The floor caved in and Scott plummeted down a twenty-foot hole. There he found the amulet which gave him the power to see the dead.

The amulet cannot be destroyed, given away or discarded. If it is, it magically returns to its owner. Although Scott is the unfortunate owner of the amulet, Jane and Vaughn are also cursed to see ghosts. Each ghost they encounter requires their help. If they refuse to help any spirit, they will be haunted by that spirit. The amulet is theirs for life, and death is the only known escape (a release from its grip).

Jane has a coffee mug that reads "Bad Hair Day." She wrote the song "Copper Wire"; Vaughn wrote the song "Little Blue Pills." Nathan Larson composed the theme.

50. **Hawaiian Eye** (ABC, 1959–1963)

Hawaiian Eye — Investigation-Protection is a private detective organization located in the lobby of the Hawaiian Village Hotel in Honolulu, Hawaii. The agency is also called a security firm and was also said to be at the Hilton Hawaiian Village Hotel. Tracy Steele (Anthony Eisley), Tom Lopaka (Robert Conrad) and Gregg MacKenzie (Grant Williams) are "The Eyes," as they are called, who provide the hotel security and hire out their investigative services to help people in trouble.

Chryseis Blake (Connie Stevens), called Cricket, is a singer who runs Cricket's Corner, the hotel's gift shop. Phil Barton (Troy Donahue) is the director of special events at the hotel. While not detectives, both assist "The Eyes" on cases when needed.

Cricket is 20 years old and in love with life. She is five feet two inches tall and measures 37-20-36. She was born in San Francisco and enjoys jazz music. When she was a teenager, she would hang out at Fisherman's Wharf to hear a trumpet player named Joey Vito perform. She now frequents the Blue Grotto Club on Kalakalu Street in Honolulu to hear her idol perform. Cricket performs in the Hawaiian Village Hotel's Shell Bar (also seen as the Shell Lounge) and is an amateur photographer. She hopes to make it big one day by selling her pictures to newspapers. Phil was born in Florida and calls Cricket "The original do-gooder" as she will help people she believes are in trouble. When Connie Stevens left the series for a short time in 1963, she was replaced by Tina Cole as Sunny Day, a hopeful singer who worked at the Hawaiian Village Hotel's information booth.

Gregg was born in Los Angeles and had originally planned to become a police officer. After graduating from UCLA he became interested in private investigating and worked briefly in California before relocating to Hawaii. His car license plate reads LPQ 401. Tom, born in Hawaii, is the son of a fisherman. His car license plate reads 643 421. Tracy, born in New York City, had studied law but yearned for a life of danger and intrigue. He worked briefly in his chosen field but eventually gave it up to become a private investigator. His car license plate reads JK3 961. Cricket drives a jeep, license plate M31 071; Phil's license plate reads 15-652.

Kim Kasano (Poncie Ponce) is a cab driver and owner of Kim's Cab, who does occasional work for Tracy and Tom; 7T 403 is his license plate number. Danny Quon (Mel Prestidge) is the police lieutenant who assists "The Eyes."

The Cafe House is the diner frequented by the regulars. Hotel benefits are held in the Dome Room; an ad for United Airlines can be seen on the window next to Cricket's Corner. Tom and Tracy call Cricket "Lover"; when Tracy needs Kim to follow a suspect, he says, "Control to Kim," via a radio link.

Mack David and Jerry Livingston composed the theme "Hawaiian Eye."

51. **Heart of the City** (ABC, 1986–1987)

Wes Kennedy (Robert Desiderio) is a detective with the Los Angeles Police Department. He is a widower and the father of two children, Robin (Christina Applegate) and Kevin (Jonathan Ward).

Wes solves 24 percent of his case load, which is 10 percent higher than the rate of other cops in the precinct. He became a cop "To get the animals off the streets. It's what I do, it's what has to be done." Wes has a photographic memory and an impressive arrest record but too many shootings. Wes lives at 5503 Pacific Way and his car license plate reads ICYD 198. In the pilot episode, the house number reads 4607. Wes is dating Kathy Priester (Kay Lenz), a waitress at a diner called Trio's Grill.

Wes is still haunted by the memory of his wife Susan's death. Wes was a street cop who was chosen to head a S.W.A.T. (Special Weapons and Tactics) team for the L.A.P.D. One day, while exercising to a television aerobics show, Susan sees a bulletin about a shooting involving a S.W.A.T. team. Fearing that Wes may have been shot, Susan ignores Wes's warnings about never going to a crime scene and rushes out of the house. Susan's mind is eased when she sees that Wes is fine. Seconds later a shooting occurs between the cops and criminals and Susan is killed in the crossfire.

It is 18 months later when the series begins. Robin is 16 years old and bitter; she blames Wes for her mother's death. Robin was sweet and innocent and held the image of the pretty girl next door. She has now drastically changed her image. She has shortened her hair, developed an attitude and dresses in clothes one would attribute to a high priced call girl. "I may look like a tramp, but boys are not getting near me — no way, no chance. I dress to please myself, not some boy." Robin attends West Hollywood High School and takes dance lessons. She played Beauty in a "Beauty and the Beast"–themed rock video. Robin claims that dance is a celebration to make people feel good. Although Robin is very attractive she says, "I don't think I'm as beautiful as other people see me." As the series progressed, Robin mellowed. She became less bitter when she forgave her father for what happened to her mother.

Kevin is 15 years old. He also attends West Hollywood High and while studious, he is confused by girls and doesn't know what to make of them. He is bright and wears glasses and thinks girls want muscles not brains. Wes mentioned that Kevin gets A's and B's from his male teachers and C's from his female teachers but can't explain why.

Ed Van Duzer (Dick Anthony Williams) is Wes's superior, the watch commander. Sergeant Halui (Branscombe Richmond) is the Hawaiian-by-birth cop who calls everyone Brother. Patrick Williams composed the theme "Heart of the City."

Hell Town *See* Father Dowling Mysteries

52. Honey West (ABC, 1965–1966)

H. West and Company is a Los Angeles-based private detective organization owned by Honey West (Anne Francis), a shapely (36-24-34) blonde who inherited the company and her partner, Sam Bolt (John Ericson), from her late father. Sam made a promise that he would look after Honey and keep her out of trouble if anything happened to her father. Honey had assisted her father and Sam and has now become a much sought after detective.

Honey operates out of her luxurious apartment at 6033 Del Mar Vista in Los Angeles. She is shrewd, uncanny and capable of defending herself. Although she possesses a black belt in karate, she does take an occasional beating. Honey uses the latest in scientific equipment; for example, her lipstick, earrings and compact double as a transmitter and Sam's eyeglasses encompass a miniature receiver. She incorporates a mobile base of operations disguised as a TV repair truck (H. West TV Repairing); license plate 1406 122, later IET 974. In some scenes, the truck is seen with a name printed on its sides; in others, the sides are blank. Honey has a pet ocelot named Bruce and the wall displaying various vases in Honey's apartment is actually the secret entrance to her lab behind the living room wall. The wall is later bare. An ornament to the right of it has a secret button that opens the wall to reveal the lab. Honey carries a gun — and uses it. Her earrings also double as miniature gas bombs when thrown and broken. When Honey becomes upset, she takes her anger out on target practice figures and always hits the bullseye. "I come here for practice," she says, "not therapy" as Sam thinks. "If you say so," Sam says. Honey is not always successful and does let clients down. She often risks her life by going undercover to solve a case such as a society woman or wealthy playgirl. She and Sam try to cooperate with the police but Honey can't promise they will always go by the book.

"That West dame and her partner, they're rough to handle," say felons. Some say, "Honey West, the girl private eye. Well, well, well. Don't you know a lady's place is in the home?" Sam is always there for Honey although he does sometimes arrive too late to save Honey from being roughed up. He thinks Honey is a born cynic as she believes every case is connected to a murder. Sam also feels Honey is not as effective as her father when he ran the company. Honey has a tendency to let cases pile up and becomes too focused on a case when it gets the best of her. Sam has a collection of guns in the truck and chooses one that he feels is right for the job at hand. Sam also does undercover work, usually posing as a chauffeur or playboy to fool confidence men. The innocent looking ball point pen Honey gives to certain clients is actually a miniature transmitter she uses for tracking purposes.

The pilot episode, "Honey West: Who Killed the Jackpot," aired on *Burke's Law* on April 12, 1965. Here Honey and Sam seek the person who killed their client three days after he hired them to protect him. Joseph Mullendore composed the opening theme "Wild Honey" and the closing signature "Sweet Honey."

53. Hudson Street (ABC, 1995)

Precinct Number 7 on Hudson Street in Hoboken, New Jersey, is home to Tony Canetti (Tony Danza), a conservative homicide detective. He is divorced from Lucy (Shareen Mitchell) and the father of Mickey (Frankie J. Galasso). Tony was born in New Jersey and attended Hoboken High School. His late father owned a shoe store, Canelli's Discount Shoes; it was here that Tony worked after school and on weekends. A botched robbery attempt cost Tony's father, Victor, his life, but made Tony realize he had to do something about it — become a cop. He graduated from rookie school and became a beat cop. He upheld the law and he made people feel safe. He made friends and acquired snitches he could trust — and who could trust him. Tony lives near the precinct on Hudson Street and frequents a diner called the Pool Hall. Tony calls his snitches "information engineers."

Melanie Clifford (Lori Loughlin) is a young woman who dreams of becoming a reporter for the *New York Times*. She was born in New Jersey and lives with her parents at 11 Wilson Street. She is liberal and works as the obituary editor for the *Hoboken Reporter*. After several years on the job she receives a promotion to the Metro Desk (police reporter) and finds a new hangout — the press room of Precinct 7. A short time earlier, Melanie and Tony met on a blind date. They were opposites who were attracted to each other but barely able to stand each other. They agreed not to see each other again. Circumstances place them together again and their bickering love-hate relationship is the actual focal point of the series.

Kirby McIntire (Christine Dunford) is the gorgeous police detective who works with Tony. She is well endowed and when someone says "Nice bust," she takes it the wrong way, believing they are referring to her breasts. Kirby is the precinct's Jill of all trades. She always manages to get the cases nobody else wants — for example, catching a lingerie thief — and the work nobody else will do — for example, filing, filling out reports, making coffee. Jennifer Bassey and Steven Gilborn played Melanie's parents, Betsy and Nelson Clifford. Jonathan Wolff composed the theme.

54. Hunter (NBC, 1984–1991; 1995; 2002; 2003)

Rick Hunter (Fred Dryer) is a detective sergeant with the Los Angeles Police Department, Division 122. The department is also called Central

Division, the Parker Division, the Parker Center Police Station and Metro Division. Rick is an honest but tough cop who has a skeleton in his closet: he is the son of a mobster but has rejected a life of crime to uphold the law. Hunter, unlike previous TV detectives, seems to enjoy violent confrontations, especially when he is forced to use his gun. Unlike so many prior series where bullets fly and no one seems to get hit, Hunter's bullets are often fatal to criminals. Hunter resides at 5405 Ocean Front Drive and drives a car with the license plate IADT 89, later 2IQ 1584; his car code was originally 1-William-56, then 1-William 156 and L-56.

Over the course of the series run, Rick was partnered with three women: Dee Dee McCall (Stepfanie Kramer), Joann Molinski (Darlanne Fluegel) and Christine Novak (Lauren Lane). Dee Dee, a detective sergeant, was teamed with Rick from 1984–1990. Like Rick, she was tough and honest and those qualities earned her the nickname "The Brass Cupcake." Dee Dee resides at 8534 Mezdon Drive and her car license plate reads IGO45 48, later IGOQ 458. Her car code was originally 1-Adam-43, then Charles Albert 420 and finally L-59. Dee Dee, a widow, had been married to Steve McCall (Franc Luz), a sergeant killed in the line of duty.

In the episode "Street Wise" (May 7, 1990), Dee Dee accepts the marriage proposal of her old flame, Dr. Alex Turner (Robert Conner Newman), a college professor. In part two of the episode (May 14), Dee Dee leaves the force to marry Alex. The episode of September 19, 1990, "Deadly Encounters," teams Rick with a tough rookie cop, Officer Joann Molinski. Joann lived at 4535 North Sheridan and drove a car with the license plate 2GEE 645. Her badge number was 1836 and R-21-Charles was her car code. Joann is written out in the episode of January 9, 1991 ("Fatal Obsession") when she is killed (shot three times) by a psychotic woman named Loreen Arness (Ellen Wheeler). Rick remains without a steady partner until September 9, 1991, when he is teamed with Christine Novak, a sergeant who prefers to be called Chris. Chris is the mother of a young daughter named Allie (Courtney Barilla) and lives at 6341 West Beverly Drive; Allie attends the Worster Avenue Grammar School. She and Chris shop at a store called One Life. Chris's mobile code is R-30-Charles and she is divorced from Al Novak (Robin Thomas), Allie's now estranged father.

Rick's superiors also varied throughout the series. Lester Cain (Michael Cavanaugh then Arthur Rosenberg) was the first captain. He was replaced by Captain Dolan (John Amos); Dolan by Captain Wyler (Bruce Davison); and Wyler by Chief Charles Devane (Charles Hallahan). Sporty James (Garrett Morris), owner of the somewhat shady Sporty James Enterprises, is Rick's information man (snitch). Mike Post and Pete Carpenter composed the "Hunter" theme.

TV Movie Updates

1. The Return of Hunter (NBC, April 30, 1995). Rick Hunter (Fred Dryer) is now a lieutenant with the Parker Division of the L.A.P.D. He is as tough as ever but now works alone. He is engaged to Vickie Sherry (Beth Toussant) and Charlie Devane (Charles Hallahan) is still his superior. The movie, which has the subtitle "Everyone Walks in L.A.," finds Hunter taking on a personal vendetta: finding Jack Valko (Miguel Ferrer), a madman who killed Vickie and now taunts Hunter to catch him. Joseph Conlan composed the new "Hunter" theme.

2. Hunter: Return to Justice (NBC, November 16, 2002). Rick Hunter (Fred Dryer) is a lieutenant with the L.A.P.D. He has the car code L-22 and has been involved in seven shootings in the past three years. Dee Dee McCall (Stepfanie Kramer) is now a sergeant with the Juvenile Division of the San Diego Police Department. Dee Dee was not a part of the prior TV movie. Dee Dee is also engaged to Roger Prescott (Sam Hennings), a wealthy drug company owner who is running for mayor. The story, also promoted by NBC as *Hunter: The Movie*, reunites Rick and Dee Dee when Dee Dee invites Hunter to her engagement party. Trouble begins when Roger's past is uncovered — a Russian KGB agent and traitor to the U.S. — and Dee Dee is kidnapped by members of the Russian Mafia seeking to trade her for secret lists of former KGB agents possessed by Roger. Rick intervenes and in a violent confrontation with the mafia, rescues Dee Dee but is unable to save Roger's life. The program ends with Rick and Dee Dee parting company. "Don't be a stranger" are Dee Dee's final words as the story ends. No mention is made of what happened to Alex, the man Dee Dee left the force to marry in 1990.

Series Revival

Hunter (2003). A six-episode continuation of the prior TV movie. The first episode, "Back in Force" (April 12, 2003) finds Lieutenant Rick Hunter (Fred Dryer) becoming a member of the San Diego Police Department when he leaves Los Angeles following the shooting death of his partner. Sergeant Dee Dee McCall (Stepfanie Kramer), formerly with the Juvenile Division of the San Diego P.D., is now partners with Hunter in the Robbery-Homicide Division. Their superior is Captain Gallardo (Mike Gomez).

Rick has not mellowed with age; he is more prone to violent confrontations than before. When he speaks to a suspect he warns him, "The worst part of your day is not when I show up but when I come back." A visual of an FBI computer file on Hunter revealed the following information:

Date of Birth: February 3, 1941; Social Security Number: 991-022-2042; Police I.D. Number: 179; Address: 1229 Riverside Drive, San Diego 92125-0922; Telephone number: 619-555-0142. His and Dee Dee's car code is 930-Sam. Rick's license plate was first seen as 9999042, then E9999028. Dee Dee, who drives a car with the plate 9999027, teaches children music at the Juvenile Center in her spare time. Her badge number is 794. Christopher Franke composed the new series "Hunter" theme.

55. I Had Three Wives (CBS, 1985)

"Just about every client I ever had wants to kill me," says Jackson Beaudine (Victor Garber), a three times divorced private detective who owns Jackson Beaudine Investigations at 1163 Vandover Street in Los Angeles. His office phone number is 555-3112. Jackson is not your typical private detective. While he does investigate cases and tries to help people in trouble, he has a knack for asking the wrong questions of the wrong people and constantly puts his life in jeopardy. "I need all the help I can get," he says, and he relies on the assistance of this three ex-wives — Liz Bailey (Shanna Reed), Samantha Collins (Teri Copley) and Mary Parker (Maggie Cooper). Liz, Samantha and Mary are career women. Jackson claims each of the marriages failed "because we got in the way of each other's career and stopped each other's personal growth."

Elizabeth is a reporter for the Los Angeles *Chronicle*. She lives at 6 Preston Drive. Samantha, called Sam by Jackson, is an aspiring actress. Her claim to fame is the starring role in the horror film *Hatchet Honeymoon*. She lives in an apartment at the Roxbury Apartment Complex. Mary is a lawyer with the firm of Maxwell, Cooper and Associates. She is the mother of their son, Andrew (David Faustino) and they live at 12718 Kenmore Road in Brentwood.

Jackson drives a car with the license plate TUB 285 and lives in an apartment near the waterfront. Bill Conti composed the theme "I Had Three Wives."

56. In the Heat of the Night (NBC, 1988–1992; CBS, 1992–1994)

Sparta, Mississippi, is a small southern town with a considerable amount of crime. William O. Gillespie (Carroll O'Connor) is the town's white police chief and Virgil Tibbs (Howard Rollins) is his black chief of detectives.

William, called Bill, was born in Mississippi. He resides at 11 Vanover and has a hunting dog named Roscoe. Bill first mentions he was married to a woman named Anna Caterina but never had any children. Anna died in childbirth. "I lost him when I lost her." Later, Bill mentions he was married to a woman named Georgia Farren, who deserted him shortly after the birth of their daughter, Lana (played as an adult by Christine Elise). In 1988, Bill dated JoAnn St. John (Lois Nettleton), a cashier at his favorite eatery, the Magnolia Cafe. Ten years earlier, JoAnn was a $100 a night call girl known as Kelly Kaye. Their romance ended a short time later. In 1991, Bill began a romance with Harriet DeLong (Denise Nicholas), a younger woman who was also a black city councilwoman. Bill's office is in the City Hall Building and he drives a squad car with the license plate M-7246, later M-7555.

Virgil was born in Philadelphia and was a member of the state police department before relocating to Sparta. He tends to go by the book and often objects to Bill's sometimes unorthodox investigative procedures. Bill feels you have to think like a criminal to catch a criminal. Virgil and his wife, Althea (Anne-Marie Johnson) live at 4602 Cherry Lane and 555-2002 is their phone number. Althea's maiden name was Peterson and she is a teacher at Sparta Community High School. They are later the parents of a son they name William Calvin Tibbs. Virgil's license plate reads M-1320.

In 1989, when Carroll O'Connor entered the hospital for by-pass surgery, the former police chief, Captain Thomas Dugan (Joe Don Baker) was brought out of retirement to replace him. Bill's absence was explained as the Chief attending a month-long symposium on domestic terrorism in Washington, D.C., as the representative from Mississippi. Another change occurred in 1994 when the City Council objects to Bill's relationship with Harriet and declines to renew his contract. As Bill steps down to become the county sheriff, Hamilton Forbes (Carl Weathers), a former police inspector from Memphis, Tennessee, is brought in as Sparta's new police chief. It is at this time that Virgil also leaves to complete school and become a lawyer. The series ended shortly after.

Other officers working under Bill are Parker Williams (David Hart), Bubba Skinner (Alan Autry), Wilson Sweet (Geoffrey Thorne), Chris Rankin (Sheryl Lynn Piland) and Lu Ann Corbin (Crystal Fox). Parker has three cats (Fuzz Face, Old Man and Wrencher) and his favorite watering hole is the Big T Truck Stop. The series is based on the 1967 feature film of the same title. Bill Champlin sings the theme "In the Heat of the Night."

57. Jake and the Fatman (CBS, 1987–1992)

Jason Lochinvar McCabe (William Conrad), called J.L. for short, began his TV career as the District Attorney of an unnamed Southern California city (1987–88). He next became a prosecuting attorney for the Honolulu Police Department (1988–90), then the D.A. of Costa Del Mar, a small city in California. Jake Styles (Joe Penny) is the stylish investigator who assists him in all locales. He was joined in 1991 by Neely Capshaw (Melody Anderson), an investigator for the Costa Del Mar D.A.'s office.

J.L. is somewhat overweight and has earned the nickname Fatman. He is a tough prosecutor and will use every means at his disposal to convict a felon. J.L. was born in Atlanta, Georgia, and began his career as a lawyer, then as a prosecuting attorney for the D.A.'s office. He has also been called "Buster" and he has a somewhat lazy (appears to always be sleeping) dog named Max. J.L.'s favorite watering hole is Dixie's Bar in first season episodes; Ann Francis plays Dixie, the bar owner. Only one base of operations was given for J.L.—building 310 of the Costa Del Mar Municipal Court House.

Jake was born in California and as a kid had the nickname Butchie. His childhood hero was Tom Cody, star of the mythical TV series "Sky Hawk." An address for Jake is not given. He drives a car with the license plate 2VAK 087 and 555-4796 is his phone number in first season episodes. Neely lives at 5440 Canyon Drive with her daughter, Sarah (Taylor Fry). Neely drives a station wagon, license plate 2VT MOV3. Sarah has a teddy bear named Georgie Bear and attends the Folger Park Grammar School.

Each episode is titled after a song; for example, "It Had to Be You," "The Tender Trap," and this song is played over the episode's after-theme opening credits. Dick DeBenedictis composed the theme "Jake and the Fatman."

58. The Job (ABC, 2001–2002)

Mike McNeil (Denis Leary) is a detective with the 21st Precinct of the N.Y.P.D. in Manhattan. He is Irish and "The only thing I like is being a cop." He breaks the rules, or, as he says, "bends them," to solve a case. Mike drives a car with the license plate HORL 931; people say he drives like a maniac. Mike lives in the suburbs and works in the city. He smokes, drinks like a fish and is totally unfaithful to his wife, Karen (Wendy McKenna). He is a womanizer and is secretly dating a woman named Toni (Karyn Parsons). While Toni knows about Karen, Karen is unaware of Toni. Karen eventually discovered Mike's mistress, but the series ended without any resolutions.

Mike takes pain killers even though he has no pain. He is not very friendly, sometimes looks the other way instead of arresting a suspect and believes he is unlucky, not only at gambling but with women. Mike works with Frank Harrigan (Lenny Clarke), Jan Hendrix (Diane Farr) and Terrence Phillips (Bill Nunn). It took Terrence five years to figure out what a 12-year-old girl figures out while spending only 20 minutes with Mike — He's not nice. Terrence is nicknamed Pip and is mystified as to why he has that nickname. He believes people think he resembles one of singer Gladys Knight's Pips, but he feels he doesn't look like any one of them — "It's hard to tell because your eyes tend to look at Gladys Knight." Jan is the only regular female cop in the squadroom. She was born in the Bronx and attended Cardinal Spellman High School where she was called Duck — "because I had a voice like a duck." Jan is single and looking for Mr. Right but feels the pressures of her job will never make that happen. She believes women of all ages hate Mike because of his nasty attitude about everything. Frank is the overweight cop who appears to be the only person in the precinct who can stand being Mike's patrol car partner. He enjoys eating — at home, in the squad room, in the car, on the street — wherever and whenever a free moment allows him to indulge in his favorite activity. Before becoming a cop, Frank felt he had a calling to become a priest — "But the celibacy thing got me. I couldn't imagine giving up sex." The series is rather light on facts and concentrates heavily on Mike's day-to-day activities on a job he appears to like, then hate, then like again.

59. John Doe (Fox, 2002)

"Who am I? And where did I come from," says John Doe (Dominic Purcell), a man of mystery who knows everything about everything — except who he is. Is he a government experiment? An extraterrestrial? John Doe simply does not know. Life for John Doe, as he knows it, began when he awoke on a deserted island (Horseshoe Island). With no apparent means of escape, he dove into the ocean possibly hoping to swim to a mainland. This failed and he attached himself to some floating driftwood and let the tides guide him. He was found by Asian fishermen and rescued. He was put ashore in Seattle, taken to a hospital and given the name John Doe.

On the day of John's appearance, satellite photos indicated that it was a clear day and there were no atmospheric disturbances. No distress calls were logged by the Coast Guard and no loved ones were reported as missing persons fitting his description — "No nothing," he says. The first episode reveals two clues to John's possible identity. The first is a symbol on his right shoulder — "a circle in a K," as John calls it. The symbol of ancient Egyptian hieroglyph from 29 BC shows slight similarities. It is also the symbol of a defunct Asian publishing house's logo — is it a birthmark or a branding?

The second clue comes at the end of the episode when it shows John standing on a pier. A ferry is passing and a woman is seen looking toward the pier. She apparently recognizes John Doe and calls out the name Tommy. John turns and looks, but doesn't recognize the woman. He attempts to find her but is unable when the ferry docks. Is Tommy his name? Does someone finally recognize him? John's search for the mysterious woman is a continuing aspect of the series.

John is not only unaware of who he is, but he is color blind. He sees everything in black and white as does the viewer when a scene is seen through his eyes. However, when something he sees is related to his life (a clue) he can see in color as what happened with the girl on the ferry. And "did I mention I know everything from the contents of a box of Applejacks to the mating habits of the zebra to everything in between?" However, John is not a psychic; "I can't predict things" and "for a guy who has all the answers, I don't have the one that means the most."

To help him find out who he is, John begins his life by acquiring money. He has an amazing ability to calculate odds and wins a great deal at a race track; he later acquires money by investing in the stock market. John next finds an apartment through Evergreen Realty and, to make the best use of his abilities, establishes himself as a consultant to help the police solve crimes or, as he says, "I'm a privately funded think tank." He next hangs posters on telephone poles reading "Have You Seen Me? I'm Missing." He has also contacted 150 police precincts across the country reporting himself missing. His phone number is 206-555-0167.

John drives a sports car with the license plate 793 QLF. He hires a homeless teenage girl named Karen Kalwalski (Sprague Grayden) as his secretary and office organizer. John lives above a bar, The Sea, and plays piano in its lounge. A character named Digger (William Forsythe) is the apparent bar owner. About his name he says, "Don't even ask." The song "My Funny Valentine" by Rogers and Hart "means something to me, but I don't know what it is." "I don't know things I'm supposed to know" (like why he likes hot dogs) "but I know things I'm not supposed to." The Sea is located at 148 Fourth Avenue in Seattle. John resides in Apartment 205.

While watching the game show *Jeopardy* on TV and giving the answers before they are asked, the show is interrupted for a news bulletin about a kidnapped young girl. John sees the news bulletin in color and figures the girl must be a connection to his past. He offers his help to Detective Frank Hayes (John Marshall Jones) and solves the case. He rescues the girl but is unable to connect her to his past. Lieutenant Jamie Avery (Jayne Brook), Frank's superior, is skeptical of John and rather reluctant to work with him or let Frank associate with him. But John has the unique ability to find clues even the best forensic scientists overlook and his help becomes beneficial to the police department, especially Frank. Frank is married and the father of two children. He is with the Seattle, Washington, P.D. and drives a car with the license plate 314 GNN. Karen is currently studying art, but she is a foster child and has been in trouble with the law. She also works two days a week as a tour guide at the Art Museum.

Before the series ended without revealing who or what John Doe is, he found one other clue to his identity — the plastic figure of a Phoenix. He saw this in red and a Phoenix is the ancient Greek symbol of rebirth. Danny Lux composed the theme.

60. Johnny Midnight (Syndicated, 1960)

Johnny Midnight (Edmond O'Brien) is a former actor turned private detective who says, "Broadway is the world of make-believe, but I found out that the curtain never comes down on the real things that happen on the Street of Dreams. That's why I gave up acting to become a private investigator." Johnny lives in a penthouse on West 41st Street and Broadway; "My favorite street in my favorite town — New York City."

Johnny owns his own theater, The Midnight Theater, and still frequents the actors' hangout, Lindy's Bar, where he likes to eat and keep in touch with his show business friends. Cost doesn't matter much when it comes to his clients. If he sees that a person is in real trouble, the money becomes secondary. Johnny also works on behalf of the Mutual Insurance Company and uses his skills as a former actor to help him solve cases. His favorite disguise is Gearhart Houtsman, the Old German.

Aki (Yuki Shimoda) is Johnny's houseboy; he calls Johnny "Mr. Johnny Midnight." Lupo Olivera (Arthur Batanides) is Johnny's police department contact, a sergeant with the Homicide Division of the N.Y.P.D.

A jazz adaptation of the song "The Lullaby of Broadway," played by Joe Bushkin, is the show's theme song.

61. Just Cause (PAX, 2002)

Alexandra DeMonaco (Elizabeth Lackey) is a young woman seeking to begin a new life. She has just been released from prison after serving three years of a five year sentence for insurance fraud. During her time at the Mendincino's Women's Prison, Alexandra, called Alex, studied law via Bay City college's internet program. Although Alex acquired her degree, she is a felon and is thus unable to practice law. Alex was framed but she can't prove it. Alex was working as the office manager for her husband, a lawyer. Unknown to Alex, her husband was working with unethical doctors to defraud insurance companies. When an investigation into her husband's business affairs showed that Alex had manipulated the books, she was arrested and her husband disappeared, taking their daughter with him. Alex decided to use her time in prison to become a lawyer to help people.

Burdick, Whitney and Morgan is a prestigious San Francisco law firm. It is here that Alex hopes to find a job and get her name cleared by a pardon from the governor. Her meeting with senior partner Hamilton Whitney III (Richard Thomas) nets her a job as his researcher when he becomes impressed by her enthusiasm. "I want to become a lawyer to help people who need help," Alex tells him, "not to make rich clients richer." But Whitney is doubtful he can have her case overturned, which would allow her to practice law, due to a lack of evidence.

Alex is not your typical researcher or paralegal. She is a bright and determined woman with the mind of a detective. Her enthusiasm and sleuthing skills immediately change Whitney's way of thinking when Alex proves two cases of corporate suicide were actually murder. Whitney feels his life has changed in another way also: he changes the focus of the law firm from civil litigation to criminal defense when he realizes the true meaning of Alex's words. At the end of the first episode, Alex presents Whitney with her book — recommendations as to why she should be pardoned. Whitney rejects it. "The governor is my friend and I have to tell the truth. No embellishments, no exaggerations." Whitney then places a folder on his desk and tells Alex, "If it's not what you want, I'll understand." As Whitney leaves the office, Alex picks up the folder and opens it. A smile crosses her face as she reads it: "Dear Governor Romero. I'm writing you this letter on behalf of Alexandra DeMonaco to request that you pardon her crime. Her passion for a just cause has spirited me to rediscover the reason why I became a lawyer in the first place. She has reminded me that the true purpose of the law is the pursuit of justice. In this book you will find many who share my voice that she will make an excellent lawyer.... Edmond Burke said 'The only thing necessary for the triumph of evil is for good men to do nothing.' Alexandra DeMonaco stands up and fights with the angels. We need her on our side." It appeared that Alex was granted her pardon, but subsequent episodes reveal that her pardon was not granted and she is continuing to seek justice.

Alex was a model prisoner and has been released on parole. Terms of her parole include no staying up past 11:00 PM except for employment; no leaving the city and no association with known felons. Upon her release from prison Alex was given a cross by her cellmate — "You're an ex-con now. You're gonna need all the help you can get." Alex wears it as part of a necklace. Alex, an army brat, was born in East Los Angeles and attended Roosevelt High School. She now lives at 1196-B Hayes Avenue. Alex's case is numbered B096301. In prison she worked kitchen detail and says, "I developed a talent for reading people." Although she is not supposed to associate with felons, Alex does break parole by visiting her prison friends for help in solving crimes. Alex, middle name Sandra, is allergic to dust. She wears expensive ($15 a pair) sheer pantyhose and is persistent once she is on a case. She likes to do her own detective work but becomes too emotionally involved in cases.

Alex, called Miss DeMonaco by Whitney, believes her boss is rich and stuck up as he appears to be all work and no play. Whitney, a graduate of Harvard Law School, has an undergraduate degree in Asiatic languages. Whitney comes from a family of professionals: his father was a surgeon; his uncle, the author of a book called *Just Cause*, was a criminal lawyer. Whitney will not violate a court order ("I have a code of ethics"). He loves San Francisco and hates to see it dragged through the mud. He says of Alex, "She's a bully. She won't listen. She irritates the hell out of me." He also believes her emotions cloud her judgment. Whitney says of his career, "I like fishing, but I throw the little ones back. I like to wade out deep and catch the big ones." Whitney has been married three times and maintains a working relationship with his third wife, Rebecca, an FBI agent whom he met when she interrogated him during a case.

62. Kate Loves a Mystery (NBC, 1979)

Kate Columbo is the wife of the famed homicide detective, Lieutenant Columbo of the L.A.P.D. On the series *Columbo* (see entry) Kate was never seen or mentioned by a first name; she was either "The Wife" or "Mrs. Columbo." Kate was never much of a detective on the *Columbo* series. Columbo would remark that when he and the Mrs. would go to the movies, she would always pick the wrong person as the killer. Kate suddenly inherited her husband's sleuthing abilities in two short lived series: *Mrs. Columbo* (February 26 to March 24, 1979) and *Kate Loves a Mystery* (October 18 to December 6, 1979). In *Mrs. Columbo*, Kate Columbo (Kate Mulgrew) lives at 728 Valley Lane in San Fernando, California, with her daughter, Jenny (Lili Haydn). "My husband" or "The Lieutenant," as Kate referred to her husband, is never seen; he is always on a case or away on business. Kate works as a writer for the *Weekly Advertiser*, a "throwaway" newspaper published by Josh Alden (Henry Jones). Jenny attends the Valley Elementary School; 555-9861, later 555-9867, is Kate's phone number and 859 KTL is the license plate number of her sedan. While hubby is away, Kate looks after his badly in need of repair 1952 Peugeot, license plate 044 APD, by driving it on occasion. Kate also cares for Fang, the lazy basset hound who was also called Dog in the *Columbo* series. Kate studied journalism in college and worked at it for a time before she gave it up for marriage and a family. Six months ago she woke up and asked herself where she was. It was then that she decided she needed to get back in the work force. The *Advertiser* goes to press at 2:00 on Tuesday. Kate takes Fang to the Parker Street Pet Hospital; Southwest Telephone services the area. Although Kate is supposed to cover events like pet shows and garden clubs, she always manages to stumble upon and solve crimes.

When *Kate Loves a Mystery* premiered, Kate was now divorced and used her maiden name. Kate Columbo was now Kate Callahan and Lili Haydn her daughter, Jenny Callahan. They lived in the same house, had the same dog and Jenny attended the same school. The Peugeot was gone and so was Kate's prior car; she now drove one with the license plate 304 MGD. Kate still worked for Josh Alden (Henry Jones) but at a different paper, the *Weekly Advocate*, in the San Fernando Valley. Kate still managed to stumble upon crimes, but solved them with the help of her friend, Mike Varrick (Don Stroud), a sergeant with the Valley Municipal Police Department.

John Cacavas composed the themes "Mrs. Columbo" and "Kate Loves a Mystery."

63. Kojak (CBS, 1973–1978; ABC, 1989–1990)

The Manhattan South Precinct of the N.Y.P.D. is an old building that is cold in the winter and hot in the summer. The detectives work long hours and overtime is a necessary part of the job. The coffee is one step ahead of suicide and the squad room detectives joke all the time—"They have to. These guys don't know what they'll find out there. It could be a killer with a .351 Magnum or a body chopped into pieces. They gotta get their laughs when they can," says Theo Kojak (Telly Savalas), a dedicated, hard-working detective whose beat is lower Manhattan.

Kojak was previously an officer with the 26th Precinct. He works on hunches which often pay off, and when he personally becomes involved in a case, he becomes fixated and doesn't care what it takes to solve it. Kojak says, "I don't care about my badge; I don't care about my pension. But somebody's gonna take a hard fall for what they did." Kojak drives a sedan with the license plate 394 AFL, later 383 JDZ, and lives at 215 River Street. He smokes pencil-thin cigars, but is famous for being the only cop on the force who loves lollipops—the round Tootsie Roll Pops. Theo is abrasive and has to be to deal with the gory cases he investigates. Because of the nature of cases, there are no female detectives in Theo's unit. Stella's is Theo's favorite restaurant and Irene Van Patten (Diane Baker) is his romantic interest. Theo is Greek and his catchphrase is "Who loves ya, baby."

Frank McNeil (Dan Frazer) is the chief of detectives, and Theo most often works with detectives Crocker (Kevin Dobson), Stavros (George Savalas), Rizzo (Vince Conti) and Saperstein (Mark Russell). While Kojak is forever yelling "Crocker!," "Saperstein!" and "Rizzo!," he calls only Crocker by a first name (Bobby). Theo refers to his men as yo-yo's when they get into arguments, and he calls Crocker and Saperstein Laurel and Hardy or Abbott and Costello when they work together. George Savalas, Telly's brother, originally worked under the name Demosthenes.

In the ABC version, Kojak is a police inspector with the 74th Precinct in Manhattan. He drives a sedan with the license plate NRV 171, and his assistant is Detective Warren Blake (Andre Braugher). Kevin Dobson reprised his role in the episode of February 3, 1990, "It's Always Something." He is now assistant D.A. Robert Crocker. Kojak's lollipops have also been changed from Tootsie Roll Pops to an unknown sugar-free brand. The pops are wrapped in clear cellophane.

Billy Goldenberg composed the original CBS theme "Kojak"; Mike Post composed the revised ABC theme version "The New Kojak Theme."

Note: Telly Savalas also played Kojak in three TV movies

1. The Marcus-Nelson Murders (CBS, March 8, 1973). The pilot film for the CBS series. Here Theo attempts to help a teenager who is being wrongly convicted for the murder of two men.

2. Kojak: The Belarus File (CBS, February 16, 1985). Kojak teams with FBI agent Dana Sutton (Suzanne Pleshette) to find the killer of elderly Russian immigrants. Dan Frazer, George Savalas, Mark Russell and Vince Conti reprised their earlier roles.

3. Kojak: The Price of Justice (CBS, February 21, 1987). Theo, now an inspector at the precinct ("They let me join the club") investigates the case of a woman accused of murdering two children.

Proposed Spinoff (Unsold Pilot)

Salathiel Harms, Bounty Hunter. Rosey Grier as Salathiel Harms, an imposing California private detective who tracks down bail jumpers. Two pilots were produced and broadcast as episodes of the CBS series *Kojak*: "Bad Dude," January 25, 1976, Harms travels to New York seeking a professional hitman; and "Black Thorn," December 5, 1976, Harms teams with Kojak to find a man with a connection to an unsolved murder.

64. Lady Blue (ABC, 1985–1986)

Katy Mahoney (Jamie Rose) is a detective with the Violent Crimes Division of the 39th Street Station of the Chicago Metro Police Department. Katy, the daughter of a cop, is street smart, street tough, and an expert when it comes to using her guns. She is young, beautiful and mean — a female version of Clint Eastwood's Dirty Harry film character. Katy is called ABC's Dirty Harriet in press information. Katy plays by her own rules. While she respects the law and has sworn to uphold it, she bends it to accomplish her goals and keep the streets of her hometown free of thugs. Her superior, Lieutenant Terry McNichols (Danny Aiello) says, "Katy can read a crime scene in progress like most guys read the sports page," although he does complain about her violent approaches and too frequent use of her gun. Katy lives at 1107 West Brandis Place and rides in a car with the license plate 4DJ 56; her badge number is 28668 (688 in the pilot episode). See also *Get Christie Love* and *Police Woman*. Arnetia Walker sings the theme "Lady Blue."

Lanigan's Rabbi *See* Father Dowling Mysteries

65. The Last Precinct (NBC, 1986)

Precinct 56 is a former county morgue turned funeral parlor turned police station that city officials use as a dumping ground for what it calls odd-ball officers — psychologically challenged cops who are part of the force but just not stable enough for regular precinct duties and assignments. They handle non-violent crimes but always manage to stumble upon real crimes that require their unique brand of justice to solve.

Rob Wright (Adam West) is the laid back, non-aggressive, easy-going, indecisive captain of Precinct 56. Rob feels he must do what is right because his last name is Wright and "I stand for right." His inability to command a regular precinct was the reason for his transfer, but Rob believes his leadership abilities made him the right man for the job. The officers under his command are Melba Brubaker (Randi Brooks), Tremayne Lane (Ernie Hudson),

Martha Haggerty (Yana Narvanna), Butch Briscoe (Keenan Wynn), Sundance (Hank Rolike), Alphabet (Vijay Amritraj) and the King (Pete Willcox).

Melba is blonde, beautiful and tough. Although it should be against the rules, Melba wears a revealing uniform, low cut top for cleavage and a miniskirt for her legs. You would never guess it by looking at her, but Melba, who likes to be called Mel, was formerly a man — Melvin Brubaker. Mel tried living the life of a man, was a star ballplayer, but felt he was meant to be a woman and underwent a sex change operation. Mel's toughness makes her a loner. Tremayne is a sergeant and is nicknamed Night Train for his love of working the night shift. Martha, a sergeant also, is from a military family and assists Rob as his second in command. She runs the precinct like an army base and is too aggressive which is the reason for her transfer. She is seeking a man but is having difficulty finding one that can meet her standards.

Alphabet is the nickname for Officer Shivoramanbhai Poonchwalla, an exchange officer from Calcutta that the police commissioner has no idea what to do with, so he assigned him to Captain Wright. Alphabet's full name is displayed on a rather large name tag on his uniform and he has little knowledge of American police procedures or what to do when on assignment. He is hoping to learn from his fellow officers and bring this knowledge back to his homeland. The King, who has no other name, is a former Elvis impersonator who "overdosed" and now believes he is the reincarnation of Elvis Presley. He dresses like Elvis, sings and talks like him and will only respond to the name King. William, the overweight officer, is nicknamed Raid for his habit of raiding the refrigerator. Butch and Sundance are elderly officers who work as a team and prefer to be called Butch and Sundance after their Old West heroes, Butch Cassidy and the Sundance Kid. Felony is the lazy precinct dog; the Honey Bunns Drive-In is the local eatery. Stacey, the waitress, is played by Nicollette Sheridan. Arnold Bludhorn (James Cromwell) is the frustrated police chief who oversees Precinct 56 and is seeking a way to disband it and its officers. Mike Post and Pete Carpenter composed the theme.

66. The Law and Harry McGraw (CBS, 1987–1988)

Harlan H. McGraw III, better known as Harry McGraw (Jerry Orbach), is the owner-operator of Harry McGraw Private Investigations in Boston. Harry is tough, disorganized and irritable. He is reluctant to tell the whole truth, or "The Straight Skinny" as he calls it. He believes he attracts the worst clients; he considers them missions of mercy clients. Harry rarely hands out a business card — "I'd give you a card but I'm fresh out. I'm in the book." He has a gambling problem and especially likes to play the horses ("I never forget a nag I lose on"). He rarely uses a gun and relies on his fists ("Okay, I get busted up a bit, but at least I get a case solved"). He claims that murder cases have a way of bringing out the worst in people and that if you need a lot of protection, he's the guy that can give it to you.

Harry drives a car with the license plate 615 RER and lives in an untidy apartment on Melrose. He has a police record — arrested by the Boston Police for suspicion of murder and burglary — and had his private investigator's license suspended four times in three years. Once on a case, Harry's seedy and abrasive side appears. He becomes relentless and a determined fact finder despite the dangerous obstacles he might encounter. He is also a master of disguise and uses such deception to trick suspects into revealing information. Harry uses the resources of the local paper, the *Morning Bulletin*, and hangs out at a bar called Gilhooley's.

Ellie Maginnis (Barbara Babcock), a criminal attorney with the firm of Maginnis and Maginnis, has the office opposite Harry's agency. The program is a spinoff from *Murder, She Wrote*, wherein the character of Harry McGraw appeared several times. Richard Markowitz composed the theme.

67. Leg Work (CBS, 1987)

Claire McCarron (Margaret Colin) is a former assistant district attorney turned owner of McCarron Investigations, a private detective agency she operates from an office at 17 West 36th Street in New York City. Claire guarantees results and charges $500 a day plus expenses. She has a dog named Clyde and drives a silver Porsche, license plate DEX 627; mobile phone number 555-4365. The car is always in need of repair and Claire must do a lot of walking to accomplish her goals, hence the title. Claire also displays her shapely legs by wearing miniskirts. Claire lives in an apartment at 765 East 65th Street and has a rare collection of pre–World War II Lionel "O" gauge electric trains that she inherited from her father. Claire often eats out and the only two foods she can prepare are oatmeal raisin cookies and coq au vin (chicken in wine sauce). When a case bothers Claire, she resorts to making cookies.

Claire works with her brother, Fred McCarron (Patrick James Clarke), a lieutenant with the Office of Public Relations at One Police Plaza in Manhattan, and Wilhelmina "Willie" Pipal (Frances McDormand), the Manhattan Assistant District Attorney. The series had two working titles: "Eye

Shadow" and "Leg Work." Margaret Colin had the choice of using either title. While she preferred neither, she chose *Leg Work*. Michael Omartian composed the "Leg Work Theme."

Leg Work is based on aspects of two former CBS projects: an unsold pilot called "Adams Apple" (August 23, 1986) and the 1985–86 series *Foley Square*. In the pilot, Sydney Walsh played Toni Adams, a private detective working out of Manhattan, or, as she called it, "The Big Apple." Carolyn Seymour was Tricia Hammond, the District Attorney, and Cherry Jones was Janice Eaton, Toni's contact at the Manhattan D.A.'s office. Toni had a dog named Mary Jo and both *Leg Work* and "Adams Apple" were produced by Frank Abatemarco. In *Foley Square*, Margaret Colin played Alex Harrigan, an assistant district attorney working out of the Criminal Courts Building at Foley Square in Manhattan. Aspects of this character were combined with those of Toni Adams to create Claire McCarron and *Leg Work*.

68. MacGruder and Loud (ABC, 1985)

Malcolm MacGruder and Jennifer Loud (John Getz, Kathryn Harrold) are patrol car officers with the L.A.P.D. Malcolm (badge number 459) and Jennifer, called Jenny (badge number 449) are secretly married. Department regulations prohibit married couples from working together. They live at 165 North Veranda—Malcolm in Apartment 2A; Jenny is Apartment 2B. The bookcase in Malcolm's apartment has been secretly converted into a revolving door to allow access to both apartments.

Jenny drives a car with the license plate IC 21501. Malcolm's license plate reads 698 917. Jenny hates a Code 3 ("They're too dangerous"); her and Malcolm's mobile code is 8-Z-11, and 275 816 is the license plate of their patrol car. Jenny's badge number was also given as 458 and Malcolm's as 445. Paul Chihara composed the theme.

69. Magnum, P.I. (CBS, 1980–1988)

Robin's Nest is an estate on Concord Road, later Kalohoa Drive, on the north shore of Hawaii that is owned by the fabulously wealthy but never seen pulp fiction writer, Robin Masters. Jonathan Quayle Higgins (John Hillerman) is the estate's major domo; private detective Thomas Sullivan Magnum (Tom Selleck) provides security for the estate in return for his living quarters off the main house.

Magnum was born in the town of Tidewater, Virginia. As a kid he was a fan of Roy Rogers' movies and would pretend to be a hero and keep the neighborhood free of outlaws. His first paying job was delivering newspapers for the *Daily Sentinel*; he earned $12 a week plus one penny for each paper he sold. He decided on a military career and attended Annapolis. After serving with the VM02 Unit in DaNang during the Vietnam War, he became a naval intelligence officer. He resigned shortly after "when I woke up one morning and realized I was 33 and never 23." He turned his attention to investigating and became a private detective. He charges $200 a day plus expenses; he will lower his fee to $175 if a client can't afford him. He is writing a book called *How to Be a World-Class Private Investigator* and also held a temporary job as house detective at the Hawaiian Gardens Hotel but was angry because he couldn't carry a gun.

Magnum enjoys working the *New York Times* crossword puzzle on Sunday and exercises by swimming, playing volleyball and running. His favorite movie is *Stalag 17* and Rosebud is his password for the estate's computer system. There are five phone lines on the estate and Magnum always calls Higgins on Robin's private line — "It's the only number I can remember." Magnum is a member of the King Kamehameha Club and drives a red Ferrari with the license plate ROBIN I (also seen as 5GE 478 and 308 TTS); 555-2131 is Magnum's phone number. He hates to be called Tommy. Magnum narrates the stories, talks to the camera, acts as a big brother toward women and hangs his head when he becomes frustrated.

Magnum claims that the relationship between himself and Higgins is "constant arguing, constant yelling, constant long, boring stories, constant not knocking on my door." Higgins always barges in on Thomas when he needs him. Jonathan served Her Majesty in five conflicts over 35 years, most notably as a member of England's MI-5 and MI-6 during World War II. His greatest embarrassment is his expulsion from the prestigious Sandhurst Academy, something he does not talk about. In 1957 he ran a hotel called the Arlington Arms which catered to the rich and famous. He has a ham radio with the call letters NR6DBZ and his hobbies are painting and building model bridges. He created his own blend of tea, Lady Ashley Tea, and is chairman — also called managing director — of the King Kamehameha Club. Higgins is also chairman of the Honolulu branch of the Britonis Seaman's Fund Charity and a member of the committee on historical preservation. And, as Magnum said, he tells endless tales of his experiences as a survival expert. He enjoys doing the Sunday *London Times* crossword puzzle and is writing his memoirs in a diary he calls *Crisis at Suez*. Higgins has two Great Danes, Apollo and Zeus, who patrol the estate grounds. The dogs, whom Higgins calls The Lads, do not like Magnum but tolerate him. Higgins has the mobile car code N6DB2 and he says about Magnum: "I don't like the way you live, I don't like the way you drive Robin's car and I don't like your friends." In voice overs, Magnum tells the audience that "I am 99 percent sure that Higgins is Robin Masters; but it's that one percent that could mean disaster." *The Serpent's Wisdom* is one of the books mentioned as being written by Robin, whom Higgins calls Mr. Masters. John Hillerman also played his half-brothers, Father Paddy MacGuinness and Don Luis Monqueo.

Orville Wilbur Wright (Larry Manetti), called Rick, and Theodore Calvin (Roger E. Mosley), called T.C., are Magnum's friends. Rick was born in Chicago and was a Marine Corps weapons expert during the Vietnam War. He came to Hawaii to open his own nightclub, Rick's Place, but gave it up to manage the King Kamehameha Club. He has numerous underworld connections and helps Magnum by obtaining information from the street. Rick's favorite song is "Feelings."

T.C., a former chopper pilot in Vietnam, now runs the Island Hopper Helicopter Service. Rates are $100 an hour; Bravo 516 is his air code. Prior to the war, T.C. was a Golden Gloves Boxer (also said to be a football player). He is divorced from Tina (Fay Hauser) and is the father of Bryant (Shavar Ross).

Carol Baldwin (Kathleen Lloyd) is the assistant D.A. who sometimes works with Magnum; she has a dog named Chelsea. Francis Hofstetler (Elisha Cook, Jr.), better known as Ice Pick, is the underworld boss Magnum turns to for help. Robin Masters, who is seen from the back only (Bruce Atkinson) is voiced by Orson Welles. Robin's Ferraris have the license plates ROBIN I and ROBIN II. His favorite charity is the Home for Wayward Boys. Tom (jersey 4), Rick (17) and T.C. (32) are members of Robin's softball team, the Paddlers. Robin's first published story was "The Last Days of Babylon." Visitors to the estate must sign the Robin's Nest Guest Book. The King Kamehameha Club was first said to be next to Robin's Nest; it is next said to be on Old Pali Road in lush surroundings. Magnum has no official office and uses the club as one.

Ian Freebarin-Smith composed the original theme "Magnum, P.I." (first and second seasons); Mike Post and Pete Carpenter composed the revised "Magnum's Theme."

Note: Three attempts were made to spinoff a series called "Luther Gillis." The project would have starred Eugene Roche as Luther Gillis, a St. Louis-based private detective whose motto is "Trouble is my business." Sheree North would have co-starred as his secretary, Blanche Rafferty. In the first pilot, "Luther Gillis: File #521 (October 6, 1983), Luther travels to Hawaii to find a missing teenage girl. "The Return of Luther Gillis" (February 16,

1984), the second pilot, finds Luther in Hawaii attending a detective convention and becoming involved in a kidnapping plot. The final pilot, "Luther Gillis: File #001" (December 6, 1984), finds Luther attempting to help a man being threatened with blackmail.

70. Martin Kane, Private Eye (NBC, 1949–1954; Syndicated, 1957–1958)

Martin Kane is a rugged private detective working out of New York City. He has an office in the Wood Building in Manhattan identified by its zone — New York 20; zip codes did not yet exist. The sign on his office door reads Martin Kane — Private Investigator. Kane charges fees that he feels are appropriate to the case at hand — as much as $500. He uses determination and force of character to achieve results. He refers to women as "Doll Face" and "Sweetheart" and his hangout is McMann's Tobacco Shop; El Dorado 5-4098 is its phone number. Kane smokes a pipe and uses Old Briar pipe tobacco at 15 cents a pouch. The shop is a vital part of the live series, as the sponsor's products are prominently displayed. In addition to Old Briar, other products of the United States Tobacco Company that are sold are Dill's Best pipe tobacco, Encore filter tip cigarettes and Sano cigarettes, no filter tips. When Kane discusses a case with shop owner Tucker "Hap" McMann, customers appear to purchase a product. Hap excuses himself and pitches the sponsor's product while Kane, or someone else involved with the case, waits patiently on the side. With the sale concluded, the show picks up from where the customer entered. When Kane places tobacco in his pipe, the camera zooms in for a closeup of the product name. Interestingly, announcer Fred Utal said during the closing theme, "And now a few seconds, friends, to remind you that your annual federal and state cigarette taxes provide almost ten times as much as it costs to operate the United States Coast Guard. So remember, in buying cigarettes, over half your packs go to tax."

William Gargan (1949–51), Lloyd Nolan (1951–52), Lee Tracy (1952–53) and Mark Stevens (1953–54) played Martin Kane. Walter Kinsella played Tucker "Hap" McMann; Frank M. Thomas was Captain Burke; and King Calder was Lieutenant Grey Redford, both of the N.Y.P.D. Homicide Squad. Hap was replaced by Don Morrow, who played himself in last season episodes, as the owner of the tobacco shop.

A revised version of the series, titled *The New Adventures of Martin Kane*, appeared in syndication in 1957 with William Gargan returning to the role of Martin Kane. Kane was now a former U.S. Air Force colonel turned private detective who operates out of London. It is a 40 minute trip from the airport to his flat. While he still works with the police, he is not the hardboiled character depicted in the earlier series: "I don't speak in fancy jargon, and I don't go around beating up beautiful women — an impression people get from seeing detectives in movies and reading about them in books." The most the "old" Martin Kane ever did to a beautiful woman was slug her if he felt she deserved it or if he needed to do so to save his life. Women were often referred to by the slang of the day — "Skirt," "Doll" and "Tomato."

Brian Reece played Scotland Yard Inspector Headley; his mobile car code was 19-C. The series is also known as *Assignment Danger*, the title used when the series was first resyndicated after its initial run.

71. Matlock (NBC, 1986–1992; ABC, 1992–1995)

Matlock and Matlock is an Atlanta, Georgia, based law firm owned by Benjamin Layton Matlock (Andy Griffith) and his daughter, Charlene (Linda Purl). It became Ben Matlock, Attorney-at-Law, when Charlene left in 1987 to begin her own law practice in Philadelphia. In the last first-run NBC episode, "The Assassination," Brynn Thayer is seen as Ben's daughter Lee Ann McIntyre. Lee Ann is a prosecuting attorney who has come to Atlanta from Philadelphia to visit her father following a legal separation from her husband, Peter. Charlene does not appear and no mention is made as to what happened to her. When the series switched to ABC with the episode, "The Vacation," Ben and Lee Ann have formed a partnership and operate a firm called Matlock and McIntyre, Attorneys-at-Law, in Atlanta. Lee Ann is still separated from her husband whom she calls "the jerk" and still uses his last name. Ben is trying to convince her to use her maiden name. When Lee Ann leaves to start her own practice in California in 1994, Ben replaces her with Attorney Michelle Thomas (Nancy Stafford) and changes the firm's name to B.L. Matlock, Attorney-at-Law, with Michelle Thomas, Attorney-at-Law appearing under his name in smaller letters. The mailing address of the firm, first season, reads simply Matlock and Matlock, Atlanta, Georgia, 30303; 555-9930 is the office phone number.

Ben charges $100,000 a case and is known for his high rate of success in defending clients. He is a Gemini and was born in the town of Mount Harlan, Georgia. Ben is a graduate of Harvard Law School and worked as a public prosecutor in Atlanta before beginning his own law practice. He attends law seminars "because you're never too old to learn" and teaches law at Eaton University. He has a doctorate degree in law from the Baxter Law School where they have also named a chair after him. Ben drives a sedan with the license plate RAF 285 and he is known for two things: eating hot dogs, usually with grape soda, and white suits; he has a closet full of them. This began in 1969 when a case brought Ben to Los Angeles. He became ill after eating several pieces of bad fish and was taken to Community General Hospital. There, he was treated by a young resident intern named Dr. Mark Sloan (Dick Van Dyke, from the series *Diagnosis Murder*). Ben was just starting his practice and Mark convinced him to invest his life savings, $5,000, in the hottest new item, 8-Track tapes. The 8-Track system proved to be a failure and Ben lost everything. Cheap white suits off the store rack and hot dogs were all he could afford, but he carried on the tradition throughout the years.

Ben sang in a church choir in his youth and occasionally plays the guitar. He despises a paper called the *Informer* because it reports on his cases and hampers his chances of freeing his clients. He also has little faith in police labs; "They're not working to help my clients." He prefers to do his own investigating. Ben doesn't make unsubstantiated charges and will occasionally take a case for free. He was voted Man of the Year by the Atlanta Chamber of Commerce in 1991 and won't allow anyone to smoke in his office — "Not even my best-paying clients." Ben is also known as a great storyteller "although he embellishes a little" says Michelle, and he knows how to appeal to a jury.

Ben rises each morning at 5:00 AM ("It's the best time for thinking") and constantly complains about paying taxes — "I owe thousands and thousands of dollars." He collects old coins — an 1804 silver dollar is his oldest — and usually defends clients at the Fulton County Court House. Ben did lose one case — his own in Small Claims Court. He bought a used 1962 refrigerator for $68.42 from a woman and sued her when it broke down. The judge ruled it was an "as is sale" and he lost. If Lee Ann sees her father walk past a hot dog vendor without looking, she knows something is wrong.

Julie March (Julie Sommars) is the prosecuting attorney with the Atlanta D.A.'s office. She was born in Nebraska and is an expert on jewelry. She considers herself one of the best legal minds in the South; Ben calls her the wildest, most ruthless prosecutor the state has. Ben also says Julie makes the best fried chicken he has ever tasted — even better than what his mother use to make. Julie and Ben take in a play or movie every Friday night. Julie left the series when she moved to Los Angeles to work as a prosecutor in the D.A.'s office.

Les Calhoun (Don Knotts) is Ben's neighbor, a retired manufacturer who prefers to be called "Ace"; he calls Ben "Benjie" or "Benje." Ace loves to shop for Christmas presents and believes "I've got great taste" in everything.

Ace, who wore lizard skin shoes and ate chop suey everyday, made plastic eyelets for sneakers.

Tyler Hudson (Kene Holliday), Ben's first investigator, was a brilliant stock market investor. He was named Young Atlanta Businessman of the Year and won $2,000 in the Junior Chamber of Commerce Chili Bake-Off. He was replaced by Conrad McMasters (Clarence Gilyard, Jr.), a police deputy who doubled as Ben's investigator. Cliff Lewis (Daniel Roebuck) is a young attorney Ben hires to assist Conrad on investigations. Cliff, a member of the Mount Harlan Volunteer Fire Department, is the son of Ben's old nemesis, Billy Lewis (Warren Frost). Billy blames Ben for breaking the heart of his sister, Lucy, many years ago. Billy claims Ben dumped Lucy after dating her for eight years; Ben claims he and Lucy mutually agreed to separate. Carol Huston appeared briefly in 1994 as Jeri Stone, the private detective Ben hired as his investigator when Charlene first left.

Cassie Phillips (Kari Lizer) is Ben's law clerk, a student at the Baxter Law School in Atlanta. Betty Lynn was Sarah, Ben's receptionist in first season episodes. In the pilot episode, Lori Lethin played Charlene and Alice Hirson was Hazel, Ben's receptionist. Flashbacks show Ben's father, Charlie Matlock (Andy Griffith) as the owner of a gas station in Mount Harlan. Steve Witting plays young Ben Matlock. Dick DeBenedictis composed the theme "Matlock."

Proposed Spinoffs

1. *McShane* (October 28, November 3, 1986). The original concept for *Jake and the Fatman* (see entry). William Conrad as James L. McShane, a former cop turned District Attorney of Atlanta, Georgia. McShane is overweight, has a German shepherd named Max and has vowed to break the back of organized crime. The pilot episode, titled "The Don," finds McShane prosecuting a man Ben Matlock is trying to prove is innocent of a murder charge.

2. *The P.I.* (March 3, 1994). Max Morgan (George Peppard) is a gambling-addicted private detective who runs Morgan Investigations in Los Angeles. Jessica Morgan (Tracy Nelson) is Max's estranged daughter, who has come to California to study art. When Jessica helps Max solve a case they become a father and daughter detective team. Elyssa Davalos plays Allison Darnell, the L.A.P.D. detective Max and Jessica assist.

72. Matt Helm (ABC, 1975–1976)

Matt Helm (Anthony Franciosa) is a former U.S. government intelligence agent for the Company turned private investigator. Matt resides at the

McGuire Beach House at 2001 Postal Road in Malibu Beach, California, with his girlfriend, Claire Kronski (Laraine Stephens), a private practice attorney. Matt drives a red Thunderbird convertible with the license plate 258-8PP; 555-2040 is his telephone number. Claire, called Kronski by Matt, was born in Texas. Her office address is 36 Primrose Lane and 555-1333 is her phone number. Matt claims "Kronski is the most honest lawyer who ever lived but one of the sneakiest people I have ever known."

Ethel (Jeff Donnell), who calls Matt "Matthew," runs Ethel's Answering Service; Lieutenant Hanrahan (Gene Evans), Matt's friend, is with the Homicide Division of the Parker Center of the L.A.P.D. Morton Stevens composed the theme "Matt Helm."

73. Matt Houston (ABC, 1982–1985)

Matlock Houston (Lee Horsley), called Matt, is a millionaire oil baron, cattle rancher and playboy who helps people in deep trouble. He is the owner of Houston, Inc., a conglomerate at 200 West Temple Street in Los Angeles (address later given as 100 Century Plaza South in Los Angeles) and Houston Investigations, the agency through which he enjoys doing what he likes best—solving crimes. 555-3141 is his office telephone number. Matt also owns the Houston Cattle Ranch in Texas.

Matt owns a Rolls Royce, license plate COWBOY I, and a car that he uses in his investigative work that he calls the *Excalibur*, license plate 21 VE 124. Matt calls his computer Baby and N1090Z is the identification number of the Houston Industries helicopter.

C.J. Parsons (Pamela Hensely) is Matt's assistant. She lives at 8766 West Beverly, Apartment 3C. Roy Houston (Buddy Ebsen) is Matt's uncle and assistant in last season episodes; Vince Novelli (John Aprea) is a lieutenant with the S.C.P.D. (Southern California Police Department); Vince's mother, Rosa (Penny Santon), owns Matt's favorite eatery, Mama Novelli's Restaurant; Michael Hoyt (Lincoln Kilpatrick) is a lieutenant with the L.A.P.D.; and Murray Chase (George Wyner) is Matt's harried business manager. Dominic Frontiere composed the theme "Matt Houston."

Proposed Spinoff (Unsold Pilot)

Zoey (February 1, 1985). Deborah Adair as Zoey Martin, a beautiful private investigator who uses the latest in scientific technology to solve crimes. The pilot episode, "The Beach Club Murders," finds Zoey teaming with Matt Houston to find an extortionist.

74. McMillan and Wife (NBC, 1971–1976)

The home at 345 Melrose in San Francisco is the residence of Stewart McMillan (Rock Hudson), the police commissioner, and his wife, Sally (Susan Saint James), a woman who loves to play detective and help her husband solve crimes. Their phone number is 555-8600; 376 QK6 is Sally's station wagon license plate number, and 835 CRO is Stewart's sedan license plate number.

Stewart, nicknamed Mac ("Everybody calls me Mac"), is a former lawyer and Korean War veteran (Naval Intelligence). Mac reads a paper called the *Daily Post* and at breakfast he likes his English muffins broken apart ("one breaks an English muffin; one does not cut it"). He has lunch at a health food diner called The Grainery and hates going to Sally's mother's house for Saturday brunch ("She's a terrible cook"). Mac mentioned that his grandfather, John P. McMillan, began a company in 1903 called Kenamack Alfalfa, which was designed but failed to find new uses for alfalfa. Mac played football in college and each year turns lawyer for his annual reserve duty with the Navy's Legal Service Office.

Mac is an unusual police commissioner as he actually involves himself in criminal investigations. This pleases Sally, a bright woman who believes she has the makings of a private investigator. Sally's maiden name is Hull. She works with deaf children at Century Hospital and when she has a problem, she meditates. Sally has an uncanny knack for finding trouble. She gathers evidence for Mac "by peeking" ("It's not nice to be sneaky"). Sally hopes to surpass her mother in the cooking department and takes gourmet culinary classes at the local high school. She believes she is on the right track because Mac "loved my rattlesnake bernaise and walnut casserole in goat butter." Each Halloween, Sally displays Marvin, her life-size skeleton.

Mildred (Nancy Walker) cooks and cleans for Mac and Sally. She considers herself a Jill of all trades for all the work she does — including helping Sally solve crimes. Mildred has a slight drinking problem and is trying to quit. She stores eggs in the seven day meat keeper section of the refrigerator and has all the essential kitchen utensils set for her height level, about five feet. Mac likes the items about a foot higher so he doesn't have to constantly bend when he cooks. Sergeant Charles Enright (John Schuck) is Mac's right hand man. His squad car license plate reads 261 508; Mac's limo license plate is 589 ODG. Mildred Natwick played Mac's eccentric mother, Beatrice McMillan; Linda Watkins was Sally's mother, Emily Hull.

McMillan and Wife ended after five seasons. It returned in 1976 (to 1977) for six episodes as *McMillan*. A contract dispute forced Susan Saint

James to quit. Her character was written out when viewers learn that Sally was killed in an airplane crash. Nancy Walker also left the series, quitting the McMillan household to star in her own show, *The Nancy Walker Show* (ABC, 1976–1977). Martha Raye was brought on as Agatha Thornton, Mildred's sister, who became Mac's new housekeeper. Mac, now a widower, was fully adjusted to his new life style when the revised version of the series premiered. John Schuck continued his role as Charles Enright, but now as a lieutenant and more closely involved with Mac in his investigations. The series aired as a segment of *The NBC Wednesday Mystery Movie* and *The NBC Sunday Mystery Movie*. Jerry Fielding composed the theme.

75. Me and Mom (ABC, 1985)

Morgan, Garfield and Hunnicutt is a Los Angeles-based detective agency located at 2936 Hampton Boulevard; 213-555-5613 is its phone number. Kate Morgan (Lisa Eilbacher) is a young criminologist who runs the firm with her wealthy and glamorous mother, Zena Hunnicutt (Holland Taylor) and Lou Garfield (James Earl Jones), a tough, former cop with the Homicide Division of the L.A.P.D. Kate lives in an apartment at 137 Stepford Place; Zena resides in a luxurious home at 51 Chevia Street. Amy Holland sings the theme "Me and Mom."

76. Miami Vice (NBC, 1984–1989)

James "Sonny" Crockett (Don Johnson) and Ricardo Tubbs (Philip Michael Thomas) are detectives with the vice squad division of the Miami Metro Dade County Police Department, also called the Miami, Florida, Police Department. Sonny is divorced from Caroline (Belinda J. Montgomery) and the father of Billy (Clayton Barclay Jones). Sonny lives away from the pressures of society on a boat he calls *The Saint Vidas Dance*. Sonny is "a drug dealer this week, an outlaw biker the next. I'm trying to get by on four hours of sleep a day. I go undercover for weeks at a time. It's disastrous on a marriage, hell on the nervous system." Sonny still loves Caroline but when it comes to being a cop it's strictly business.

Sonny is a former football player for the University of Miami, the Gators; he wore jersey 88. Although he had a promising career, "I traded the whole thing in for two years in Nam." After the war he became a cop. He started in plainclothes and worked his way up to vice. He gets a high from the action but suffers from a gambling and drinking problem. He prefers to do things his way and has been suspended for misconduct. Once on a case he doesn't request backup and he won't submit progress reports. He fears leaks in the department could compromise his cases.

Sonny lives on his boat with Elvis, an alligator who was the former mascot of the Gators football team. Elvis was benched for taking a bite out of a player and now works as Sonny's watchdog and dope sniffer. Elvis shows his teeth when strangers appear and ticks — he ate a clock. Elvis is also high; he devoured a bag of LSD when searching a Key West bus for drugs. Sonny has an account at the Dade County Federal Bank and says of he and Tubbs, "We're just tollbooths on the highway when it comes to bustin' drug runners." Ricardo calls it, "Sonny singing the vice blues." To protect his identity around the marina where his boat is docked, Sonny is known as Sonny Brunette.

Ricardo was born in the Bronx, New York, and was a detective with the Armed Robbery Division of the N.Y.P.D., Bronx Division. Another episode claims he was an undercover narcotics detective with the N.Y.P.D. When his brother, Raphael, is killed by a drug kingpin in Brooklyn, Ricardo tracks the killer to Miami and meets Sonny, who is seeking the same man. They solve the case and Ricardo accepts an offer to work with Sonny in vice. When Ricardo visits Sonny on the boat he is known as Ricardo Cooper to protect his identity. Ricardo, called Rico by Sonny, says his name stands for "tough, unique, bad, bold and sassy." Ricardo is single and lives in an apartment on Linden Avenue. He is not as aggressive as Sonny and prefers to take a less gung ho approach when it comes to questioning or chasing suspects. He has an account at the Security Central Bank of Florida.

Sonny and Ricardo work with detectives Gina Calabrese (Saundra Santiago), Larry Zito (John Diehl) and Trudy Joplin (Olivia Brown). Lieutenant Lou Rodriquez (Gregory Sierra) is their first superior; he is replaced by Lieutenant Martin Castillo (Edward James Olms). Last season episodes find Sonny marrying Caitlin Davies (Sheena Easton). Jan Hammer composed the theme.

77. Michael Shayne (NBC, 1960–1961)

Michael Shayne (Richard Denning) is a private detective with an office, number 322, at 483 Adams Street in the city of Miami, Florida. Mike, as he is sometimes called, often complains that his mail occasionally gets rerouted to Miami Beach by mistake. His phone number is 236-6236 and he never sees a client before ten in the morning. Mike enjoys his work despite what some people say — "Mike is practical and realistic and will never get rich at what he is doing." He is relaxed and easygoing and tries not to fly off the handle. He will avoid violence if possible, offers a cigarette to clients and suspects to relax them, and manages to sneak in a kiss when the client is a gorgeous female. Mike gathers the evidence, sorts through the clues and uses every dirty trick in the book to get the truth from both clients and suspects. He uses Brazer's Chemical Lab to do his analysis, and he is a member of the Private Investigators of America.

Angel is the affectionate name Mike uses for Lucy Hamilton (Patricia Donahue, Margie Regan), his ever faithful secretary and sometimes "legman." Lucy, who can type 90 words a minute, never lets a client get away. She lives in a respectable apartment at 8 Gower Street and her phone number is 976-6616.

Tim Rourke (Jerry Paris) is Mike's friend, a reporter-photographer for the Miami *Tribune*; Will Gentry (Herbert Rudley) is the homicide police chief based in the Municipal Justice Building who Mike says is "one of the most cooperative police officers I've ever worked with." Leith Stevens composed "The Theme from Michael Shayne."

Note: The Brett Halliday-created characters first appeared on television on September 28, 1958 in an unsold pilot called "Man on a Raft" broadcast on NBC's pilot series, *Decision*. Mark Stevens played Michael Shayne, Merry Anders was Lucy Hamilton and Robert Brubaker portrayed Tim Rourke. In the story, Mike is hired by Ann Conway (Diane Brewster) to find her husband's killer. Had the pilot sold, the series would have been called "Michael Shayne, Detective."

78. Mike Hammer (Syndicated, 1957–1959; CBS, 1984–1987; Syndicated, 1997–1998)

Original Syndicated Version (1957): Mike Hammer (Darren McGavin) is a two-fisted private detective working out of New York City. He has an eye for the girls; friends tell him, "Watch it, Mike, your fangs are showing." If there is a beautiful "doll" or "dish" in trouble, Mike will go out of his way to help her, even waive his fee if necessary. Mike uses force, his fists, to get results and considers roughing up a suspect his social call. This character, created by Mickey Spillane, takes the law into his own hands and dishes out his own brand of justice — violence — and gets away with it. Mike has an office, Room 812, in Manhattan and lives in a hotel on West 47th Street. For research, Mike uses the newspaper morgues of the real *Daily News* at 220 East 42nd Street and the mythical *Chronicle*. Mike's traditional secretary, Velda, is not present in this series, which presents Mike as a loner out to battle injustice and make a buck. The only other regular is his friend, Pat

Chambers (Bart Burns), a captain with the Homicide Division of the N.Y.P.D.'s 19th Precinct. Brian Keith was originally scheduled to play the role of Mike Hammer but was dropped when producers felt he was not right for the role. Dave Kahn and Melvyn Lenard composed the theme "Riff Blues."

CBS Version: Hard boiled New York City-based private detective Mike Hammer (Stacy Keach) was once a cop—"But I knew all the rules, that's why I'm not a cop now." He owns the Mike Hammer Agency at 304 West 16th Street in Manhattan. He has an eye for the ladies, but he is not as violent as his predecessor. Mike resides at 4100 Tenth Avenue and 212-555-6974 is his office phone number. He drives a blue 1966 Mustang and carries a gun he calls Betsy. As a kid Mike had a dog named Ike; they were called "Mike and Ike." His hangout is Marty's Bar.

Velda is present in all CBS versions. As originally created, Velda was a brunette with a gift of gab and the ability to handle a gun. For television, hair color and using a gun didn't matter; being well-endowed did. Lindsay Bloom played Velda in the CBS series (*Mickey Spillane's Mike Hammer*, 1984–1985, and *The New Mike Hammer*, 1986–1987). Velda was now agile, had the gift of gab, but strayed from using a firearm. Pat Chambers (Don Stroud) is a detective with the Homicide Division at the N.Y.P.D. Lawrence Barrington (Kent Williams) is the Manhattan D.A. and Ozzie the Answer (Danny Goldman) is Mike's information man.

The series gimmick is a character called "The Face" (Donna Denton), a beautiful but mysterious girl who is seen briefly in each episode. She appeared to be following Mike. In the final episode, Mike uncovered her to be a writer named Laura who wrote "Nick Steele" mystery novels under the pen name Frederick Flynn. She tailed Mike to get story material. Prior to this last episode, the girl playing the role had only been identified as "D.D." Earle Hagen composed the theme "Harlem Nocturne."

1997 Syndicated Version: *Mike Hammer, Private Eye* combines elements of the prior series to present a tougher, more aggressive Mike Hammer (Stacy Keach). Shannon Whirry plays Velda, Mike's buxom secretary, with Kent Williams as Lawrence Barrington, the Deputy Mayor of New York, and Rebecca Chaney as "The Face."

CBS TV Movies: Prior to the 1984 series, three TV movie pilots aired

1. Mickey Spillane's Mike Hammer: Margin for Murder (October 15, 1981) with Kevin Dobson (Mike Hammer), Cindy Pickett (Velda) and Charles Hallahan (Pat Chambers).

2. *Mickey Spillane's Mike Hammer: More Than Murder* (January 26, 1983) with Stacy Keach (Mike Hammer), Lindsay Bloom (Velda), Don Stroud (Pat Chambers) and Kent Williams (Lawrence Barrington).

3. *Mickey Spillane's Mike Hammer: Murder Me, Murder You* (April 9, 1983) with Stacy Keach (Mike Hammer), Tanya Roberts (Velda), Don Stroud (Pat Chambers) and Kent Williams (Lawrence Barrington).

Also: Prior to the New Syndicated Series, Three Additional TV Movies Appeared

1. The Return of Mickey Spillane's Mike Hammer (September 18, 1986), the pilot for *The New Mike Hammer* series that features the same cast (Stacy Keach, Lindsay Bloom, Don Stroud and Kent Williams) in the same roles.

2. Mickey Spillane's Mike Hammer: Murder Takes All (May 21, 1989). Stacy Keach returns as Mike Hammer with Lindsay Bloom (Velda) and Don Stroud (Pat Chambers).

*3. **Come Die with Me: A Mickey Spillane Mike Hammer Mystery*** (December 6, 1994). The unsold pilot episode for a new version of the Mickey Spillane character that takes Mike away from New York City and places him in a new home in Miami Beach, Florida. Rob Estes plays a younger Mike Hammer and Pamela Anderson is Mike's gorgeous, buxom secretary, Velda, who relocated so she could continue being Mike's girl Friday. Mike's office door reads "Mike Hammer, Private Eye"; his phone number is 555-9606 and his car license plate reads HAMMER. The character of Pat Chambers has also been changed — from a male to a female. Patricia Chambers (Darlanne Fluegel) is a detective sergeant with the Miami Police Department. The pilot finds Mike again helping the underdog — a pretty girl find her missing father. Ron Ramin composed the theme.

Proposed Spinoff (Unsold Pilot)

Harry (May 13, 1987). Mary Frann as Harriet Quayle, a tough but beautiful Australian private detective, nicknamed Harry, who has made New York City her new home. The pilot episode, titled "A Face in the Night," finds Harry teaming with Mike Hammer to find an elusive novelist.

79. Mr. and Mrs. North (CBS, 1952–1953; NBC, 1954)

Apartment 6A at 24 Sainte Anne's Place in New York's Greenwich Village is home to Jerry and Pamela North (Richard Denning, Barbara Britton), a happily married couple who often help the police solve crimes. Jerry is a former World War II Navy Lieutenant turned private detective who relinquished his career of murder and mayhem for what he believed would be a peaceful existence as a publisher (company name not revealed). Pamela appears to be a typical wife. She cares for the house, organizes quiet dinner parties, but believes she has the mind of a detective and has set her goal to solve murders. Pamela, while beautiful and fashion conscious, doesn't go out of her way to find a crime; a crime seems to have a way of finding her. She is forever stumbling upon them and when she sees something that is wrong, she immediately associates it with foul play. While she would like to solve what she finds on her own, Pamela often feels she needs help and drags Jerry into her little murder mysteries. Jerry finds himself turning detective again and does so because it's easier to give into Pam than to argue with her when she has her mind set on something.

Pamela and Jerry have been married for five years when the series begins. Pamela, called Pam, was a secretary and Jerry a detective when they married on a Friday afternoon and honeymooned in Paris. On the occasion of their first wedding anniversary, Pam gave Jerry a pocket watch with the inscription "To Jerry, With Love, Pam." Jerry claims that Pam has a suspicious mind and that her curiosity often gets her into trouble. He fears for her safety and always changes his plans to accommodate her; "Since I married Pam, disrupted plans are the one thing in life that I can positively depend on." While Jerry likes to relax and take it easy every once in a while, Pam always seems to be fully of energy — "I use to go to parties and dance and stay up all night and work the next day and go to another party that evening. I'm just as young as I ever was."

Pamela does solve crimes on her own. She is so unassuming that culprits are unaware of her brilliance and are caught by surprise. Pam is very proud of herself at these moments and tells Jerry "that if I hadn't used by brains, I'd be dead. You'd have a corpse for a wife." Unfortunately, Pam tells Jerry this when he is trying to sleep or is involved with a manuscript. The remark falls on virtually deaf ears — "Yes honey, that's nice dear." Occasionally Jerry's subconscious hears what Pam is saying. When he realizes what Pam has said, he shows great concern and tells her not to do it again. She agrees — until the next episode.

The Norths address was also given as 23 Sainte Anne's Place, Apartment 408, even though Apartment 6A is seen in the opening theme. Their phone number was given as GRamercy 3-4098, GRamercy 3-8099 and GRamercy 3-4370. Their car license plate reads NN 1139. Bill Weigand (Francis DeSales) is their friend, a lieutenant with the Homicide Division of the N.Y.P.D. He was best man at their wedding; PE 6-0599 is his phone number. The series is based on the characters created by Frances and Richard Lockridge.

Two Pilots were Produced Prior to the Series

1. *Mr. and Mrs. North*, NBC, May 19, 1946. John McQuade played Jerry North with Maxine Stuart as Pamela North. Here the Norths try to solve the mystery of who killed a man and placed the body in their apartment. Vinton Hayworth played Lieutenant Bill Weigand with Millard Mitchell as his assistant, Detective Mullins.

2. *Mr. and Mrs. North*, NBC, July 4, 1949. Joseph Allen, Jr. and Mary Lou Taylor play Jerry and Pamela North. Here the couple attempt to help a lawyer find the culprit who is killing heirs to a large estate.

Mrs. Columbo *See* Kate Loves a Mystery

80. The Mod Squad (ABC, 1968–1973)

The word "mod" is defined as "young people noted for their emphasis on stylish dress; often as a symbol of their alienation from conventional society." Pete Cochrane (Michael Cole), Julie Barnes (Peggy Lipton) and Linc Hayes (Clarence Williams III) are three such people — young adults arrested on minor charges and offered a choice by Captain Adam Greer (Tige Andrews) of the L.A.P.D.: spend time in jail or perform specific undercover assignments for him as the Mod Squad. "Times change and cops have to change with it," says Adam. "They can get into a thousand places that we can't. Who is going to suspect kids." Pete, Julie and Linc were headed for nowhere and Adam gave them a chance to change the course of their lives. They are not permitted to carry guns and rely on their street smarts to accomplish their goals.

Pete is from a wealthy family and lived in a 14 room, five bathroom Beverly Hills mansion. He simply met the wrong kind of people and was kicked out by his parents for being anti everything. Pete rejected all the efforts his parents made to help him. He was arrested for taking a joy ride in a stolen car.

Julie had no address. Her father had deserted the family and Julie lived with her mother in San Francisco. When Julie discovered her mother was a prostitute, she ran away. She was arrested in Los Angeles for having no visible means of support. Julie couldn't handle her mother's life of one night stands and just "split." She has lost track of her mother and does not know where her mother is or if she is still alive. Recalling her life with her mother depresses Julie; she becomes bitter and cries. She now lives in a 1½ room apartment on LaCentra Drive.

Lincoln, nicknamed Linc, was born and raised in the Watts section of Los Angeles. He lived in a three room apartment with 13 people and grew up bitter and disillusioned. He believed in the Black Cause but during the Watts riots, he started a fire and was arrested for arson. He has now come to respect people of all races, and color doesn't matter when arresting criminals although he does say, "I hate to fink on a soul brother."

The whole idea behind the Mod Squad is for Linc, Julie and Pete to melt in, not stand out. Adam believes this is possible although his superior, Chief Barney Metcalf (Simon Scott) believes the Mod Squad are just kids on probation. Adam becomes upset when the squad is arrested as part of a bust. He feels their attitudes will expose their undercover operations. Julie screams, "Police brutality"; Linc uses the Uncle Tom bit and Pete sounds off with his big mouth. At first the cases were tough and Julie said, "How did we get into this?" "We made a deal," says Pete; "And it beats walking the streets," says Linc.

Julie, Pete and Linc break all the rules — from stealing and breaking and entering — to get the job done. Each feels they are now part of something important for the first time in their lives. Although they like Adam, they feel he is too hard to please. Julie is restless during assignments; Pete is impatient and too anxious to make things happen; Linc is the calm one and usually brings focus to the group. Pete drives an old woodie, license plate 198 543, and the squad's mobile code is W-6-0. Adam enjoys fishing and 10–12 is his car code.

On May 18, 1979, ABC ran a TV movie/pilot called *The Return of the Mod Squad* that was a failed attempt to revise the series. The story finds Pete, Julie and Linc (Michael Cole, Peggy Lipton, Clarence Williams III) reuniting after a seven year absence to help Adam (Tige Andrews), now the Deputy Police Commissioner, find a mysterious assailant who is threatening to kill him. Had the series sold, the squad would have performed special assignments for Adam.

Pete, who was anti-establishment, returned to his home in Beverly Hills to take over his late father's business. Julie finally found happiness when she married Dan Bennett (Roy Thinnes), a rancher in northern California. Linc had moved to New York to complete his college education and is now working as a school teacher in Los Angeles. He is also the father of an adopted son named Jason (Todd Bridges).

81. Monk (USA/ABC, 2002)

Adrian Monk (Tony Shalhoub) is a brilliant detective with the 14th Division of the San Francisco Police Department. He is married to a woman named Trudy and lives in a house on Cole Street. Trudy, an investigative reporter for the *Examiner*, was killed in 1998 when she became the victim of a car bombing. Was she working on a story? Did she get too close to something? These are the questions that drive Adrian to continually review the facts of the case in the hope that he will one day find her killer. He often returns to the site of the bombing — Parking Space 5-B in a building garage — looking for inspiration. Trudy's death also affected Adrian in another way. It triggered a rare anxiety disorder that makes him germ phobic and afraid of virtually everything. The condition immediately interferes with Adrian's work and he is given a 315 temporary suspicion (a psychological discharge).

Adrian regularly sees psychiatrist Dr. Kroger, played by Stanley Kamel, and is aided by his full time nurse, Sharona Fleming (Bitty Schram). Adrian needs to keep busy, but he is still "too nuts," as people say, to return to the force, something he desperately misses. With the help of Sharona, the only person he feels comfortable with, Adrian begins a private consulting business and together they set out to help people in trouble. Even the police use Monk's unique abilities when they are stumped. Monk's fee is $500 a day plus expenses.

Monk has encyclopedic knowledge of strange and obscure facts. He cleans to think and notices everything about people. He has a photographic memory and the deductive skills of Sherlock Holmes. He can spot things at a crime scene that even the most highly trained specialists overlook. Monk can tell the brand of cigarette a person smokes simply by the odor; he can study a crime scene and deduct, quite accurately, whether the killer was a man or woman, black or white and even height and weight. He can rearrange shredded documents and everything must make sense in order for him to perform properly. A person who is neat and tidy impresses Monk. When Adrian goes to a restaurant, he orders separate plates for the various foods — foods that touch upset him — and he brings his own silverware.

Heights, germs, crowds, the dark and even milk are only a small fraction of the fears Monk must overcome. Sharona says, "He's making good progress on the milk." Monk is a compulsive cleaner and doesn't like to be touched. If he must shake someone's hand, Sharona gives him a Lever Brothers 2000 Moist Towelette. He is also superstitious and afraid of cars. When he must ride in a car, he prefers that Sharona do the driving. Monk worries about everything ("Did I turn the gas off?" "Did I leave the coffee pot on?")

and sometimes has great difficulty thinking because he is always worrying. Monk needs a five watt night light to sleep (any brighter and he can't sleep) and takes three showers a day. He sleeps with Trudy's picture on his night stand and sometimes has trouble making decisions. He is allergic to tomatoes and is use to certain meals on certain days; chicken pot pie was mentioned for Tuesday. He becomes upset if Sharona changes the menu. Monk places his everyday clothes in individual plastic bags, fixes pillows on couches, straightens pictures and makes sure that any desk or bulletin board he sees is in perfect order. He also needs to touch things as he walks to feel secure; for example, every fire hydrant, every fence rail, every mail box. After first meeting Monk, people say, "That's the famous Adrian Monk, the living legend? He's nuts." Sharona assures them, "He's not." In a flashback sequence, it is learned that in high school Monk was on the track team but was even compulsive then. Willie Nelson is Monk's favorite singer and Adrian is capable of playing the clarinet.

When Monk studies a crime scene, Sharona says, "He's doing the zen Sherlock Holmes thing." Sharona, a practical nurse, is very devoted to Adrian, but his disorder sometimes gets to her and she exclaims, "I quit," but she always comes back "because I miss Monk." When asked why she works for Adrian, Sharona says, "It's the worst job I ever had but it's also the best job I ever had. I'm having adventures, I'm putting bad guys behind bars, I feel like Lois Lane. How many practical nurses can say that? Not many." Sharona does act like Lois Lane and puts her life on the line to help Monk, who becomes her "Superman" when he overcomes a fear only momentarily to save her life.

Sharona is divorced and lives at 308 Valencia at 28th Street with her young son, Benjy (Kane Ritchote). Benjy is in the sixth grade and loves to draw comics. Sharona mentioned that before moving to San Francisco she worked as a ballroom dancer in Atlantic City, New Jersey. Sharona cannot take a vacation because Adrian cannot live without her. Sharona interned at Medista General Hospital and has an account at North California Bank. Her car license plate reads 4GBI 462. Sharona believes in psychics; "I can't tell you how much money I wasted on those TV psychics." Monk does not believe in psychics—"only in what I can see." Sharona believes Monk is a psychic who doesn't believe in psychics.

Adrian carries a good luck charm with him at all times—a key chain given to him by Trudy. When Monk assists the police, it is on "Observer Status" only. His former captain, Leland Stottlemeyer (Ted Levine) is the one who seems to need Monk's help the most. Leland is often amazed by Monk's abilities. "How does he see what he sees? I have two eyes and see everything he sees, but I don't see what he sees." It was Leland, who was worried about Monk, who found him Sharona — "She showed up one day and never left," says Monk.

Jeff Beal composed the theme.

82. Moon Over Miami (NBC, 1993)

The Walter Tatum Detective Agency, also called Walter Tatum, Inc., is a private investigative firm located at 668 Strand in South Beach in Miami, Florida. Walter Tatum (Bill Campbell) owns the agency; Gwen Cross (Ally Walker) assists him. The agency charges $200 a day plus expenses; 555-3666 is its phone number and Walter drives a car with the license plate WCU 72N.

Walter was raised by his grandparents, Nate and Adelaide Tatum (George O. Petri, Pat Gellar) since he was two years old, at which time his parents were killed in a plane crash. Nate was a famous musician and played sax with the Benny Goodman Band. Walter was fascinated by police and detective shows on television and this influenced his decision to become a lawyer to help people. One summer while working as an apprentice for the Legal Aid Society, Walter's life changed. He saw private detective Gavin Mills (Elliott Gould) help an old lady get her hot water turned back on. The detective did more for the lady than a whole team of lawyers. Walter quit law school and became an apprentice to Mills. He later opened his own agency.

Gwenevere, called Gwen, is the spoiled daughter of Arthur Cross (Chelcie Ross), a wealthy businessman. Arthur has babied Gwen all her life. When he felt the time was right, he arranged a marriage for her — to a man Gwen disliked. Feeling that "My life has no meaning," Gwen refused to get married and deserted her father and fiance. In an effort to find Gwen, Cross hires Walter Tatum. Walter finds Gwen, but takes her side and tells Cross he is unable to find her. Gwen, without any money and desperately in need of a job, finds employment as Walter's receptionist. She later doubles as Walter's investigator when she helps him solve a case of bank fraud.

Gwen originally lived in the office, then in an apartment on Lomax Drive. She is a graduate of the University of Miami and very careful about what she eats ("I don't eat desserts because they are an unnecessary indulgence"). Gwen adapts quickly to her new life style but fears her father will one day find her and she will be forced to go back to live a life she hates. The series ended abruptly three months after its premiere with Gwen's relationship with her father still uncertain. She and Walter began a relationship, but this too was left unclear. Delfeayo Marsalis composed the theme.

83. Moonlighting (ABC, 1985–1989)

Blue Moon Investigations is a Los Angeles-based private detective organization owned by Maddie Hayes (Cybill Shepherd). David Addison (Bruce Willis) is her chief investigator and the agency's manager. Agnes DiPesto (Allyce Beasley) is the agency's receptionist; and Herbert Viola (Curtis Armstrong) is Agnes's romantic interest and the agency's bookkeeper.

Madeline, who prefers to be called Maddie, was a beautiful and sophisticated model who suddenly found herself penniless when her business manager embezzled her funds. With no intent on working for a living, Maddie begins to sell off her business interests, one of which is a detective agency called City of Angels Investigations. Fearful of losing his job, David Addison sweet talks Maddie into saving the company. They become partners and lovers in the reorganized Blue Moon Investigations, also called the Blue Moon Detective Agency, which is located in an office (206) of an unnamed building.

Maddie is said to be one of the world's most glamorous and most photographed models. She was born in Chicago on October 11 and as a child had a sheep dog named Sport. Her face has graced the covers of such magazines as *Fashion*, *Glamour*, *Vanity Fair* and *Vogue* and she appeared in television commercials as the Blue Moon Shampoo Girl. Maddie has a perfect driving record and her car license plate reads 28 0018.

David was born in Los Angeles on November 27. He is a graduate of UCLA and is optimistic about everything. He constantly jokes, makes lewd sexual remarks and sings whenever the opportunity permits, even when it doesn't. He calls Maddie "Blondie Blonde" and says, "I'm a capitalist — I take my capital wherever I can get it." "Do bears bare? Do bees be?" is his catchphrase and he drives a car with the license plate 2900 LB.

Maddie is totally honest and forthright; she believes in people despite what has happened to her. David is immature, deceitful and totally distrustful of people. He'll take any case as long as it means money and often goes behind Maddie's back to find clients. Maddie and David constantly bicker about everything, especially the agency, which appears to be a losing proposition for Maddie. "Addison, we need a client, a client we can depend on; a bread and butter client who can help us pay our light bill." David insists that "we have clients" and "we must create our own opportunities. We're sitting on a money machine; we only have to figure out how to turn it on." Maddie feels just the opposite — "We're standing on the decks of the *Titanic*. No one calls, no one comes in and it's bankrupting me. Why am I living this life? I don't deserve this!" Maddie's first sigh of relief came in the episode "Portrait of Maddie" when the agency showed its first profit of $2,035.76.

Despite Maddie's complaints, David does find clients—all of whom Maddie finds unsettling. She especially hates infidelity cases because they are too full of deception and dirt. She also complains about the clients who walk in off the street: "I should have known when a client walks in off the street she'd be nuts"; for example, a girl claiming to be a Leprechaun who hires them to find her pot of gold.

A series like *Moonlighting* comes along once in a blue moon. It was something different at the time but production problems abounded and eventually caused its cancellation. When a new episode could be had, it was heavily promoted by ABC. Despite the fact that Maddie and David have nothing in common, they were brought together in the final few episodes of the 1986–87 season. The following season finds Maddie returning to her parents home in Chicago to sort out her relationship with David. Here, she discovers she is pregnant (to reflect Cybill's real life pregnancy with twins). Maddie had been unfaithful to David and was not sure if the baby was David's or her friend Sam Crawford (Mark Harmon). In a strange turn of events, Maddie marries Walter Bishop (Dennis Dugan), a man she met on a train. The series totally lost its charm and audience and was soon cancelled. The episode, "A Womb with a View," suggested that David is the father. Bruce Willis appeared as Maddie's unborn child and commented on David's relationship with Maddie.

"Blue Moon Detective Agency. If persons are missing; if objects are lost, we'll find them for you at a reasonable cost" or "Blue Moon Investigations. Get in some trouble, we'll be there on the double. Wife a philanderer, don't worry, we'll handle her" are but two of the many phrases Agnes uses to answer the agency's phones. Agnes talks in rhymes and lives at 633 Hope Street, Apartment 723. Eva Marie Saint and Robert Webber appeared as Maddie's wealthy parents, Virginia and Alexander Hayes. Paul Sorvino was David's father, David Addison, Sr.; and Imogene Coca played Agnes's mother, Clara DiPesto.

Al Jarreau sings the theme "Moonlighting."

84. Murder, She Wrote (CBS, 1984–1996)

The Victorian house at 698 Candlewood Road in Cabot Cove, Maine, is home to Jessica Beatrice Fletcher (Angela Lansbury), a widowed mystery novelist better known as J.B. Fletcher. Jessica, maiden name MacGill, is a former high school English teacher who was married to Frank Fletcher, a real estate broker responsible for establishing the Cabot Cove Democratic Society. During a summer vacation from college Jessica worked as an apprentice at the Applewood Playhouse; it was here that she first met co-worker Frank Fletcher. They dated and later married. They had a faithful marriage but were never blessed with children. After Frank's death from natural causes in the early 1980s, Jessica quit her teaching job of 19 years to devote full time to her one indulgence — writing. The publication of her first novel, *The Corpse Danced at Midnight*, became a best seller and began a new career for her as a mystery novelist and amateur sleuth. To always have Frank near her, Jessica wears a pendant near her heart that contains a picture of Frank.

The population of Cabot Cove is 3,560; its zip code is 03041. Jessica's mother had come from Kilclier, Ireland, and Jessica grew up in New England. As a child, Jessica would skinny dip at the lake in the back of the family house. Jessica's fascination for writing could be attributed to a college break when she worked as a reporter for a newspaper wire service. The Cabot Cove Bus Lines, later called Tri-County Bus Lines, services the area. Other businesses are the Light House Motel, the Cabot Cove Boat Works and the local eatery, the Cabot Cove Diner. The *Globe Gazette*, also seen as the *Cabot Cove Gazette*, is the town's newspaper and the Cabot Cove Cemetery was established in 1710.

Jessica enjoys jogging, gardening, cooking and helping with local charities. She rarely drinks, but when she does, it's a glass of white wine. Jessica is friendly, talkative and uses her bicycle to get around town. She dislikes driving and refuses to get a license. In later episodes, Jessica acquires a job in New York City as a criminology teacher at Manhattan University. She resides in Apartment 4B at the Penfield Apartments, 941 West 16th Street; 212-124-7199 is her phone number. In New York-based episodes, Jessica also teaches creative writing in Inner City High School and does volunteer work on behalf of the Museum of Cultural History and the Liberty Foundation. Jessica also became a world traveler and wherever she goes she is willing to help a stranger in trouble; she is also eager to help the police figure out "who done it," all of which give her inspiration for her books.

Jessica is an expert on poisons due to her research and often says, "I think I know who the murderer is. Now to prove it!" Angela Lansbury also played her look-alike British cousin, Emma MacGill, a veteran music hall entertainer living in London.

Jessica's original publisher was Covington House; later it is Sutton Place Publishers then Harper Publishers and finally Consolidated Publishers, all in New York City. Two of Jessica's lead fictional detectives are Inspector Dison and Inspector Gelico. Damain Sinclair is the debonair jewel thief she created. The following is an alphabetical listing of the books mentioned as being written by J.B. Fletcher, most of which are offered as "Murder of the

Month" book club selections: *Ashes, Ashes, Fall Down*; *The Belgrade Murders*; *Calvin Cantebury's Revenge*; *A Case and a Half of Murder*; *The Corpse at Vespers*; *The Corpse Danced at Midnight* (made into a book on tape for the blind); *The Corpse Wasn't There*; *The Crypt of Death*; *The Dead Must Sing*; *Dirge for a Dead Dachshund*; *The Killer Called Collect*; *A Killing at Hastings Rock* (made into a virtual reality game); *The Launch Pad Murders*; *Love's Revenge*; *Messenger at Midnight* (made into a movie); *Murder at Midnight* (Jessica's favorite book "because I didn't know who the killer was until the last 12 pages"); *Murder at the Asylum*; *Murder at the Digs* (suggested by her friend, Dr. Seth Hazlett); *Murder at the Ridge Top*; *Murder Comes to Maine*; *Murder in a Minor Key*; *Murder on the Amazon*; *Murder Will Out* (made into a virtual reality game); *Runaway to Murder*; *Sanitarium of Death*; *The Stain on the Stairs*; *Stone Cold Dead*; *The Triple Crown Murders*; *The Umbrella Murders*; *The Uncaught*; *The Venomous Valentine*; and *Yours Truly, Damain Sinclair*.

According to Seth Hazlett (William Windom), the town's elderly doctor, Cabot Cove leads the nation in the sale of live bait. Doc Hazlett, as he is called, has been practicing medicine for 37 years and lives in a 120-year-old house. Doc is a widower, a bit cantankerous and has a penchant for talking. He has a natural curiosity about life and enjoys fishing off his boat, *Cavalier*. He drives a car with the license plate 60062 and when in Boston, he enjoys a meal at a restaurant called Clams 'n' Claws. He plays pool at Haggerty's Pool Hall.

Amos Tupper (Tom Bosley) was the original town sheriff. He was a bus driver before he joined the police department and is a bit inept at his job — a better talker and eater than he is law enforcer. He was replaced by Sheriff Mort Metzger (Ron Masak) when Amos retired and went home to Kentucky. Mort was a football player with the LA Rams whose career ended when he injured his knee. He then became a police officer with the N.Y.P.D. but quit for the job of sheriff in Cabot Cove because "I couldn't handle the politics." He also says he came to Maine "because I like it here." Mort calls Jessica "Mrs. F" and rides in patrol car 103, license plate number 0170 702. The Joshua Peabody Inn is his favorite eatery.

A reformed jewel thief named Dennis Stanton (Keith Michell) is featured in nine episodes that have Jessica Fletcher acting as the host rather than the principal player in the story. In the introductory episode, "A Little Night Work" (October 30, 1988), it is learned that Dennis became a thief to get even with the insurance company, Susquehana Fire and Casualty, that refused to pay for his late wife's medical bills. He would steal jewelry insured by that company. Stanton's second episode, "When the Fat Lady Sings" (November 19, 1989) found him reformed, now working as a claims investigator for the

Consolidated Casualty Insurance Company in San Francisco. He is employed by Robert Butler (James Sloyan) and receives assistance from his secretary, Rhonda Markowitz (Hallie Todd). His nemesis is Perry Catalano (Ken Swofford), the police lieutenant who balks at Stanton interfering in police matters.

While the Dennis Stanton character was not spunoff into a series of its own, one series did evolve from *Murder, She Wrote—The Law and Harry McGraw* with Jerry Orbach recreating his role as a Boston-based detective (see entry for information). The episode of November 7, 1993, "Bloodlines," reunited on screen Angela Lansbury and Mickey Rooney for the first time since 1944 when they both appeared with Elizabeth Taylor in the film *National Velvet*.

John Addison composed the theme "Murder, She Wrote."

Note: Angela Lansbury returned as Jessica Fletcher in the following TV movies: *Murder, She Wrote: South by Southwest* (1997), *Murder, She Wrote: A Story to Die For* (2000), *Murder She Wrote: The Last Free Man* (2001) and *Murder, She Wrote: The Celtic Riddle* (2003).

85. Murphy's Law (ABC, 1988–1989)

Daedalus Patrick Murphy (George Segal) is an insurance investigator who not only solves cases of insurance fraud but murders as well. He is a recovering alcoholic and lives in a loft at 3116 Hillside with Kimiko Fannuchi (Maggie Han), a beautiful Eurasian model.

Murphy works for Wes Hardin (Josh Mostel), the claims manager for the First Fidelity Casualty Insurance Company in San Francisco; he originally worked for Triax Insurance. Murphy came from a troubled past. His parents had an unsteady relationship. When Murphy was ten years old his father walked out on him; his last words to Murphy were "Go to hell, kid." Murphy's mother struggled to raise him on what little money she made as a waitress. Murphy became part of the work force at an early age, taking whatever odd jobs he could find. According to Murphy, even meals played havoc with his life; he called the breakfast his mother made for him from leftovers "Dangerous Eggs."

Murphy eventually married a girl named Marissa (Kim Lankford) and they had a daughter named Kathleen. They lived on Baker Street and Marissa called Murphy "Paddy." The pressures of work caused Murphy to take up drinking and this, in turn, caused Marissa to divorce him. Ten years later Marissa married Charles Danforth (Bruce Gray), a wealthy lawyer, and has totally raised Kathleen (Sarah Sawatsky). Murphy now feels he wants to become a part of Kathleen's life and is in a fierce battle with Marissa to win visitation rights.

Murphy's battles with Marissa is also affecting his relationship with Kimiko, who is caught in the middle. Kimiko, who prefers to be called Kim, is much younger than Murphy. She was born of an Italian father and Japanese mother and often helps Murphy solve cases, most often by going undercover. Kim's claim to fame is being the calendar girl for Morgan Power Tools. While blessed with stunning good looks and a gorgeous figure, Kim can't seem to achieve the status of a model with lesser assets. She refuses to do nude layouts and spreads featuring her in string bikinis. Kim drives an old Saab; Murphy has a sedan, license plate SPM 162.

Morgan DeSade (Elizabeth Savage) is Murphy's nemesis, his old boss at Triax Insurance, and Victor Beaudine (Charles Rocket) is Murphy's rival, a sleazy agent for First Fidelity, who uses underhanded methods to solve cases. Al Jarreau sings the theme "Murphy's Law."

My Partner the Ghost *See* Haunted

86. Naked City (ABC, 1958–1959; 1960–1963)

The program opens with these words spoken by the producer, Herbert B. Leonard: "Ladies and gentlemen, you are about to see the Naked City. This story was not photographed in a studio; quite the contrary. The actors played out their roles in the streets and buildings of New York itself." *Naked City* appeared as two separate series: a half-hour version (1958–1959) and a longer running hour version (1960–1963). Each version was filmed in black and white and focused on the gruelling investigations of police officers as they solved crimes.

1958 Version: Jim Halloran (James Franciscus) and Dan Muldoon (John McIntire) are detectives with the 65th Precinct in Manhattan. Jim is married to Janet (Suzanne Storrs) and is the father of Evie (Dorothy Dollivaine). He wore badge number 41367 and lived at 39 West 64th Street. Dan, an older detective, drove a car with the license plate 8T 5657. He was killed off in the episode "Ten Cent Dreams" (March 10, 1959) when his car blew up after hitting a gasoline truck during a high speed car chase. He was replaced by Mike Parker (Horace McMahon), a somewhat gruff lieutenant who now worked alongside Jim. Also assisting Jim and Mike was Sergeant Frank Arcaro (Harry Bellaver). George Duning and Ned Washington composed the theme "This Is the Naked City."

1960 Version: Lieutenant Mike Parker (Horace McMahon) and Sergeant Frank Arcaro (Harry Bellaver) reprised their roles with Detective Adam Flint (Paul Burke) becoming their new partner.

Adam was born in the Bronx and lived at 166th Street and McClelland Avenue; he attended P.S. 11 near Yankee Stadium. He now lives in Manhattan at 393 West 48th Street, Apartment E. He is romantically involved with Libby Kingston (Nancy Malone), an actress who works at an unidentified television studio in Manhattan. Libby lives at 362 East 65th Street and takes the 8th Avenue IND subway line to work; 346-3593 is her phone number. Adam drives a car with the license plate 6N 7878 and, as Libby says, "He always forgets to clean out his pockets when he takes his suits to the cleaners."

Like the prior version, the series is a character study of people in trouble with the law and very little trivia information is given. Frank's license plate is 2G45 45; Mike's is 4T 893. It takes 28 minutes for a police van to travel from the 65th Precinct to the Tombs Holding Cell in Manhattan. Before it became known by the initials N.Y.P.D., P.D.N.Y.C. (Police Department of New York City) appears on police vehicles. Mike walked a beat on Fordham Road in the Bronx in 1931; to celebrate his thirtieth anniversary (April 1, 1961) on the force, Mike was given a trophy that said "The Mike Parker Fan Club." Libby was listed as the cheerleader.

Each episode ended with one of the most famous lines in television history: "There are eight million stories in the Naked City. This has been one of them." Billy May composed "The Naked City Theme" (1960–62); Nelson Riddle composed "The New Naked City Theme" (1962–1963).

Related Series

N.O.P.D. (Syndicated, 1956). Many sources claim that *Naked City* was the first weekly series to move out of the studio to film entirely on location. A very rare and virtually forgotten series called *N.O.P.D.* (New Orleans Police Department) did just what *Naked City* did — but two years earlier. It dealt with the investigations of Victor Beaujac (Stacy Harris) and John Conroy (Louis J. Sirgo), homicide detectives with the N.O.P.D. Stories were based on official N.O.P.D. files and the series followed the format of *Dragnet* (see entry) in its presentation with Stacy Harris acting like Sergeant Joe Friday. The series is filmed on location and it appears that actual citizens were used in the dramas; acting is not their forte. The writing is also sluggish and the camera work not particularly good.

Stories are narrated by Beaujac, who also questions the suspects while Conroy, whom Victor calls "John-O," takes notes. Victor resides in an apartment on Bourbon Street; John was said to live on Shady Pine Avenue. Only the two stars receive credit; other officers appear to be men associated with the N.O.P.D. *N.O.P.D.* is one of the truly lost series of early television and, even after screening the only known episodes to have been found, information is still evasive.

87. Nancy Drew (ABC, 1977–1978; 2002; Syndicated, 1995)

Teenage sleuth Nancy Drew was created by Edward Stratemeyer in 1930. Stratemeyer also created the Hardy Boys, the Bobsey Twins and the Tom Swift mystery stories. As with the Hardy Boys, Stratemeyer suggested plot lines and hired ghost writers to compile the stories under the pseudonym Carolyn Keene; Mildred Benson is the best known of these. Since publication of the first book, *The Secret of the Old Clock*, Nancy has solved over 350 mysteries.

Nancy is pretty, smart and adventurous and has become a heroine to millions of American girls. Nancy attends River Heights High School in the town of River Heights and is being raised by her widowed father, Carson. Nancy's mother died when Nancy was three years old. Nancy has her own car, a blue Roadster, and enjoys solving mysteries, making her the most famous of the literary detectives. All *Nancy Drew* books carry the same identical face type and the familiar Nancy Drew profile — Nancy with a magnifying glass. Nancy is accompanied on her adventures by her tomboyish girlfriend, George; George's somewhat neurotic cousin, Bess; and Nancy's true but dull boyfriend, Ned. Only recently, in 1996, did 16-year-old Nancy turn 18 and graduate from high school to attend college.

A series of four Warner Bros. feature films brought Nancy Drew to life in 1938 and 1939: *Nancy Drew, Detective*; *Nancy Drew and the Hidden Staircase*; *Nancy Drew, Reporter*; and *Nancy Drew, Troubleshooter*. Bonita Granville was perfectly cast as Nancy Drew with John Litel as her father, Carson, and Frank Thomas, Jr. as her boyfriend, Ted — not Ned. George and Bess were not a part of the movies. Here, Nancy attended the Brinwood School for Girls in River Heights and was planning to become a lawyer ("I think every intelligent woman should have a career").

The books were first adapted to television in 1977 as *The Nancy Drew Mysteries* and in 1978 as *The Hardy Boys/Nancy Drew Mysteries*. Pamela Sue Martin, then Janet Louise Johnson, played Nancy Drew with William Schallert as her father, attorney Carson Drew. The series is set in the town of River Heights. Nancy has been out of high school for five years and is now working for her father as a part time investigator. Her ambition is to become a private detective, but in the meantime she researches legal files and checks driving records. However, when a case turns into a mystery for Carson, Nancy becomes a detective and tries to help Carson solve it. Nancy constantly takes chances and often places her life in jeopardy. "Nancy is a girl with a very inquisitive mind who loves to solve a mystery," says Carson. "But the day she began part time investigative work for me was the start of my gray hairs."

Carson, a widower, has offices in the Municipal Building next to the Essex Smoke House. He and Nancy live at 8606 Bainbridge Street. Nancy dislikes being told she is wrong; it angers her and sets her into motion to prove what she saw or feels is right. While Nancy does do investigating, she doesn't consider what she does prying—"I just observe." Nancy donates toys to the Children's Hospital and is capable of trick motorcycle riding.

Nancy is assisted on all her cases by her best friend, Georgia "George" Fayne (Jean Rasey, Susan Buckner). George, who attended River Heights High School with Nancy, lives at 16 River Street. A job is not mentioned for George but she does want to become a detective. Nancy feels George is not ready and lets her practice by doing undercover work for her. While Carson is shrewd and can read people, George is often in a daze as to what is going on when she and Nancy are on a case. George often comes up with "clues that don't seem to mean anything except to Nancy," she says. George loves to shop and is usually frightened by everything she feels is dangerous. She often paints a graphic picture of what could happen if she and Nancy go any further. Bess is not a part of the series.

The character of Ned Nickerson was first played by George O'Hanlon, Jr. He was Carson's assistant and Nancy's shy boyfriend although Nancy was never quite sure what Ned's intentions were. Ned believes in psychics, palm readers and tarot cards. Ned is afraid to ask Nancy for a date and George believes "Nancy has turned your brains into mush. Your mistake was to become her friend. She thinks of you as a big brother." Ned also believes "Nancy is not interested in romantic things like moonlit rides. She's a very serious girl." This indecisive Ned was dropped in favor of a more forceful Ned (Rick Sprinfield). Here Ned, who had an eye for Nancy, was an investigator for the Boston D.A.'s office who worked with Carson.

In the opening theme, the following Nancy Drew books are seen: *Nancy Drew and—The Quest of the Missing Map, The Clue in the Crossword Cipher, The Spider Sapphire Mystery* and *The Sign of the Twisted Candle*. Glen A. Larson composed the theme.

Nancy Drew returned to television in 1995 in a new version called *Nancy Drew* that took Nancy away from her traditional setting of River

Heights in Illinois. Nancy (Tracy Ryan) is 21 years old and lives on her own in Apartment 603 of the Callisto Hotel at 306 Marsh Avenue in an unidentified city. While still hoping to become a detective, she works at various jobs as an employee of the Temp Agency. She is also attending an unnamed college and studying criminology. Like in the prior series, wherever Nancy goes, mystery follows. Nancy is just as slim and attractive as her predecessors, but she has been given the ability to pick locks and defeat alarm systems. Nancy likes ketchup on her hot dog and drives a car with the license plate NDY 7M2.

Nancy is assisted in her capers by her best friend, Georgia "George" Fayne (Joy Tanner) and George's cousin, Bess Marvin (Jhene Erwin). George and Bess share Apartment 3 over a store called Phillips Shoes. Nancy, Bess and George left River Heights to attend college. George is studying film — she hopes to become an editor — and works part time as a messenger for Quick Draw Couriers. Bess is studying journalism and works part time on a newspaper called *The Rag*, the city's alternative newspaper. Bess writes a column called "Ask Me Anything." The character of Ned Nickerson (Scott Speedman) appears occasionally as Nancy's boyfriend. John Tucker composed the theme.

On December 15, 2002, ABC aired *Nancy Drew*, the pilot for a prospective series. Nancy has graduated from high school and, at age 18, is attending River Heights University close to Boston. Maggie Lawson plays Nancy Drew with Lauren Birkell as George Fayne, Jill Ritchie as Bess Marvin, Brett Cullen as Carson Drew and Nick Stabile as Ned Nickerson. New to the story is Marieh Delfino as Christina Louisa Maria Timkins, Teeny for short, Nancy's new friend, a rich debutante from Rockport, Texas.

Nancy is still smart, pretty and adventurous. She drives a blue sports car, license plate AV655 22; 65859 is her university parking permit number, and she has been spoiled by the latest in technology, a cell phone. Unfortunately, Nancy breaks several laws: she drives without a seat belt and talks constantly on the cell phone — one hand on the steering wheel, the other holding the phone. Nancy's car is registered in Illinois and it is mentioned for the first time on TV that when Nancy was three her mother died of a heart attack. The Drews also have a dog named Butch.

While Nancy apparently lives close to home, as she visits her father, she lives on campus in the Kelly Hall Dorm. She has a picture of herself with her parents and a picture of her inspiration, Sherlock Holmes, on her desk. Nancy is studying journalism and is a member of the school's newspaper, *The Gazette*. Nancy was apparently a writer for her high school newspaper, the River Heights High *Inkwell*, which reported many of the crimes she, Bess and George solved. Richard Marvin composed the theme.

88. Nash Bridges (CBS, 1996–2001)

Nash Bridges (Don Johnson) is an inspector with the San Francisco Police Department. He is partners with Joe Dominquez (Cheech Marin) and the father of Cassidy (Jodi Lynn O'Keefe). He is twice divorce and lives with his father and Cassidy at 855 Sacramento Street.

Nash was born on December 7, 1955. He had a dog named Old Jimbo, was interested in magic, especially slight of hand, and was on the football team (jersey 55) at Bay High School. He attended the San Francisco Police Academy and was the youngest cop to ever receive a Gold Star. Nash has a tendency to call people "Bubba." He wears badge number 22 and 5-George-31 is his mobile car code. Nash drives a 1971 yellow Plymouth Barracuda convertible with the license plate GQD 685. Only 14 such cars were made and he calls his The Cuda. It has a 426 Hemi engine and can put out 490 torque at 425 horsepower. In some episodes, Nash claims the car was made in 1970. Nash has a photographic memory and loses his temper when he becomes angry.

Lisa (Annette O'Toole) is Nash's first ex-wife; Kelly (Serena Scott Thomas) was the second Mrs. Bridges. Lisa, the owner of a catering company, is Cassidy's mother. Though divorced, Nash and Lisa are still close; he and Kelly are further apart.

Nash is first an inspector, then Captain, and heads the S.I.U. (Special Investigative Unit of the S.F.P.D.). Headquarters was first located in a building in downtown San Francisco. When an earthquake partially destroyed the building, operations were transferred to a docked ferry boat called the *Eurika* on Hyde Street. Two years later, the ferry is replaced by a 177 foot barge that once housed the Allied Cannery Company, then a rave club. The barge is believed to be haunted by "The Phantom D.J." Mysterious music plays at various times and no one can find the reason or source for its happening. Nash often breaks the rules to get the job done and takes the heat for doing so. He prefers to work with his team and balks at sharing cases and information with the FBI. "They're too damned sure about everything," says Nash.

Joe was originally introduced as Nash's ex-partner who quit the force to become a private detective. He is semi-retired when the series begins and helps "The Nashman," as he calls Nash, solve crimes. He is later back on the force, first as an inspector then lieutenant. He is married to Inger (Caroline Langerfelt) and lives in an apartment at 4665 Laguna. In last season episodes, he and Inger become the parents of a girl they name Lucia.

Joe is the owner of a gay bar called the Tender Loin through a get-rich scheme that backfired and partners with Nash in a moonlighting business called Bridges and Dominquez—Private Investigators. They have offices at 427 Grey Street in a building full of psychiatrists. They often become involved in private capers while working on departmental matters. Joe also began a company called Loco Joe's Salsa wherein he tried to market his family's secret recipe for salsa sauce. After the family became involved, he and Inger received one percent of the company.

Cassidy, Nash's only child, first attended Bay High School then Berkeley College. She originally had aspirations to become an actress but later found an interest in law enforcement and attended the police academy. As an actress, Cassidy appeared topless in an avant garde play called *Tears of the Monkey*. Cassidy became a police officer and was first assigned to the Seacliff section of San Francisco. She was later reassigned to Nash's unit as a uniformed officer. Cassidy is rarely defiant and loyal to her father. If she does get angry, she takes her frustrations out on the police gym punching bag. Nash was uneasy with Cassidy becoming a cop as he was with her doing nude scenes in plays. Cassidy was involved in a fatal shooting and exonerated but quit the force when she felt her father was against her becoming a police officer. The series ended with an unresolved cliff hanger on May 4, 2001 when Cassidy is seen weighing the possibilities of returning to the force or leaving to begin a new life in Paris. Cassidy revealed that chocolate is her favorite flavor of ice cream.

Nick Bridges (James Gammon) is Nash's father, a former longshoreman who lived at the Three Oaks Retirement Home before he came to reside with Nash. Nick could not get along with "management" as he calls it. Nick served aboard the USS Phoenix during World War II and now cares for the house and does the cooking. He owns a race horse named Mr. Woody, stall 241 at the Golden Gate Stables, and is suffering from the early stages of Alzheimer's disease. Nash's sister, Stacey Bridges (Angela Dohrman), is an assistant district attorney.

Inspector Caitlin Cross (Yasmine Bleeth) is a beautiful internal affairs officer Nash calls "The Grand Inquisitor." Caitlin has been assigned to perform an audit investigation of the S.I.U.'s prior cases. She first worked for the FBI but quit "when I couldn't tell lies from truths." She next worked as an analyst for the CIA, Russian Intelligence Division; "I analyzed Russian documents all day long." As a result, she can read and speak Russian. She resigned after five years. The mayor of San Francisco then hired her to oversee S.I.U. procedures. Caitlin lives in an apartment at 440 California Avenue. Her eyes are listed as "Sultry Blue" on her driver's license and she is totally self-sufficient. Caitlin has a difficult time asking for help and hates it when

Nash calls her "Sister"; for example, "I've got a hot lead for you, Sister, trust me." Caitlin drives a Xebra Roadster electric car with the license plate XEBRA. She is the coach of a Police Athletic League soccer team called the Cougars (green uniforms) and often plays against Joe's team, the Palominos (red uniforms).

Caitlin says, "I find things out, that's what I do." She becomes angry when Nash tries to keep something from her; "I'll find out," she says. After working with Caitlin for a while Nash said, "She's a hell of a lot better than people give her credit for, but when it comes to solving crimes, she's not better than me."

Harvey Leek (Jeff Perry), Evan Cortez (Jaime P. Gomez) and Antwon Babcock (Cress Williams) are other members of Nash's team. Harvey is a Grateful Dead music fan; he has a collection of 155 ticket stubs from every concert he attended. He is divorced from Bonnie (Julianne Christie) after five years of marriage. He drives a 1991 Ford Ranchero. Evan was formerly an officer with the S.F.P.D. for seven years before being reassigned to the S.I.U. He had a brief relationship with Cassidy that was frowned upon by Nash who didn't want his daughter dating a cop because of the risks involved. Evan also calls Nash "Nashman." Antwon is a tough black inspector whose attitude has fostered his transfer to five different investigative units in three years. He is street smart and appears to have found a permanent station with the S.I.U.

Nash is the only cop at the S.I.U. with his personal guardian angel — Angel (Tracey Walter), an apparent homeless person who dresses in white with a pair of wings. He came from out of nowhere to save Nash's life during a case and has now taken it upon himself to watch over Nash. Angel, as Nash calls him, has no apparent means of income and no background after 1958. As best as Nash can determine, Angel is really Peter Spellman. He was born at Saint Mary's Hospital on January 27, 1949. He was adopted by Dr. Alvin Spellman and his wife Helen. After Helen's death, Peter was sent to a foster home where he lived until the age of nine. In the summer of 1958 his records stopped. He became non-existent. He never paid taxes, never had a job, has no social security number, was never in the service. No school records exist either. Angel says he cannot lie to anyone. He likes honey on his English muffins.

Elia Cmiral composed the original theme "Nash Bridges." Eddie Jobson composed the revised theme "I've Got a Friend in You" and Ray Bunch composed the final season "New Nash Bridges Theme."

89. Nero Wolfe (NBC, 1981; A&E, 2001–2002)

Nero Wolfe is an overweight master criminologist, gourmet cook, horticulturist and connoisseur of fine wine. He is also wealthy, reclusive, abrupt, insulting and arrogant. He lives in a New York brownstone but seldom leaves the house to solve crimes. His legman, private detective Archie Goodwin, collects the evidence for him. Nero considers the evidence Archie gathers to be pieces of a puzzle. When a case is solved in Nero's mind, he gathers all the suspects at his home. He recaps the crime, questions the suspects and reveals the culprit. While operating as a private investigative agency, Nero also helps the police, namely Inspector Cramer, solve crimes. On NBC, Nero's address was given as 918 West 35th Street; on A&E, he resides at 454 West 35th Street in Manhattan.

Nero raises orchids and enjoys sitting "in my nice big easy chair and enjoying a delectable glass of beer." Nero claims he doesn't leave the house "because I hate traffic." When a circumstance forces Nero to leave his home, he immediately misses the comforts of his home and avails himself to the comforts of other people's homes. It is at these times that Nero hopes for one thing — a meal prepared by a gourmet cook. These occasions also give Nero the opportunity to pick up minute details the police often overlook. He solves cases by hard facts not by imagining who did it. Nero usually sets a trap to catch a killer — "We can't go to him, so we have to make him come to us."

Nero depends on Archie and Archie depends on Nero. "I do nothing without Archie," says Nero. "He's inquisitive, charming, impetuous, alert and forceful. He gets me what I need to solve crimes." Archie lives at 237 East 46th Street and doesn't take notes when he questions a suspect — "I have a photographic memory." Nero sometimes believes Archie's last name should be Wolf because he has an eye for the ladies. Nero is not a judge of women, but of Archie he says, "Your insatiable interest of the female seems to sometimes border on the psychotic." Deep down Nero fears that Archie is going to leave him when he meets the right girl and marries. Archie believes Nero has only two passions — orchids and beer. Both versions are based on the character created by Rex Stout.

NBC Version: William Conrad plays Nero Wolfe with Lee Horsley as Archie Goodwin. George Voskovec is Fritz Brenner, Nero's gourmet cook; Robert Coote is Theodore Hortsman, Nero's horticulturist; and Allan Miller is Inspector Cramer of the N.Y.P.D.'s 18th Precinct.

A&E Version: Maury Chaykin plays Nero Wolfe with Timothy Hutton as Archie Goodwin. Colin Fox is Fritz, Nero's personal chef; and Bill Smitrovich is Inspector Cramer of the N.Y.P.D. This version is set first in the 1950s, then the 1960s although Archie's outlandish wardrobe places him in the 1940s. Discounting the brightly colored suits he wears, his appearance is reminiscent of Jack Webb's Sergeant Joe Friday character on the series *Dragnet*.

Note: On December 18, 1979, ABC aired a pilot film called "Nero Wolfe" with Thayer David in the title role. Tom Mason was Archie Goodwin; Biff McGuire was Inspector Cramer; and David Hurst was Fritz Brenner. The pilot story, based on the Rex Stout book, *The Doorbell Rang*, finds Nero attempting to solve a puzzling murder involving a young tycoon under secret investigation by the FBI.

N.O.P.D. *See* Naked City

90. Over My Dead Body (CBS, 1990–1991)

Maxwell Beckett (Edward Woodward) and Nikki Page (Jessica Lundy) are an unlikely pair of crime solvers: Maxwell is a former Scotland Yard Inspector turned mystery story writer; Nikki is a newspaper obituary writer seeking a position as a crime reporter.

Maxwell actually pretends to be a retired Scotland Yard inspector to give credibility to his books. He has written six books, but only three were a success: *All That Glitters* (four weeks on the best-seller list), *The Fire Confrontations, Hanging Crimes, Hooker by Crook, Over My Dead Body* and *Taking the Heart*. Maxwell is constantly seen arguing with his unnamed publisher about his books. The publisher feels Maxwell's books are bombing because they have no grit. When Maxwell gets upset over these conversations, he goes to the local park to argue with himself.

Maxwell was called "Beckett of the Yard," or so he has led his readers to believe, and "The Catcher of Uncatchable Thieves, the Solver of Unsolvable Crimes." In 1981, he claims to have worked for the Anti-Terrorist Squad of the New Scotland Yard. Maxwell also wrote a series of children's books—*M Mongoose*—under the pen name A.J. Edison. He drives a Rolls Royce, license plate 2915 AJ; Alotta's is his favorite restaurant; and he donates money to a charity called the Fog City Shelter. Max's mobile phone number is 555-4242. Carolyn Seymour appeared as Maxwell's ex-wife, Diane; she has a dog named Woody.

Nikki is a pretty, brash, street-smart young woman in her late twenties who aspires to bigger and better things. She is a Pisces and works under the name Miss Black. While she does write the obit column for the San Francisco *Union*, her actual job is a journalist trainee. It was her fascination with Maxwell Beckett stories that enabled her to become an amateur sleuth. One night while nursing a cold, Nikki saw a man strangle a woman in the apartment across from hers. When no evidence of a crime could be found, the police dismissed the case. Nikki knows what she saw and believes a great sleuth like Maxwell Beckett is the man she needs. When Beckett dismisses Nikki as a flake, she prints his obituary in the paper. The prank almost costs Nikki her job, but it accomplishes her goal: she is able to convince her hero that a murder occurred and together set out to prove it; a political figure killed a prostitute to prevent his affair becoming a matter of public record. The investigation stirs Maxwell's creative juices; Nikki feels she is acquiring the experience she needs to become a reporter. The two find they need each other and remain a team. Nikki is a graduate of San Francisco High School and State College where she majored in journalism. She lives in Apartment 307 at 5045 Hode Street and rides a motorcycle. Her unseen father, a football coach, leaves messages on her telephone answering machine that predict her every move.

Lee Holdridge composed the theme "Over My Dead Body."

91. Partners in Crime (NBC, 1984)

Carole Stanwyck (Lynda Carter) and Sydney Kovack (Loni Anderson) are beautiful, amateur private investigators who run their late husband's company, the Caulfield Detective Agency in San Francisco. The company is also called the Raymond Dashill Caulfield Detective Agency. Both women married Raymond Caulfield and both women divorced him.

Carole, Ray's first wife (1972–1975) was owed $62,000 in back alimony. Sydney, Ray's second wife (1976–1978) was owed $56,000 in back alimony. Ray proposed to both women at the Top of the Mark Restaurant. When Ray is killed during a case assignment, Carole and Sydney meet for the first time at the funeral. They inherit his company, a mutual mother-in-law (Jeanine), a housekeeper (Harvey) and a heavily mortgaged mansion. They became "Partners in Crime" after solving Ray's murder and deciding to remain a team.

Carole, a former New York debutante and teabag company heiress, lost her money through bad investments. She is brunette, measures 38-25-37 and works as a freelance photographer. She lives at 654 Verona Drive and drives a car with the license plate IFL 896. Carole wears a medium size dress and is always elegantly attired. She sometimes worries that she wears the wrong outfits for undercover assignments. Carole admits to one bad habit ("I'm always losing keys") and despises wearing an electronic bug on an assignment, which she places in her bra; sometimes in her pants pocket. Carole is very concerned about her figure and will not eat junk foods ("Too many carbohydrates, fats and calories"). She has a strict dating rule and will never call a man for a date ("I never did and I never will").

Sydney is a stunning, street-wise blonde and measures 36-24-36. She grew up in the Mission District of San Francisco where she learned all the tricks of the trade — from lock picking to picking pockets. As a kid, she ran numbers for her father and had a mean left hook; she sent three school bullies to the dentist. She is now an aspiring but struggling musician — bass fiddle — who hopes to one day play with the San Francisco Symphony Orchestra. Her biggest break came when she played in a band for singer Rochelle Robins. Sydney has been studying the bass for 20 years and has played professionally for 15. She wears a size small dress and lives at 921 Hayworth Street, Apartment 3C. Sydney can hot wire a car, carries lock picks with her at all times and only plays tennis because she feels she looks fabulous in a tennis outfit. She drives a car with the license plate IPCE 467.

"We're not exactly Sherlock Holmes and Dr. Watson," says Carole, "but we get the job done." Sydney adds, "We call the cops a lot." To ease the minds of troubled clients, Carole tells them "We already have a plan, we're professionals, we can handle it," to which Sydney gives a puzzled look, knowing it's Carole's way of stalling for time.

When Sydney asks, "My car or yours," for an assignment, Carole always replies, "Yours. Mine's low on gas." Sydney then remarks, "Why did I even ask that question. Of course it's low on gas, it's always low on gas." When Carole volunteers to carry Sydney's bass, she says, "Boy this is heavy." Sydney, a blonde, likes to wear wigs when she goes undercover; brunette is her favorite, and she asks, "Carole, am I sexy as a brunette?" Carole responds with lines like "Sophia Loren better watch out." The Sausilito Bar is their favorite watering hole.

Jeanine Caulfield (Eileen Heckart), Carole and Sydney's mutual mother-in-law, is the unpublished author of 57 books. She owns the Partners in Crime Book Store, later called Jeanine's Book Store, and lives with Carole and Sydney at the mansion. She fancies herself as an amateur sleuth, but does not involve herself with the girls or their cases. Harvey Shain (Walter Olkewicz) cares for the mansion. His claim to fame is that he met Rock Hudson on Fisherman's Wharf.

Ken Heller and Nathan Sassover composed the theme "Partner's in Crime."

92. Pete Kelly's Blues (NBC, 1959)

"The period was called the Roaring Twenties," says Pete Kelly (Jack Webb), a cornet player and leader of a jazz band called the Big Seven. "Americans were told they had to stop drinking but thirty million of them stayed thirsty and ate salted peanuts to make sure. It was an age of jazz music, speakeasies, rum running, bathtub gin, murder, reprisal and organized disorder. Everything was on sale — from wood alcohol to immortal souls — and down the street was a guy who would give a discount on either one. Those were the accents of 1927 and the music, it was jazz. From the start it had kind of an epileptic charm. It fitted the times but it was more than the times. It said more, it made jokes and it wept. It laughed out loud, it dosed and sometimes spoke with regret."

For Pete Kelly, it began in Chicago. As a kid he became fascinated with the cornet and set his goal on becoming a musician. In one episode, Pete mentions that musician Gus Trudeaux taught him how to play the cornet. They became friends but when Gus became involved with the mob, Pete left Chicago and headed for Kansas City, Missouri, the series setting. Later, Pete mentions he was a struggling musician who befriended Gus at a union meeting. However, he also befriended a piano player named Augie and he and Augie drifted to Kansas City where Pete later formed the Big Seven.

Pete lives in a small room on Grand Avenue near Washington Square; in Chicago, he lived at 18th and Halstead. Pete would like to do nothing else then play the cornet, but that was not meant to be as trouble seems to find him no matter where he goes. While not an official private detective, Pete becomes a somewhat unofficial source of law and order when he risks his life to help people in trouble.

Pete and the Big Seven play regularly at Lupo's, a brownstone turned funeral parlor turned speakeasy at 17 Cherry Street. "It's a standard speakeasy," says Pete. "The booze is cut but the prices aren't. The beer is good and the whiskey is aged — if you get there later in the day. We play here from 10 PM to 4 AM, with a pizza break at midnight. The hours are bad, but the music suits us. There's one other thing about 17 Cherry Street and that's trouble. You can get it by the yard, the pound, wholesale and retail."

George Lupo (Phil Gordon) owns the speakeasy. "He was the only kid in Linback County who got turned down for reform school," says Pete. "He later fought in the war with the 102nd Infantry and he pays scale — with a five dollar kickback." Other regulars are Savannah Brown (Connee Boswell), Pete's friend, a singer at Fat Annie's, a speakeasy on the Kansas side (Annie says, "It's easy to sing the blues — all you need to do is be born when there is rain on the roof") and Johnny Cassiano (Anthony Eisley), an officer with the Kansas City Police Department. Dick Cathcart is the offscreen cornet player for Pete; the Matty Matlock Combo provides music for the club scenes. Connee Boswell sings the theme "Pete Kelly's Blues." The program opens with these words: "This one's about Pete Kelly. It's about the world he goes around in; it's about the big music, the big trouble and the big Twenties."

Note: The program is based on the radio series of the same title (NBC, 1951) with Jack Webb as Pete Kelly and Jack Kruschen as George Lupo. The singer at Fat Annie's in this version is Maggie Jackson, played by Meredith Howard. Dick Cathcart is also the offstage cornet player for Jack Webb. A 1955 theatrical version, called *Pete Kelly's Blues*, with Jack Webb, Peggy Lee and Ella Fitzgerald appeared next.

93. Peter Gunn (NBC, 1958–1960; ABC, 1960–1961)

Peter Gunn (Craig Stevens) is a former cop turned private detective who operates out of Los Angeles, California. He resides at 351 Ellis Park Road; KR2-7056 is his phone number; and JL1-7211 is his mobile car phone number. His company is known as both Gunn Investigations and Peter Gunn's Private Detective Agency, established on July 5, 1957. Peter Gunn is actually the first private detective created for television. Prior detectives, like Mike Hammer, Richard Diamond, Ellery Queen and Martin Kane, were all based on characters appearing in books, on the silver screen or on radio.

Peter Gunn was a bit more sophisticated than his predecessors. He was always well dressed and more reserved and polished. He spoke more respectfully and frequented a classy hangout. However, like those before him, Gunn inherited a flare for violence — whether it was with his fists or gunplay. Mother's, a waterfront nightclub owned by a woman known only as Mother (Hope Emerson, Minerva Urecal) is the classy hangout Gunn chose to frequent the most although he was seen entering such dives as the Green Cafe, Nate's Hot Dogs and Cooky's, a beatnik coffee house.

Edie Hart (Lola Albright), the glamorous and sophisticated singer at Mother's, is Gunn's romantic interest. She lives at the Bartell Hotel, Apartment 15, at 1709 Ver Banna Street, and later became the club's owner; she changed the name to Edie's; KL6-0699 is her phone number.

Lieutenant Jacoby (Herschel Bernardi) of the 13th Precinct of the L.A.P.D. Homicide Squad, is Gunn's police department contact; 366-2561 is his desk phone number. Babby (Billy Barty) is one of Gunn's snitches, a diminutive pool hustler he often tells Peter to "think tall." When he sees that Gunn is troubled, he says, "You've got that eight ball look." Gunn pays his snitches $10 for information. Emmett (Bill Chadney) plays the piano at Mother's. Henry Mancini composed the series jazz score and theme "Peter Gunn."

Note: In 1967, Craig Stevens recreated his role as Peter Gunn in a theatrical film called *Gunn*. Laura Devon was Edie; Edward Asner, Lieutenant Jacoby; and M.T. Marshall, Mother. On April 23, 1989, ABC aired the TV movie *Peter Gunn*. Peter Strauss was Peter Gunn; Barbara Williams was Edie;

Peter Jurasik was Lieutenant Jacoby (given the first name of Herschel); Pearl Bailey was mother; and David Rappaport played Spec, Gunn's diminutive snitch.

94. Picket Fences (CBS, 1992–1996)

Rome, Wisconsin, is a small town characterized by strange citizens and unusual crimes. There is Peter Breck (Michael Jeter), a man fascinated by frogs and called "The Frogman." K.C. McDonald (Jessica Tuck), called "The Snake Lady," collects snakes and carries a boa with her at all times. Frank Tucker (David Provall) is a man obsessed with potatoes and carries a five pound bag of Idaho potatoes with him wherever he goes; he has earned the nickname "Frank the Potato Man." There is the mysterious and unknown "Serial Bather," a man who breaks into people's homes when they are out to take a bath; and Louise Talbot (Natalija Nagulich), the town's transsexual schoolteacher; before her sex change, she was Walter Souder.

Dealing justice to anyone who breaks the law is Jimmy Brock (Tom Skerritt), the local sheriff, and his deputies, Maxine Stewart (Lauren Holly) and Kenny Locas (Costas Mandylor). Jimmy is married to Jill (Kathy Baker) and the father of three children: Kimberly (Holly Marie Combs), Matthew (Justin Shenkarow) and Zachary (Adam Wylie). The Brocks are Protestant and live at 211 Willow Road.

Jimmy, the son of criminal attorney Walter Brock (James Coburn), was previously married to a woman named Lydia (Cristine Rose), who is Kimberly's birth mother. A year after divorcing Lydia, Jimmy married Jill and moved to Rome because it was safe. Jill is a private practice doctor who is also on call at Norwood Hospital, later said to be Thayer Hospital. Jill drives a stationwagon with the license plate 857 JXV. Kimberly is 16 years old and attends Rome High School. She plays the piano and has aspirations of becoming a singer, changed in later episodes when she became a clerk to the town's legal eagle, Douglas Wambaugh, and set her sights on becoming a lawyer.

Kimberly likes to dress provocatively to impress boys but is stopped from doing so by Jill, who refuses to let her leave the house in attire such as ripped jeans and bosom-revealing blouses. The series took a bold step forward in the episode of April 29, 1993, "Sugar and Spice," when Kimberly begins to question her sexuality. She is talking to her girlfriend, Lisa Fenn (Alexondra Lee), when Lisa brings up the prospect of what it would be like to kiss a girl. Kimberly is reluctant to try it until Lisa tells her how erotic she read it was. They become curious and kiss, possibly the first such erotic kiss on TV. Both appear to like it, but Kimberly has a serious side effect: is she a lesbian or is she straight. The series ended without really resolving Kimberly's dilemma.

Matthew and Zachary attend the Fisher Elementary School. Matthew envisions himself as a detective while Zachary shows promise of becoming a musician — he plays trombone. Jimmy is also musically inclined and plays the saxophone.

The sheriff's department is located in the Rome City Hall Building in Hogan County. Maxene, called Max, and Kenny ride in a patrol car with the code 2181. Max is famous for ending the murdering careers of "The Green Bay Chopper" and "The Cupid Killer"; she was forced to shoot them. In her youth, Max had sexy lingerie pictures of her taken so that when she becomes old she could see how beautiful she once was. Although supposed to be for her eyes only, the photos appeared in the girlie magazine *Boudoir* when the photographer sold copies for money. Kenny was born in Illinois and was a former Golden Gloves Boxer. Their squad car license plate reads 82203.

Douglas Wambaugh (Fyvush Finkel) is the town's outspoken Jewish attorney. He will take any case "because Wambaugh is on the side of principle" and requires two things: The truth and a $1,000 retainer. At Christmastime, Douglas organizes the Multi-cultural Wambaugh Singers to perform holiday carols and bring people of all religions together. Ann Guilbert, then Erica Yohn, played Douglas's nagging wife, Myriam.

Carter Pike (Kelly Connell) is the town's medical examiner or "Chief Pathologist" as he calls himself. He yearns to become a detective but finds he is unable due to his uncontrollable urge to perform autopsies. Rachel Harris (Leigh-Taylor Young) is the town's ultra-sexy mayor. She suffers from an inferiority complex and when she becomes troubled she dresses in her cheerleader outfit — "It gives me confidence," she says. She was the Rome High School Cheerleading Champion in 1967. Henry Bone (Ray Walston) is the tough, no nonsense judge who rules from the Hogan County Court House. Stewart Levin composed the theme "Picket Fences."

Proposed Series Spinoff (Unsold Pilot)

The Dancing Bandit (March 3, 1995). Marlee Matlin as Laurie Bey, a beautiful, hearing impaired, modern-day Robin Hood who steals from the rich to give to the needy. Her nonviolent methods include dancing to ease her victims, thus earning her the nickname The Dancing Bandit. The proposed series would have taken Laurie out of Rome, Wisconsin, where she was captured, tried and sentenced to 3,000 hours of community service, and place her in the hands of the U.S. government, where she would use her unique skills to capture criminals.

95. Police Squad! (ABC, 1982)

An unidentified city, called "The Tuba Capital of the World," is home to Frank Drebin (Leslie Nielsen), a detective lieutenant with an unnamed special unit of what is called the Police Department, headquartered, as Frank says, "at the Police Station." Frank has an office in the squad room and is also referred to as Captain Drebin. Frank cares about people. He believes it is necessary to break the law to help people threatened by evil. Although he does his best to follow the rules, he is plagued by an uncanny presence that dulls his sense of reality and makes him somewhat of a buffoon when justice calls. Although Frank enjoys his coffee, too much caffeine makes him edgy. He shoots to kill, although he more often misses, and will not question the wife of a murder victim until he is sure the husband is dead. Frank appears to be a 24-hour-a-day cop; he rarely relaxes and seems to have made the squad room his second home. He lives at 14 Cherry Street at Galena Avenue next to the Military Millinery Store. Frank's license plate reads NAQ 758 in the opening theme; YM 4875 and TW 4305 are seen as his license plates in actual episodes. Frank appears to have only one snitch—a man named Johnny (William Duell) who works as a shoeshine "boy." Johnny knows everything about everything and will tell what he knows for $20. Priests and fire captains are also seen using Johnny's services.

Frank's superior is Captain Ed Hocken (Alan North). Officer Norberg (Peter Lupus) of the Undercover Unit assists Frank. Ted Olson (Ed Williams) is the sleazy police chemist who appears to enjoy performing hazardous experiments on children but is never given the chance; he is always interrupted by Frank.

Only six episodes were filmed and each features a special guest star (Lorne Greene, Georg Stanford Brown, Florence Henderson, William Shatner, Robert Goulet and William Conrad) who is killed off in the opening theme. Rex Hamilton as Abraham Lincoln is announced as a regular in the opening theme but never appears in the show. The series is based on the comedy style of the movie *Airplane* that just didn't work on TV, although the series did spawn two theatrical films: *The Naked Gun* and *The Naked Gun 2½: The Smell of Fear*. Ira Newborn composed the theme.

96. Police Woman (NBC, 1974–1978)

Pepper Anderson (Angie Dickinson) is an attractive police woman with the Criminal Conspiracy Division of the Los Angeles Police Department. Pepper's real name is Lee Ann, also given as Suzanne, but likes to be called

Pepper "because it's my nickname." Pepper lives at 102 Crestview Drive and 514-7915 is her phone number. Pepper rarely talks about her family and it is only known that she has a much younger sister named Cheryl (Nicole Kallis). Cheryl is autistic and attends the Austin School for Learning Disabilities; Pepper mentioned that she was caring for Cheryl. Pepper was a high fashion model who quit her glamorous job when she became bored with it. She attended the Los Angeles Police Academy and first worked in vice before her promotion to her current position as a sergeant. She drives a sedan with the license plate 635 CIN.

Pepper is the only woman on a squad that includes her superior, Sergeant William "Bill" Crowley (Earl Holliman), and investigators Joe Stiles (Ed Bernard) and Pete Royster (Charles Dierkop). Pepper seems to attract seedy characters while working on a case and often acts as bait. Her least favorite assignments are posing as Bill's wife. As Bill tells her, "It was either you or Joe or you and Pete." While Pepper is careful not to reveal too much cleavage, an inside joke said Pepper needed a pair of forty-fives to protect her thirty-eights. Although Pepper gets shot at, hit, punched and often finds her clothes getting ripped, she takes it all in stride — "It comes with the territory." There is a picture in Pepper's bedroom with the word "Pepper" spelled out in capital letters. Bill is a career cop and still in love with his ex-wife, Jackie (Bebe Besch). Joe was a former medic during the Vietnam War. Morton Stevens composed the theme "Police Woman."

The original pilot episode, titled "The Gamble," aired on *Police Story* (NBC, March 26, 1974). Here Angie Dickinson played Lisa Beaumont, a vice squad detective with the L.A.P.D. Bert Convy was Sergeant Bill Crowley and Ed Bernard and Charles Dierkop played the roles of Detectives Styles and Royster. The story finds Lisa posing as a prostitute to expose the leader of a gambling syndicate.

After the cancellation of *Police Woman*, Angie Dickinson became Cassidy "Cassie" Holland, a former L.A.P.D. officer turned private detective and owner of Holland Investigations on the 1982 NBC series *Cassie and Company*. Angie next played Ann Cavanaugh, an officer with the San Diego Police Department in the NBC TV movie *Police Story: The Freeway Killings* (May 3, 1987). She was next Kelly Mulchaney, a sergeant with the N.Y.P.D. in the NBC telefilm *Prime Target* (September 29, 1989).

Angie attempted a return to regular series work with "Angie, the Lieutenant," an unsold pilot that aired on NBC (February 1, 1992). Here, Angie Dickinson played Angela "Angie" Martin, a newly appointed lieutenant with the Metropolitan Division of the Washington, D.C. Police Department. She heads an all-male division consisting of detectives Elliott Chase (Jesse

Dabson), Carl Kanick (Michael MacRae), Ernesto Mendez (Geoffrey Rivas) and Oliver Jackson (Harold Sylvester). The pilot story finds Angie investigating the rape of a TV anchorwoman.

Proposed Spinoff (Unsold Pilot)

Task Force (March 2, March 9, 1976). The work of Michelle (Cynthia Sikes), Bobbo (Don Stroud) and Jesse (James A. Watson, Jr.), an L.A.P.D. motorcycle task force. The pilot finds the team seeking a hit and run killer.

97. Pros and Cons (ABC, 1991–1992)

The Bird and O'Hannon Agency at 1122 North Plaza in Los Angeles is a private detective organization owned by Gabriel Bird (James Earl Jones) and Mitch O'Hannon (Richard Crenna). Their office phone number is 555-6464.

The character of Gabriel Bird was originally featured on the series *Gabriel's Fire* (ABC, 1990–91). Before becoming a private detective, Gabriel served in Korea and was decorated four times. In 1959, after attending junior college, he enrolled in the Chicago Police Academy. He was a beat cop for nine years and was dedicated to the force. Neighborhood people felt safe and looked up to him. In 1969, Bird was assigned to the state's attorney prosecuting team. On December 21, 1969 at 4:45 AM, the unit raided an apartment on Hampton Street, an address believed to be the armed headquarters of the Black Liberation Army. Gabriel was unaware that he was on a witch hunt. Three members of the Elner family, the residents of the apartment, were killed before Gabriel realized what was happening. As Bird's partner was about to shoot a woman and her child, Gabriel killed him. The police department disowned Bird and considered him a Black Liberation supporter. He was convicted of murder and sentenced to life in prison.

Victoria Heller (Laila Robins) is a lawyer who becomes interested in Gabriel's case and files a writ of habeas corpus when she learns what happened to him. Case number 2266 is reopened and after serving 7,271 days in prison, Gabriel is released. Victoria then offers Gabriel a job as an investigator for her law firm, Heller and Klein. The first thing Gabriel did after being released from prison was to have two hot dogs with everything on them. He then returned to his old neighborhood on Emerald Street. Josephine Austin (Madge Sinclair) owns a restaurant called Empress Josephine's Soul Food Kitchen on Emerald Street. Gabriel was the cop on the beat when Josephine's husband died. He helped provide for her and her children when they were in need. Josephine repays a favor she never forgot by giving Gabriel free room and board in the attic room above her restaurant.

In 1991, Victoria leaves her practice to become a judge; Gabriel opens his own agency, Gabriel Bird Investigations. On his first case, Gabriel is hired by a woman to follow her husband whom she believes is having an affair. The suspect is actually a hit man who has been hired to kill Los Angeles private detective Mitch O'Hannon. In Los Angeles, Gabriel saves Mitch's life when he prevents the hit from taking place. The two join forces (and eventually become partners) to solve the case. It is learned that Mitch's secretary used information to blackmail a client; the client thought Mitch was the blackmailer and hired the hit man.

Gabriel loves gardening and owns a house at 808 Magnolia Drive in Los Angeles episodes. Josephine relocates to Los Angeles when Gabriel asks her to marry him. The wedding occurs in the episode of October 10, 1991. Josephine acquires a job as the manager of a restaurant called the Angel Grill. Gabriel goes to extremes to get the job done and keeps a diary of everything he does. His car license plate reads 2PEK 674.

Victoria is a tough, dedicated attorney who will fight for any cause she believes in. Her offices are located at 14301 North La Salle Street in Chicago; 555-4748 is her phone number; and K87 463 is her car license plate number.

Mitch lives in Apartment 705 at 455 Lane Street. He served in Korea and was with the 40th Sunburst Unit; Gabriel was with the 24th Infantry. Gabriel thinks Mitch is too careless and calls him "a lunatic; he acts like a teenager." Mitch feels that acting on impulse is the best way to get the job done. Mitch was previously partners in a firm called Pryor and O'Hannon. He drives a car with the license plate 2NR 1853, later 2GAT 123. The series was originally titled "Bird and Katt" and featured James Earl Jones and Richard Crenna as squabbling private detectives named Gabriel Bird and Peter Katt. William Olvis composed the theme.

98. P.S. I Luv U (CBS, 1991–1992)

Cody Powell (Greg Evigan) and Dani Powell (Connie Sellecca) are an unusual pair of private detectives. They are in the Federal Witness Protection Program, pretend to be married and operate P.S.I. (Palm Springs Investigations), a small security firm in Palm Springs, California, as a cover to protect their real identities.

Dani is actually Wanda Talbert, a beautiful con artist who moves from town to town pulling scams. Cody is really Joey Paciorek, a detective with the N.Y.P.D. When a con by Wanda goes wrong and she is captured by Joey, he offers her a chance to avoid jail by helping him expose a drug lord. During the assignment, Wanda is exposed as an undercover agent. The drug lord escapes but Wanda is now in jeopardy: if the mobster is caught, Wanda's testimony can convict him. To protect Wanda, it is decided to give her a new identity. Matthew Durning (Earl Holliman), a former Justice Department federal marshal, arranges for their new life style. He reassigns Joey as Dani's bodyguard and "husband." The marrieds, who dislike each other, first live in a mobile trailer home; then in the Parker Mansion when the owners leave for Europe and entrust its security to P.S.I., the telephone number of which is PSI-LUVU or 774-5888.

Dani originally worked as the receptionist for P.S.I. She is later a case worker when she helps Cody apprehend a big time mobster. Dani was born in the Bronx and grew up on the streets. She learned at an early age how to con people but was taught how to perfect her craft by her uncle, Ray Barkley (Patrick Macnee), an international rogue and confidence man. Cons have given Dani the life she loves, and spending money is her favorite hobby. She is a size 6 and is always fashionably dressed. She hates housework, cooking and especially children ("Kids are like fingernails on a blackboard. I can't take them"). Dani is not only an expert at relieving people of their money, but is capable of opening safes and picking locks. She carries a lock pick with her at all times; "It's in my bra. It's the safest place I know." Her sports car license plate reads 2YAR 133.

Cody, born in New York City, had the badge number 346 and was a street cop for 12 years before becoming a plainclothes detective. He was an honest cop and did virtually everything by the book; he objects, at times, to Dani's habit of pulling cons to get the job done. Cody comes from a long line of police officers and would like to return to the force one day with a clean record. Cody's license plate reads 2DQ 1876; PSI-5 is his car code.

Jayne Frazer plays JoJo, the P.S.I. radio dispatcher; Sonny Bono appeared as himself, the mayor of Palm Springs. Greg Evigan and Suzanne Fountain sing the theme "P.S., I Love You."

99. Quincy, M.E. (NBC, 1976–1983)

Dr. Quincy (Jack Klugman) is a medical examiner with the mind of a detective. He works for the Los Angeles County Coroner's Office and believes in investigating for himself the circumstances surrounding a victim of crime. Quincy was a surgeon before becoming a pathologist; his specialty is now forensic pathology. He lives on a boat docked at the Marina Del Ray "which I'm thinking of selling and moving into the lab" where he spends a great deal of time. Quincy has no first name; people refer to him as Quincy or

Dr. Quincy. A camera shot of his I.D. card revealed that his first name has the initial R; his job related station wagon has the license plate 899995; and the coffee kitty in the office lab asks for 25 cents per cup of coffee.

Quincy refuses police protection when working on a case. He is stubborn and will not back down. His 17 years experience as a medical examiner has made him confident in his findings "and I will risk my reputation on my findings."

When the series begins, Quincy is a widower. He and his first wife, Helen (Anita Gillette in flashbacks), honeymooned at Lake Tahoe. She called him Quince. Helen dreamed of having children — four boys and three girls — but Quincy, who had just started to practice, wanted to wait until they were more financially secure. He was afraid children would deny him his commitment to medicine. Helen died from a brain tumor before she could realize her dream. Quincy's second wife, Emily Hanover (Anita Gillette) was a doctor Quincy married in the episode of February 23, 1983. There was no mention of the fact that Emily was a dead ringer for Helen and she too apparently never knew his first name as she called him Honey, Quince and Quincy. Helen appeared in the episode of March 1, 1979 ("Promises to Keep"); Emily was introduced in the episode of September 29, 1982 ("Rattlesnakes").

Dr. Robert Astin (John S. Ragin) is Quincy's superior, the assistant deputy coroner. Dr. Sam Fugiyama (Robert Ito) assists Quincy. Danny Tovo (Val Bisoglio) owns the local bar hangout, Danny's Place. Frank Monihan (Garry Walberg) is a lieutenant with the Homicide Division of the L.A.P.D.; his car license plate reads 236 SXQ. Lee Potter (Lynnette Mettey) was Quincy's girlfriend in first season episodes. She is also the bikini-clad girl seen sharing a drink with Quincy on his boat in the opening theme.

Glen A. Larson composed the theme. See also *Crossing Jordan*.

100. Raven (CBS, 1992–1993)

Jonathan Raven (Jeffrey Meek), a private detective based on Oahu, Hawaii, uses his skills as a martial arts expert to battle crime. He is assisted by Herman "Ski" Jablonski (Lee Majors), his military buddy, a former hard-drinking security analyst.

Jonathan was raised in Japan. His father, an agent for Interpol, and his mother were killed by the Black Dragon Society when Jonathan's father got too close to exposing a drug trafficking operation. Jonathan, a teenager at the time, became bitter and vowed to avenge their deaths. He infiltrated the society and learned the martial arts. When he felt the time was right, he killed those responsible for murdering his parents. He is now sought by the Black Dragons for betraying them. Before Jonathan left Japan he had an affair with a Japanese girl named Aki Moshirho. Unknown to Jonathan, Aki was two months pregnant when he left Japan to protect her from the Black Dragons. At seven months, complications set in and Aki died shortly after childbirth. Sometime later, Jonathan received a letter from the girl's sister, Nuko Mohihiro (Patricia Ayama Thompson), telling him about the birth of his son, whom Aki named Hikatti ("Sparkling Light"), but not saying where he was. Jonathan is now in a desperate race to find his son before the Black Dragons do; Jonathan believes they will kill his son.

Jonathan drives a jeep with the license plate R2H 103. He also has a special talent for touching people on the back of the neck and instantly knocking them out. Big Kahuna's Bar is Jonathan and Ski's favorite hangout. Ski, a former army special forces agent, has a boat called the *Brew-Ski*, which he docks at Pier G-22 on Big Kahuna's Diamond Head Marina. Ski loves pastrami on rye, carries four guns (one on each side of his hips, one in his boot, one in the back of his belt), brass knuckles and a knife with him at all times. His car license plate reads M8B 730. Osata (Cary Hisoyuki Tagawa) is the Black Dragon leader seeking to kill Jonathan. Josh C. Williams played a young Jonathan in flashbacks. The TV show "America's Most Dangerous" broadcast a story about a wife killer called "The Cincinnati Shredder" with a picture of the culprit, who looked exactly like Ski, but of course, wasn't. Christopher Franke composed the theme.

Reasonable Doubts *See* Sue Thomas, F.B.Eye

101. **Remington Steele** (NBC, 1982–1986)

Remington Steele is a man who does not actually exist. It is a name that was made up by private investigator Laura Holt (Stephanie Zimbalist) to save her floundering business, Laura Holt Investigations. By taking the first name of a typewriter and combining it with the last name of her favorite football team, Laura finds a surge in business when she changes the name of the company to Remington Steele Investigations. She portrays Remington, whom she always calls Mr. Steele, as charming, suave and sophisticated. When a client asks to see Mr. Steele, Laura explains that "Mr. Steele never involves himself in a case; he functions best in an advisory capacity." If a client insists on seeing Mr. Steele, Laura passes on the case.

A routine assignment to protect the fabulous Royal Lavulite Diamonds changes Laura's life forever when the man she invented materializes in the form of a thief seeking the diamonds. Laura uncovers the thief's plot but instead of turning him in to the police she allows him to use Remington's identity to avoid capture. He later convinces Laura to make him her partner.

"The mysterious Remington Steele" is just that — mysterious. He was born in Ireland on September 6, 1952 and was apparently an orphan. He grew up on the streets and was taught the fine art of crime by master con artist Daniel Chalmers (Efrem Zimbalist, Jr.). The man, now officially known as Remington Steele (Pierce Brosnan) was 12 years earlier making the rounds as a professional boxer called "The Kilkearney Kid." He now lives at 1594 Rossmore Street, Apartment 5A, and has two cars: a 1936 Auburn, license plate R. STEELE, and a blue Mercedes, plate IDR 0373. His address is also given as 5594 Rossmore.

The Honeymooners is Remington's favorite television show and he is a fan of movies from the 1930s and '40s. He often associates motion pictures with real life and solves crimes based on their plots. His living room wall has posters from *Casablanca, Hotel Imperial, Notorious* and *The Thin Man.* He claims that old movies are for therapeutic value as they relax him. Remington has five passports with five different names from five countries. They are, in addition to Remington Steele, all characters played by Humphrey Bogart: Michael O'Leary (Ireland), Paul Fabre (France), John Morrill (England) and Richard Blaine (Australia). The episode, "Etched in Steele," finds Remington negotiating a deal with Forsythe House publishers for a book called *Remington Steele's Ten Most Famous Cases.* It is not disclosed, however, if the book will be published, or even written. Remington was voted one of the five most eligible bachelors by *Upbeat* magazine.

Laura Holt weighs 110 pounds and lives at 800 Tenth Street, Apartment 3A, in a building owned by the Commercial Management Corporation. She has a cat named Nero and 555-6235 is her phone number. Her car license plate reads JEL 1525, later IEY 9463, and T-7328 is her mobile phone number. "Atomic Man" was her favorite television show as a kid and she had the nickname Binky. For relaxation, she listens to radio station KROT; her clock radio alarm rings at 6:00 AM. While seemingly perfect, Laura is plagued by "The Holt Curse," a craving for chocolate.

Laura has had a fascination for crime since she was a little girl. She majored in criminology at Stanford University and was a member of the glee club. She shared a fourth floor dorm room with three girls and they were known as "The Four East." After graduating, Laura became an apprentice detective at the Havenhurst Detective Agency. She quit when she felt she could start her own business. Most people believed that because of her sex, Laura was not built for the job. "It takes more brains than brawn to make a detective," she says. When she finally believed that perhaps a female private detective is too feminine, she invented her mythical boss. Laura never carries a gun ("I never found the need to use one"). She is practical but intuitive, logical and brilliant. No matter how bleak the situation, Laura never loses her sense of humor. The reading glasses that Laura is seen wearing date back to her college days. She bought them to impress her calculus professor "to make me look brainy."

"Who are you? Where did you come from?" are two questions Laura constantly asks of Remington, but she never gets a response. Remington Steele Investigations is located in Suite 1157 of a skyscraper at 606 West Beverly Boulevard in Los Angeles; its phone numbers are 555-9450, 555-3535 and 555-9548. Canary yellow memo pads are used in the office. Laura constantly complains about the amount of money Mr. Steele squanders on a case, mostly to wine and dine women. Laura believes that Remington solves cases quite by chance. When he interferes in a case she is working on, Laura explains to a client that it is one of Mr. Steele's brilliant tactics. And when Mr. Steele takes a case without telling Laura, she always brings up the bargain they made — "I do the work, you take the bows." The comic strip *Blaster* used the images of Remington and Laura as Dashing Dave and Doll Face.

Murphy Michaels (James Read) was Laura's original assistant in first season episodes, and Bernice Foxx (Janet DeMay), whom Remington called Miss Wolf, was her receptionist. Mildred Krebs (Doris Roberts) replaced both characters from the second season on. Bernice was said to have run off with a saxophone player and Murphy left to start his own firm in Denver, Colorado. Mildred is a former IRS auditor who finds excitement being a secretary and amateur sleuth. She bowls on a team called the Dragon Ladies and has an uncontrollable urge to attend seances. She sometimes upsets Mr. Steele, whom she calls "Boss," if she does not have his hot coffee and paper on his desk at 9:00 AM She calls Laura "Miss Holt." Mildred's last name is seen as *Krebs* in the credits; when Laura spells her name during a case it's *Krebbs*.

George E. Mulch (Michael Constantine) is the "idea man" who complicates Laura's life with his wacky ideas; Norman Keyes (James Tolkan) is the Vigilance Insurance Company detective seeking to uncover Steele's true identity.

Henry Mancini composed the theme.

102. Richard Diamond, Private Detective (CBS, 1957–1959; NBC, 1959–1960)

Richard Diamond (David Janssen) is a handsome, New York-based private detective with an office (306) in mid–Manhattan. Diamond, a former officer with the 5th Precinct of the N.Y.P.D., charges $100 a day plus expenses; if a beautiful girl is in trouble and can't afford that, he lowers his price to $50 a day. Diamond lives at the Savoy Hotel, reads the New York *Chronicle* and doesn't come to the office on Tuesdays. He claims that a private eye is only as good as his snitches and pays these people as much as $10 for information.

Diamond drives a convertible and has a phone in his car; ZM1-2173, then ZM1-2713 were given as its calling numbers. Richard doesn't have a secretary but he does have an assistant — Sam (Mary Tyler Moore, Roxanne Brooks), a gorgeous, sexy-voiced girl who operates the Hi-Fi Answering Service. Richard has never seen Sam; "the only thing I know about her is what she tells me — and that ain't much." Samuel, as Richard sometimes calls Sam, is situated in a dimly lit room near her switchboard that is designed to accentuate her shapely legs, slim waist and well developed bust. Sam's face is never clearly seen; she wears tight blouses and sweaters and slit skirts or dresses raised just enough to show the needed bit of thigh. She wears the then famous "torpedo bra" (38B) and size ten stockings, medium length.

Sam answers Richard's office calls on the fourth ring. When Sam calls Richard she says, "It's me, Mr. D." Richard concludes his conversations with her with "As usual, Samuel, thank you." Diamond also receives clients from Sam; "Richard, I have a friend who needs help — a female friend." Murray Hill 4-9099 was Sam's answering service phone number when Mary Tyler Moore played the role; OL 4-1654 was the number when Roxanne Brooks took over the role.

Richard dines at the Lunch Counter and often goes undercover, for example, as Fred Grebble, when he has to — "Because some people are allergic to my profession." The series is later set in Los Angeles, where Richard has an office (117) in an unidentified building. His police department contact is Pete Kile (Russ Conway), a lieutenant who calls him Rick. In New York episodes, Diamond's former superior, Lieutenant Dennis "Mac" McGough (Regis Toomey) was his contact. Last season episodes also feature Barbara Bain as Karen Wells, Richard's girlfriend.

Pete Rugolo composed the theme "Richard Diamond."

Note: The series was syndicated in the 1960s as *Call Mr. D*. The theme and its entire musical background were changed. There is no credit for the revised music and the opening visuals were also changed. In *Richard Diamond*, Diamond is seen running here and there as the theme music plays. He approaches the camera and lights a cigarette. In *Call Mr. D.*, a figure is seen in a darkened alley. As the new theme plays, he walks forward and lights a cigarette; we see that it is Richard Diamond.

Richie Brockelman, Private Eye *See* The Rockford Files

103. The Roaring 20's (ABC, 1960–1962)

Pinky Pinkham (Dorothy Provine), Pat Garrison (Donald May) and Scott Norris (Rex Reason) are three friends who live and work in New York City during the 1920s.

Pinky, real first name Delaware, is a beautiful singer who owns the Charleston Club, a fashionable speakeasy (nightclub) on East 52nd Street in Manhattan. The club is also called Pinky's and Pinky's Club. The club serves a legitimate scotch called Highland Dew but is typical of the times and fashions its own bathtub gin (homemade beer). The club is characterized by a life-size photo of Pinky, dressed as a flapper and mounted on a wooden backing. Although Pinky is called a flapper, she is not typical of the word that describes a girl who drinks, smokes, dances to jazz music and throws caution to the wind in her pursuit of a good time. Pinky is just the opposite and tries to stay away from trouble. But trouble always seems to find her as bootleggers, mobsters, local crime bosses and crooked politicians find the Charleston Club the perfect hangout.

Pinky lives at the Grently Apartments, Room 21, and Skylar 2-098 is her phone number. Twelve o'clock noon is her normal wakeup time. When Pinky does fall in love, usually with men with links to the criminal world, the song "Someone to Watch Over Me" is heard playing in the background. Watching over Pinky are Scott Norris and Pat Garrison, crime reporters for a newspaper called both the *Daily Record* and the *New York Record*. Scott and Pat each earn $40 a week, later $60, and play detective, often with Pinky's help, to get front page stories by solving crimes and putting crooks and racketeers in jail. While Pat and Scott frequent the Charleston Club, they were also fond of Clanccy's, the bar located next to the Record Building. In second season episodes, the bar name was changed to The Pit. Wally Brown played Chauncey, the bar owner. The *Gazette* is the *Record's* competition.

Second season episodes dropped the character of Scott Norris and added John Dehner as Jim Duke Williams, a reporter who was also the city editor of the *Record*. Tension was introduced as Duke did whatever he could to beat Garrison to the stories, but the format just didn't work and the series was cancelled four months later.

Chris Higbee (Gary Vinson), a graduate of Cornell University, was originally the paper's copyboy, then a reporter. He lived at the Hallmark Hotel.

Joe Switolski (Mike Road) is the cop Scott and Pat help, a lieutenant with the 7th Precinct of the N.Y.P.D., also seen as the Bell Street Police Station. Spring 3-100 is Joe's direct dial telephone number.

Each episode features at least one club song by Pinky. A group called The Playboys provide Pinky's musical backing while two girls, Cindy (Gayla Graves) and Dodie (Roxanne Arlen) provide vocal backup. Cindy and Dodie are billed as "And the Girls"; they and Pinky are officially called Pinky and the Girls. Dixie (Carolyn Komant) is the hat check girl at the Charleston Club and Andre (Gregory Gay) is the maitre d'. Over at the *Record*, Louise Glenn plays Gladys, the switchboard operator.

Mack David and Jerry Livingston composed the theme "The Roaring 20's."

104. Robin's Hoods (Syndicated, 1994–1995)

McKenzie Magnuson (Claire Yarlett), Stacey Wright (Julie McCullough), Maria Alvarez (Mayte Vilan), Anatasia Beckett (Jennifer Campbell) and Eddie Bartlett (David Gail) are former law breakers who now work for Brett Robin (Linda Purl), a former assistant district attorney who oversees their activities as the owner of Robin's Nest, a night club that doubles as a private detective organization.

Robin's Nest was owned by Brett's late husband, Jake, a police officer who was killed in the line of duty. Jake was with Metro Police and believed in giving people a second chance — a way of repaying a kindness that was done to him. When Jake was 12 years old he stole some car tires. He was caught but spared the ordeal of juvenile hall when the arresting officer talked the judge into giving him a second chance. The incident changed Jake's life; it made him want to be a cop. Years later he set up the night club and had first-time offenders McKenzie, Stacey, Maria, Anastasia and Eddie released to him on parole to give them a second chance by working for him at the club. Brett had distanced herself from Jake's work at the club. When she learned what Jake had been doing in his spare time (helping people in trouble), Brett decided to continue in that capacity and run Robin's Nest full time by using Jake's "hoods" to solve crimes.

Very little information is given about the characters. Brett lives at 6 Menton Street. She had office 318 as an assistant D.A. She is not as aggressive as Jake was as the head of Robin's Nest. She does not actively involve herself in cases and acts more like a coordinator. Brett worries about finances and fears a bank will take action against her because she has five ex-cons working for her. Brett was pregnant by Jake before he was killed. Shortly before the series ended, Brett gave birth to a son and was written out when she left to care for him. She was replaced by Nick Collins (Rick Springfield), the club manager who suddenly appeared to run the club, the agency — and assure the bank that their mortgage will be paid.

Stacey is 23 years old and was arrested for possession of drugs; her police booking number is Q2470843. Stacey is blonde and beautiful and has a soft spot in her heart for people she meets who swear they are telling the truth but nobody believes. She was in the same position herself; she claimed she was framed for drug possession but couldn't prove it; no one believed she was innocent. She works as a waitress at the club and uses her assets for distraction purposes. Maria is 25 years old and was arrested for armed robbery, booking number G-2016440. Maria is Cuban and believes that is one strike against her. When she came to America at an early age, she changed her name to Mary Astor and learned to speak English so no one would know her true heritage. She later fell in with the wrong crowd, became Maria Alvarez again and was caught red-handed during a robbery attempt. Prison time mellowed the bitter Maria and she now uses her self-taught expertise with weapons and thievery to help the team. Maria also works as a waitress at the club.

McKenzie, booking number G-6769423, is 27 years old and was arrested for writing bad checks. She is always in need of money and is the schemer of the group. If something is needed, Mac, as she is called, will find a way to get it without paying for it. She drives a car with the license plate AX0 103. Eddie, originally the only male member of the group, is the most aggressive. He was arrested for aggravated assault, booking number VT-345-2514, and works as the club's bartender. He often risks parole violation by engaging in fights with suspects. Anastasia, called Anne, is 22 years old. She was arrested for breaking and entering, booking number G-4242450, and is a master at getting into places without being detected. She risks being sent back to prison if she is caught in places where she shouldn't be. While Jake kept a strict eye on his charges, Brett is sometimes lax, allowing her hoods to use their skills to accomplish a goal. Although she does warn them not to break the law, she is not in the field and the hoods, led by Anne, do what is necessary to please their clients.

John E. Nordstrom composed the theme.

105. The Rockford Files (NBC, 1974–1980)

James Scott Rockford (James Garner) is a tough private detective who takes the law in his own hands "because I don't like the alternatives." He is bitter because he was falsely convicted of robbery and sentenced to 20 years at San Quentin. He was later given a full pardon when new evidence cleared him. It is also the one thing he refuses to talk about with anyone. Jim, as Rockford is often called, now operates the Rockford Private Detective Agency, also called the Rockford Agency, from his mobile home at the Paradise Cove Trailer Colony in Malibu Beach, California, address given as 29 Palm Road, 29 Cove Road and 2354 Pacific Coast. His fee is $200 a day plus expenses and he can be reached by phone at 555-2368, later 555-9000. His gold Firebird car license plate reads 853 CNG, later OK 6853 and 853 OKG. Jim is six feet one inch tall, later said to be six feet two inches tall, and weighs 200 pounds. He was an army corporal during the Korean War and began his agency in 1968. Scotch is his favorite drink and Casa Tacos his favorite eatery. He always gives a ten percent tip because it seems like ten percent is enough. Jim lies to get what he needs from suspects and uses the alias Jerry Vanders, reporter for the L.A. *Sun*, to get into places his P.I. identity won't allow. Jim also worked briefly as a reporter named Jim Hanley for the rag sheet, *National Investigator*, while on a case. The title refers to the original concept of the series: Jim's efforts to solve cases that are considered unsolvable and labeled inactive by the police. As the series progressed, Jim took any case that came his way. He also does investigative work for the Boston Casualty Insurance Company.

Joseph Rockford (Noah Beery, Jr.), called Rocky, is Jim's 68-year-old father, a retired big rig truck driver. Rocky drove for 45 years and was a member of Truckers Union Local 214. He only uses his license now and then to help Jim. The mythical TV series "Falcone" is Rocky's favorite private eye show. Robert Donley played Rocky in the pilot episode.

Evelyn Martin (Stuart Margolin) is a con artist and friend of Jim's who prefers to be called by his street name of Angel. While Angel is helpful, Jim calls him a "transformer" ("someone who rats on someone to save his own neck"). Angel mentioned that he previously wrote the Miss Lonely Hearts column for his brother's newspaper.

Dennis Becker (Joe Santos) is a homicide sergeant with the Wilshire Division of the L.A.P.D. who is hoping to become a lieutenant. Becker has a desk in the squad room (418) and believes Rockford enjoys visiting crime scenes and other human disasters. He also fears his association with the ex-con is preventing him from getting his promotion. Dennis's wife, Peggy (Pat Finley) attends evening classes at UCLA. Beth Davenport (Gretchen Corbett) is Jim's romantic interest, a lawyer with the firm of Hardcort and Lowe. Mike Post and Pete Carpenter composed the theme "The Rockford Files."

Seven television movies were also produced that reunited James Garner, Joe Santos and Stuart Margolin: *I Still Love L.A.* (1994), *A Blessing in*

Disguise (1995), *If the Frame Fits* (1996), *Godfather Knows Best* (1996), *Friends and Foul Play* (1996), *Crime and Punishment* (1996) and *Murders and Misdemeanors* (1999).

Spinoff Series

Richie Brockelman, Private Eye (NBC, 1978). Office 24 of the Bromley Building at 4th and Alameda in Los Angeles is home to the offices of the Brockelman Detective Agency, although Richard Brockelman — Private Detective is printed on the door. Richie (Dennis Dugan) is 23 years old and has more nerve than know how. He charges $200 a day plus expenses, lives at 8410 North Turtle Dove Drive and drives a red Mustang with the license plate EDU 887, originally 238 PCE. Sharon Peterson (Barbara Bosson) is his secretary; and Ted Coopersmith (Robert Hogan) is the L.A.P.D. sergeant Richie calls Smitty. The original TV movie pilot, *Richie Brockelman: Missing 24 Hours*, aired on NBC on October 27, 1976. The character then appeared occasionally on *The Rockford Files*.

Proposed Spinoff (Unsold Pilot)

Nice Guys Finish Dead (November 16, 1979). The pilot for a series called "Lance White" with Tom Selleck as Lance White, a handsome, rich and elegant private eye who does everything wrong but still gets the glory for solving crimes. The pilot story finds Jim and Lance seeking a killer.

106. Serpico (NBC, 1976–1977)

In New York City in 1976, hot dogs were 85 cents; a pastrami on rye cost $1.85, and crime was down by 40 percent. Frank Serpico (David Birney), an undercover N.Y.P.D. officer, is one of the many men and women responsible for lowering the crime rate. Frank is with the 7th Precinct and 21049 is his police identification number; his patrolman's license expires on December 31, 1978. The 22nd Precinct was also mentioned as Frank's base of operations.

Frank is a Catholic and attended St. Michael's Grammar School. It was in high school, St. Michael's, that Frank, an altar boy, became interested in becoming a priest. He attended St. Joseph's Seminary in preparation for becoming a priest but soon after found "I wasn't cut out for it." It is not stated how or why, but Frank turned his attention to helping people in another way — as a police officer. Frank lives on West 66th Street and knows verses of the *Bible* by heart; he often recites them when on assignments. Tom Atkins plays Frank's superior, Lieutenant "Sully" Sullivan. Elmer Bernstein composed the theme "Serpico."

107. 77 Sunset Strip (ABC, 1958–1964)

Bailey and Spencer, Private Investigators is a detective agency located at 77 Sunset Strip in Hollywood, California. Stuart Bailey (Efrem Zimbalist, Jr.) and Jeff Spencer (Roger Smith) head the agency. They are assisted by Rex Randolph (Richard Long), Gerald Lloyd Kookson III (Edd Byrnes) and Suzanne Fabray (Jacqueline Beer).

Stuart, called Stu, occupies office 101. He was a former OSS (Office of Strategic Services) agent and now lives in Apartment 301 at the Sunset DeVilla; Olympia 1-3792 is his office phone number. He drives a convertible with the license plate number PAZ 184, later AVE 424, JPN 300, RTU 020 and NPO 614. Stu is a bit reluctant to use force and relies on his intelligence training to accomplish his goals during a case.

Jeff occupies office 102 and Olympia 6-1116 is his home phone number. He lives in Apartment 517 of an unidentified building and drives a car with the license plate PYB 767, later GBC 101. He reads *Playboy* magazine (surprisingly "not for the articles") and $50 is the top price he pays a snitch for information. Jeff and Stu have an eye for the ladies, and girls often tell Jeff "You're too cute to be a snoop." Jeff is more adept at physical heroics than Stu, whom he sometimes calls "The Professor" for his intelligence and ability to speak several languages.

Gerald Lloyd Kookson III, better known as Kookie, is the parking lot attendant at Dino's Lodge, the supper club next to 77 Sunset Strip. Kookie lives at 18026 Valley Hart Drive with his unseen mother, Helen Margaret Kookson, a public stenographer; his father is deceased. Kookie drives a hot rod with the license plate JOY 038, later K-3400, and uses hip talk; for example, "Squaresville, Man"; "Like Man, let's get out of here" and "I don't dig it." He refers to Jeff and Stu as "Hey, Dad" and pretty girls are "Dreamboats." Trouble is "Troublesville." The Cool Dragon Cafe and the Chez Paulette Coffeehouse are his favorite hangouts. Kookie had a way of combing his hair that drove teenage girls in the viewing audience crazy; the song, "Kookie, Kookie, Lend Me Your Comb" became a hit. In fourth season episodes, Kookie quits the parking lot business to become partners with Jeff and Stu. J.R. Hale (Robert Logan) replaced Kookie as the new parking lot attendant at Dino's. Chic Hammons (Sue Randall), a beautiful college girl studying art, became, as Kookie said, "The only girl to appeal to my intellectual side." Kookie is usually seen with gorgeous girls who are a bit kookie — today referred to as "airhead" or "bimbos."

Suzanne is a gorgeous French girl who operates the Sunset Answering Service from office 103 at 77 Sunset Strip. She is also a public stenographer, as seen in printing on the left side of the door, and lives in Apartment 217 at 152½ North Maple Street, later address given as 236 North Maple, Apartment B; 354-4567 is her phone number. Suzanne's switchboard phone number for Bailey and Spencer is Olympia 4-0992, later Olympia 5-1656. Kookie gives Suzanne two doughnuts and a cup of coffee each day to refuel her energy. Suzanne works occasionally for Stu or Jeff in an undercover capacity; for example, as a swimsuit model at Rainbow Models to discover who is stealing designs for Jeff's client, Surf 'n' Sun Styles.

Roscoe (Louis Quinn) is a stool pigeon who provides information to Stu and Jeff. He was born in the Bronx, New York, and is addicted to gambling. He calls Suzanne "Frenchy" and bets on horses at Hollywood Park. He owned a Greyhound racing dog named Genevieve, which he purchased for $500 in a claiming race, and calls girls "Fillies." Bourbon and ginger ale is his favorite drink.

Roy Gilmore (Byron Keith), called Gil, is a lieutenant with the Homicide Bureau of the L.A.P.D. He sometimes regrets the job and says, "I should have taken my father's advice and studied air conditioning instead of Nick Carter books."

Stu and Jeff sometimes work for the Pacific Casualty Insurance Company in San Francisco and Pacific Orient Insurance in Los Angeles. Dino's Lodge closes at 2:00 AM. The Frank Ortega Trio provides the music at Dino's Lodge. Kookie keeps a spare dinner jacket in the hatcheck room at Dino's for emergencies. In the back of the lodge is Dino's Poodle Palace where the pampered poodles of patrons stay.

How did Stu and Jeff come to 77 Sunset Strip? It's all a matter of who to believe. According to Jeff, it began when he arrived in Los Angeles and opened a successful private eye business in Beverly Hills. While driving one afternoon his car experienced a flat tire and he received help by a kid in a hot rod named Kookie. In gratitude, Jeff gave him his business card and said, "If I can ever repay the favor, let me know." A short time later, a struggling detective named Stuart Bailey was hired by Pacific Orient Insurance to crack an auto theft ring. During his investigation Stu meets Jeff, who is also on the case to help Kookie, whose friend has been kidnapped by the ring. Kookie suggests that Jeff and Stu work together. With Kookie's help, the trio break up the ring. When Kookie realizes that Stu and Jeff would make a good team he tells them that offices are for rent at 77 Sunset Strip.

Stu tells a slightly different version. In his scenario, Stu is successful — Bailey, Private Investigator — while Jeff, owner of Jeff Spencer Investigations, is struggling to stay in business. Here, it was Stu who got the flat tire and it was he who gave the good samaritan, Kookie, the business card.

Pacific Orient hired Jeff to crack the auto theft ring while Stu agreed to help Kookie.

Kookie tells it a bit differently. "If it hadn't been for me, they wouldn't have made the scene at all. It all started when my wheels went out on the blink. I was makin' with the tools when Jeff just happened to be driving by and stopped to help." Kookie said, "If you ever need help, just ask." When Kookie's friend is kidnapped by the auto theft ring, Kookie figures to help Jeff and his struggling private eye business by letting him crack the ring. Pacific Orient had hired Stuart Bailey, a down-on-his-luck investigator, to do the same thing. The three meet and together break up the ring. Kookie tells Jeff and Stu, "You make a great team and I've got just the place for you to get started — 77 Sunset Strip."

In 1963 (to 1964) the format changed to focus on Stu Bailey as a private detective on his own. Although the title remained unchanged, Stu now had an office in downtown Los Angeles in a building called both the Bradbury Building and the Bedford Building. The theme also changed from a snappy vocal composed by Mack David and Jerry Livingston to a musical composition by Bob Thompson. Stu now had a secretary named Hannah (Joan Staley) and stories were told in a flashback manner. As Stu talked to Hannah, a flashback was used to tell the story. When the flashback ended, Stu and Hannah returned to sum up the case.

The Series Is Based on Two Pilots

1. ***Anything for Money*** (ABC, April 16, 1957 as an episode of *Conflict*). The first appearance of Efrem Zimbalist, Jr. as private detective Stuart Bailey. Here, he is hired as a bodyguard to protect a yachtsman on a pleasure cruise to Havanna.

2. ***Girl on the Run*** (ABC, October 10, 1958). Stuart Bailey (Efrem Zimbalist, Jr.) attempts to locate a missing cabaret singer who disappeared after witnessing a murder. This 90-minute episode was broadcast as the first episode of the series but is often not part of the syndicated package. Edd Byrnes appeared as killer Kenneth Smiley before he became Kookie on the second episode of the series, which is usually seen as the first episode.

Proposed Spinoff (Unsold Pilot)

The Reluctant Spy. The episode of October 12, 1962 was the test program for an untitled series of dramas about international intrigue that was to feature a different cast and story each week. The pilot story finds Lucy Norton (Randy Stuart) hiring Stuart Bailey to prove that her husband's accidental death was actually a cleverly conceived murder by foreign agents.

Shades of L.A. *See* Haunted

108. She Spies (NBC/Syndicated, 2002)

Cassie McBain (Natasha Henstridge), D.D. Cummings (Kristen Miller) and Shane Phillips (Natashia Williams) are three beautiful girls recruited by an agent named Jack Wilde (Carlos Jacott) to form She Spies, a government organization designed to battle crime and corruption.

Cassie, D.D. and Shane are a new millennium version of the 1970s *Charlie's Angels* (see entry). Jack is a combination of John Bosley and Charlie Townsend; he formed the group and now oversees their operations. Unlike the girls of *Charlie's Angels*, who were ex-cops recruited by Charlie, Jack's "Angels" are bad girls gone good — all felons who were released from prison to serve their country.

Cassie was born in Aspen, Colorado. She is a Phi Delta Gamma who earned her way into college by conning bankers and CEOs. Cassie was raised by her father, a con artist, after her mother's death. Cassie's father taught her how to lie, steal, cheat and con; she became a part of his schemes and it eventually cost her her freedom when one of her cons backfired and she was captured. She is a brilliant career criminal and the self-proclaimed ring leader of the She Spies. Cassie is an expert at bugging and loves pretending to be someone else to get information from suspects. She enjoys walks on the beach and relaxes by playing pool.

D.D. was born in Washington, D.C. She is an expert in computers, foreign languages and explosives. She loves volleyball and dancing to the rhumba. Her father was a CIA agent who was framed for spying. D.D. knew he was innocent and the only way she could prove it was to hack into the government's database. She managed to prove her father was innocent, but she was arrested for six counts of stealing state secrets; her police booking number is 83-7648-8.

D.D. attended St. Mary's Middle School where she learned to speak French. In high school, she was voted most likely to coordinate talent; "Weird, isn't it," she says. She also played Shell Number 1 in the school production of *The Little Mermaid*. D.D. is a graduate of Harvard University (she hacked her way into the school's computer system to arrange for a diploma) and worries about "the increasing National Debt and its effects on our health and welfare program." D.D.'s favorite drink is a banana cream — one shot of banana liquor; one shot of vodka; a smidgen of orange juice and a splash of nonfat milk. She also has a fear of beets — "I try to stay away from beets. It reminds me of my grandmother's borst and that reminds me of staying in her house and that reminds me of the time my grandfather's teeth fell in my soup bowl." While each of the girls takes a turn cleaning the house in which they live as a family, it is D.D. who does the most complaining; for example, "The bulletproof windows Jack had installed — they're not easy to clean." D.D. has a plush teddy bear, Uncle Blue Bear, and a talent for what she calls "wall walking" (balancing herself between two walls in a horizontal manner).

Shane, police booking number E8045-33, was born in Los Angeles. She is African American and from a rich family. She rebelled against her parents and made good by becoming a master thief. She was eventually caught and sent to prison. Another episode claims that Shane was an only child who was raised by her father after her mother's death. Her father wanted a boy and raised her as though she were his son. Shane became "macho," as she says, and was taught things like boxing. She used what she was taught for all the wrong reasons — crime. "I wish I would have spent more time as a girl," she says. Shane is an expert in Brazilian jujitsu and is happy to kick, body punch or slam her way into a situation. She is tough in a fight and will use any means possible to defend herself. Shane is an expert on explosives, safe cracking and alarm systems. She reads *Spy* magazine and makes a wonderful peach cobbler.

Jack had the idea to recruit three girls from prison with specific skills to fight crime for the government as undercover agents; "I fought long and hard to turn that vision into a reality." He is seen bribing his superiors when he tells the story as they believe Jack "has lost it." Jack's superior (although not the one he is seen bribing) is the mysterious, unseen Chairman. Jack is now the liaison between his She Spies Program, its official title, and the unnamed government agency that backs him. Their secret base of operations is called She Spy Headquarters. Jack's van serves as the She Spies Mobile Command Center and encompasses the VX1-82 wireless phone system developed exclusively for them, but it is prone to busy signals and line interference. The team is based in Los Angeles and the girls live together in a house provided for them by the government. In some episodes the girls call it Jack's House.

Jack, a history major in college, briefs the girls before each assignment. He constantly complains that the girls are clumsy and argumentative and wreck havoc and destruction wherever they go. "We live to do it," says D.D. Shane claims, "We do it for the American Way." Jack constantly takes the heat for the girls and is determined to make an honorable crime fighting team out of them.

Jack often feels like "a desk jockey, the man in the van" and would like to become more active and do field work like his girls. He has four instant dial buttons on his phone: Chairman, Girl's House, Pizza and Chinese Food.

D.D. says, "We're part of a candlestein government organization and out to rid the world of evil doers." The girls do not carry guns because D.D. doesn't believe in guns; "We're setting an example because you never know when kids are watching." Jack says, "Technically, you're felons. You're not even out on parole. The agency won't even allow me to give you guns." When the girls oppose an assignment, Jack gets them back in line by saying simply, "Who would like to go back to prison?" The girls also complain that Jack makes a production out of each assignment literally. He makes a film — all jobs credited as "Jack" — that details the girls' assignment on "The Plasma Screen." When Shane and D.D. have a disagreement and engage in a cat fight, the viewer sees them fall to the ground, but the camera remains where they stood. Cat sound effects (fighting) are heard over the scene.

Episodes usually begin with the girls on a case. When the time is right, the theme song is played. If Cassie thinks it is not the right time to run the credits, she stops the theme and the action resumes. While the girls constantly complain to Jack about the long hours and dangerous work, they seem to only complain to each other about the bruises, sprains and cuts they get as part of the job. The girls are seen applying makeup to cover obvious blemishes, and Cassie believes a waitressing job would be easier. If the girls have to go undercover and use a mansion, Cassie says, "I'm not use to being in a mansion unless I'm robbing it."

The episode of November 24, 2002, "Spies vs. Spy," reveals that before Jack formed the current She Spy Program, a test program was conducted with a single girl named Tonya (Claudia Christian). Tonya, however, "had issues," as Jack says. She didn't fit the program and Jack had to let her go; "I fired her." Tonya escaped before she could be returned to prison and she is now "a bad girl gone good gone bad." She possesses the same skills and beauty as Cassie, Shane and D.D. and can plan and counterplan like an agent. She is also relentless and has set out to destroy the She Spy Program.

Jerry Brunskill composed the theme "She Spies." The program opens with these words: "Every once in a while an elite crime fighting team emerges, highly sophisticated, covert ops specially trained in global intelligence and maneuvers. This is not one of those teams. They're three career criminals with one shot at freedom. Now they're working for the Feds who put them away. These are the women of She Spies — bad girls gone good."

Note: Four episodes were scheduled to air on NBC. Only three actually aired (July 26–August 9, 2002); the fourth is listed in various TV programming guides for August 16. The syndicated run began in September of 2002.

109. She's the Sheriff (Syndicated, 1987)

Lakes County is a small, peaceful town in Nevada. It has its own daily newspaper, the *Bugle*, a TV station (KLCN) and the county's first female sheriff, Hildegarde Granger (Suzanne Somers). Hildegarde, called Hildy, is a widow and the mother of two children, Alison (Nicky Rose) and Kenny (Taliesin Jaffe). Hildy was married to the former sheriff, Jim Granger. She served as his deputy for two years before retiring to raise a family. When Jim dies unexpectedly, the Nevada Police Commissioner appoints Hildy as the interim sheriff to finish Jim's term.

Hildy lives on the outskirts of town at 3111 Pine Shadow Lane; 555-1515 is her phone number. She was born in Teaneck, New Jersey, and had the nickname Pepper. She and Jim met in high school and both pursued jobs in law enforcement. They became officers with the New Jersey Police Department and married. Shortly after, when an opportunity arose for Jim to become a county sheriff, he and Hildy resigned from the force and moved to Lakes County.

Hildy, maiden name Holt, is now commander of the Lake County Division of the Nevada County Sheriff's Department. People say she's prettier than Cagney and Lacey and as sexy as Pepper Anderson from TV's *Police Woman* series, but not as assertive or brash as her television counterparts. When she has the time, Hildy enjoys watching "Doctor's Hospital," her favorite TV soap opera.

Allison and Kenny attend the Lakes County Grammar School and are cared for by Augusta "Gussie" Holt (Pat Carroll), Hildy's widowed mother, who lives with them. On her first day as sheriff, Hildy captured a spy who was posing as a cuckoo clock repairman.

Max Rubin (George Wyner), Dennis Putnam (Lou Richards), Alvin Wiggins (Leonard Lightfoot) and Hugh Mulcahy (Guich Koock) are Hildy's deputies, all males who seem somewhat reluctant to take orders from a woman. Max is the Chief Deputy and the man who was in line to replace Jim until the police commissioner thought otherwise. He is bitter and schemes to get Hildy's job by discrediting her. Alvin is a by-the-books deputy and follows Hildy's commands while Hugh likes to do things his way. Dennis is second in command behind Max and often bumbles his assignments and the schemes Max has devised to dispose of Hildy. Dennis has a pet goldfish named Dwight. Priscilla Barnes was originally cast as Hildy in an unaired pilot version of the series. Bruce Miller composed the theme.

Note: The series is actually based on an unsold pilot called "Cass Malloy" (CBS, July 21, 1982). The story finds Cass Malloy (Caroline McWilliams) becoming sheriff of Burr County, Indiana, to fill the term of her late husband, Big Jim Malloy, when he dies unexpectedly. Cass is the mother of three children, Colleen, Nona and Little Big Jim (Amanda Wyss, Heather Hobbs, Corey Feldman) and faces resentment from her male deputies: Max Rosencrantz (George Wyner), Dennis Little (Lou Richards), Woodrow Freeman (Glynn Turman) and Alvin Dimsky (Dick Butkus). Tom Wells composed the theme.

110. Silk Stalkings (CBS, 1991–1993; USA, 1991–1996)

In police terminology, a Code 5 is a stakeout; a Code 3 is an emergency; a 1054 is a probable dead body; and a Silk Stalking is a murder related to members of high society. Sergeants Rita Lee Lane (Mitzi Kapture) and Chris Lorenzo (Rob Estes) are officers who investigate Silk Stalkings as members of the Crimes of Passion Unit of the Palm Springs, Florida, Police Department.

Rita Lee is a stunning girl who has a natural flair for impersonation; she pretends to be someone else to acquire information. Rita also suffers from an embolism in her brain that is located in an area that is difficult to reach and an operation could prove fatal. The swelling of the blood vessel is very minor and with medication she can live a normal life. Rita has refused to have the operation which could either kill her or paralyze her. "I'll take my chances," she says. "My philosophy is you aren't sick unless you admit you are." Chris is the only person who knows; she hasn't told her captain, fearing she would be put on medical leave and be kept busy sweeping floors.

Rita's real last name is Fontana. She was born in 1965 and raised by her father, Donald, until she was seven years old. Rita's mother died in childbirth; her father, a wealthy businessman, killed himself when he lost millions through bad investments. Rita was raised by her foster parents, Tom and Sue Lance; she took their last name because it meant so much to her. As a kid Rita enjoyed Mother Goose stories and was fascinated by "Suzy Pratt" detective books. She also enjoyed riding her Victory Flyer Tricycle. Rita is a graduate of Palm Beach High School and Florida State College. She lives at 400 East Palm Drive and 555-4793 is her phone number. Rita worked with the Vice Squad when she first joined the force. In 1995 she was promoted to lieutenant and given the title Chief of Detectives. Her car code is One-X-Ray 8.

Chris was born in Philadelphia on April 12, 1963. His parents, Anna Alexis, a former actress, and father, Ben, a lawyer, divorced when Chris was ten years old. He was sent to live with his grandmother, Rose, in Palm Beach, when he objected to his constant shifting from parent to parent. He attended the same schools as Rita, but apparently they did not know each other at the time. Rita was two years older and a senior in both high school and college when Chris was a sophomore. Chris earned a criminology degree from Florida State in 1985 and began work as a street patrol cop. In 1988 he was assigned to the robbery unit, then teamed with Rita when he made sergeant. Chris, a former Boys' League basketball coach, enjoys playing the saxophone. He lives at 4613 Fairway and drives a car with the license plate 284 736. His dream car is a 1955 Thunderbird. His car code is One-X-Ray 13, also heard as One-X-Ray 9.

Rita and Chris are not just cops. They are best friends. They call each other "Sam"; they both love golf and golfing great "Slammin'" Sammy Snead is their hero. Rita and Chris eventually became lovers. In the episode "The Last Kiss Goodnight," Chris is shot protecting Rita. When he dies at Palm Beach Memorial Hospital, Rita, pregnant with Chris's child, turns in her badge. She feared something could happen to the last piece of Chris she had — their baby.

Rita and Chris are replaced by Detectives Holly Rawlins (Tyler Layton) and Michael Price (Nick Kokotakis) in 1995. Holly is a young, tough and beautiful Southern girl with a troubled past: she grew up in various trailer parks and is on the run from an abusive stepfather. Michael left the Chicago Police Department, after a broken relationship, to join the Palm Beach P.D. as part of an officer exchange program. Both characters were dropped shortly after without explanation and replaced by sergeants Cassandra St. John (Janet Gunn) and Tom Ryan (Chris Potter). Cassandra, called Cassy, and Tom were previously homicide detectives and married. Now divorced, they have remained friends and have learned to put their feelings aside to get the job done. Cassy is savvy, totally honest and a perfectionist, making it hard for anyone to work with her. Tom is easy going and willing to break the rules to get the job done which totally contradicts Cassy's way of investigating a case. Tom is also a romantic and was a former State College football star.

Benjamin Hutchinson (Ben Vereen) called Hutch, was the first captain. He hates the FBI, which he calls Fumble, Bumble and Incompetent, for interfering in his department's cases. Hutch, a former Detroit cop, was transferred to the Fort Lauderdale division at the end of the second season. He was replaced by Robert Gossett as Vice Captain Hudson. By the end of the following season, he too was transferred to Fort Lauderdale. Harry Lipschitz (Charlie Brill) became the final captain. Called "The Lip," he was a New York cop who relocated with his wife Frannie (Mitzi McCall) to take the job with the Palm Beach P.D.

Mike Post composed the theme "Silk Stalkings."

111. Sledge Hammer (ABC, 1986–1987)

Apartment 13 at 5517 Stafford Street in an unspecified American city is home to Sledge Hammer (David Rasche), a detective with an unidentified police precinct. Sledge wears badge 6316 and drives a car with a bumper sticker that reads I LOVE VIOLENCE. He is said to be dirtier than Harry, meaner than Bronson and makes Rambo look like Pee Wee Herman. His superior, Captain Trunk (Harrison Page) calls him sadistic, barbaric, depraved and blood thirsty. He also says, "I get migraines when I have to deal with Hammer."

Hammer's weapon of choice is his .44 Magnum. He has named the weapon Gun and talks to it, sometimes imagining it talks back to him. He carries a bazooka in the trunk of his car ("for taking out suspects") and is considered a menace by the department—not only to himself and innocent civilians, but to other police officers. Sledge fires warning shots at jaywalkers, cares little about police brutality and will do what it takes to get a confession out of a suspect; for example, tying one to the back of his car and dragging him through the streets. When Hammer feels he is being watched for possibly disciplinary action, he orders a suspect to beat himself up. His philosophy is the way to fight criminals is to be wilder than they are. Hammer is divorced from Susan (Heather Lupton), a woman Sledge met through a computer dating service. She left him after three years of marriage "for a geek—someone who works for the Peace Corps."

Sledge Hammer is trigger happy and believes "all other cops are wussies—except me. I never let my guard down." He and Gun are inseparable. Wherever Hammer goes Gun goes. Sledge isn't too concerned about flesh wounds, except for the fact that they ruin good sport jackets, and crime does not seem to phase him. For example, when he and Gun go grocery shopping and a holdup takes place, Hammer shoots the suspects then goes about his business—"What I did was absolutely necessary. I had no groceries." Hammer prefers the solitude of his apartment for target practice. He is not concerned about bullets piercing the walls or being evicted and donates to a charity called Toy Guns for Tots.

Dori Doreau (Ann-Marie Martin) is a young, beautiful detective who puts her life at risk by working as Hammer's partner. The Captain is furious at Dori for doing so, but she insures him that "I know what I am doing." Dori is apparently the only other detective who can work with Sledge without being injured. While Dori is not as blood thirsty and mean as Sledge, she can handle herself. She has a background in the martial arts, top in her class in hand-to-hand combat, and is an expert shot. Hammer is not so much amazed by her beauty, but more by the fact that she can handle herself quite well. Dori's crime fighting tactics have excited Hammer and Dori always refuses his request—"I'd like to fight you sometime, Doreau." Dori is single and lives in an apartment at 102 Las Palmas Drive. Danny Elfman composed the theme "Sledge Hammer."

Related Project (Unsold Pilot)

Crazy Dan (NBC, July 19, 1986). "He's a crazy man, Crazy Dan" the theme says about "Crazy" Dan Gatlin (John Beck), a single-minded, unorthodox Los Angeles police detective with an affection for dark glasses and a knack for breaking all the rules in an attempt to get the job done. Officer Bonnie Raines (Mary Crosby) is Dan's partner, a girl who is his complete opposite and opposes his violent methods. Their superior is Captain Walker (John Hancock).

112. Snoops (ABC, 1999)

Glenn Hall, Inc. is a high tech private detective agency in Santa Monica, California. Glenn Hall (Gina Gershon) is its founder and chief operative. Dana Plant (Paula Marshall), Roberta Young (Paula Jai Parker) and Manny Lott (Danny Nucci) are her operatives. The agency charges $500 a day plus expenses plus a $5,000 retainer.

Glenn is an expert at computer hacking. She claims, "We have to be bad and break laws because we are after bad guys and it's the only way to catch them." She is 34 years old. At the age of three, her mother put her on a carousel horse at the pier and abandoned her. She was then raised in four different foster homes. Glenn is a certified pilot and hates it "when clients screw me." She gets mad at herself and takes her frustrations out on her staff. Glenn wears what she calls "a digital nipple cam" (takes stills through her bra and blouse) and has a bad habit of falling for handsome clients. Glenn claims she can go undercover better than any cop and despises skip tracing cases (apprehending escaped convicts for the reward, "It's not cost effective. There is no billing and it's dangerous").

Dana is a former detective with the Santa Monica Police Department. The detective in her never rests and her police procedures often upset Glenn. For example, Dana likes to take notes on a case. Glenn says, "No. Good detectives don't take notes. If you have to make notes, do it when we get back to the office." Glenn considers Dana to be trigger happy and is reluctant to give her a gun—even the tranquilizer gun they use to collar suspects. Dana was a straight A student in school and never broke a rule. She was the perfect child and made her parents proud. She became a good cop and always complains about how Glenn breaks the rules — "The cop in me won't let me break the law." Dana's inability to abide by Glenn's rules forced her to return to the police department, episode of November 28, 1999. "I enjoyed my job as a private detective but it's not my world." While not dropped from the series, she became Glenn's link with the police department on homicide cases. She now works with her former partner, Detective Greg McCormick of Homicide (Edward Kerr).

Roberta, 31, is more like Glenn than the conservative Dana and believes being sexy and showing cleavage is a necessary part of the job, especially when they go undercover. She has no problem breaking the law and is skilled at picking locks and opening safes. She was born in Los Angeles and is the daughter of wealthy parents. She took the job for the excitement it offers and often risks her life by taking unnecessary chances. While she is reluctant to use a gun, she does love her tube of lipstick — it doubles as a miniature video camera. Roberta lives in Apartment K at 73 Donal Road. If the occasion arises, whether at home or in the office, Roberta loves to show her sexy figure in lingerie.

Manny, short for Emmanuel, is "the gadget guy" as Roberta calls him. He relies on various electronic gizmos to keep track of people. He carries a tranquilizer gun and has a habit of shooting the wrong people and just letting them sleep where they fall. Glenn complains, but it doesn't stop him from using the gun. Manny is coach of a girl's basketball team at St. Richard's Grammar School and drives a car with the license plate LAC 0199. Blondie sings the theme "One Way or Another."

Note: An earlier series called *Snoops* aired on CBS in 1989. Tim Reid played Chance Reynolds, a criminologist and teacher at Georgetown University in Washington, D.C. He lived with his wife, Micki (Daphne Maxwell-Reid) at 30th Street in Georgetown. Micki, a protocol aide at the State Department, had a knack for stumbling upon crimes which she and Chance relished solving. Tasha Scott played their daughter, Katja; John Karlen was Stan Akers, the detective Chance and Micki helped. Ray Charles sang the theme "Curiosity."

113. Sons of Thunder (CBS, 1999)

Thunder Investigations is a private detective organization based in Dallas, Texas, that caters to people who are unable to turn to the police for help. Trent Malloy (Jimmy Wicek), the owner, charges $50 an hour for his services. He is assisted by Carlos Sandoval (Mario Sanchez) and Kim Sutter (Dawn Moxey).

Trent, a karate expert, was born in Dallas and served a hitch in the army as a Ranger where he was a hand-to-hand combat instructor. After his father's death, Trent returned to Dallas to begin a new life as a private detective and operator of the Thunder Karate School through which he also runs Thunder Investigations. Carlos, also born in Dallas, is a childhood friend of Trent's. The two, however, have dramatically different backgrounds. While it is not made perfectly clear, it appears that Trent and Carlos lived on different sides of the track: Trent on the more influential, crime-free side; Carlos on the poorer, troubled side. How they met is not related, but as a teenager Carlos joined a street gang and participated in petty crimes. When he realized what he was doing — possibly with Trent's guidance — he turned his life around and set his goal to help people. He became a police officer but quit after several years when his partner was murdered (how is not stated). He hooked up with Trent when he learned about Thunder Investigations.

Butch McMann (Alan Autry) is an ex-boxer who now owns the local watering hole, the Uppercuts Bar; he also provides information to Trent and Carlos. Kim is Trent's office manager and bookkeeper. She is an expert at pool and somewhat of a homebody as she is opposed to violence and prefers the sanctuary of the office. The series is a spinoff from *Walker, Texas Ranger*.

114. Spenser: For Hire (ABC, 1985–1988)

Spenser (Robert Urich) is a suave Boston-based private detective with a sense of chivalry and decency to all people. He lives at 357 Masave Street and drives a classic green Mustang. Spenser (no first name) first lived in an apartment that was later destroyed by fire, then in an abandoned firehouse that was later recommissioned. His original Mustang was destroyed when it blew up during a car chase. Spenser leaped out "in the nick of time" and later drives a gray Mustang.

Although Spenser helps people solve their problems and brings criminals to justice, he enjoys violence and considers himself a thug for hire. He is sensitive, romantic and a gourmet cook who enjoys a cold beer with each meal. He is an ex-boxer and keeps in shape by lifting weights. He quotes poetry and lines from books but has trouble accepting authority — a situation that causes him to leave his job at the D.A.'s office in Suffolk County and turn his talents to becoming a private detective. Spenser was born in Laramie, Wyoming. His mother died in childbirth and he was raised by his father and his mother's two brothers. He rejected the family business (carpentry) and served a hitch in the army in Korea. He was first a boxer then a Massachusetts State Trooper before becoming an investigator for the D.A.

Susan Silverman (Barbara Stock), a teacher at Smithfield High School, is Spenser's romantic interest. Hawk (Avery Brooks) is Spenser's closest friend and associate, a former enforcer (leg breaker) for the mob. Hawk drives a BMW; the car colors are seen as white, black and red. Martin Quirk (Richard Jaeckel) is the police lieutenant Spenser helps and vice versa; he was forced to leave the Boston P.D. when he suffered a heart attack. Sammy Backlin (Sal Viscusso) is a sleazy con artist turned private eye who wrote the book *.357 Justice*. He was also a friend of Spenser's whose visits caused problems. On his first visit, Spenser was stabbed and Hawk's car was stolen; on his second visit, Spenser was not only shot, but his car was stolen. The second episode, "Play It Again, Sammy," was the pilot for an unsold series (broadcast on January 30, 1988). A second pilot, for an unrealized series called *McAllister* aired on April 3, 1988, with Steve Inwood as Thomas McAllister, a tough federal prosecutor who was half Apache Indian and totally dedicated to helping the underdog. *A Man Called Hawk* (ABC, 1989) is a failed spinoff series from *Spenser*. Here Hawk (Avery Brooks) leaves Boston and returns to his hometown of Washington, D.C., to become a vigilante to assist people desperately in need of help. Moses Gunn played his mentor, a character known only as "Old Man."

Spenser is based on the books by Robert B. Parker. The Lifetime Network revised the series concept in four TV movies with Robert Urich and Avery Brooks reprising their original roles. The movies are *Spenser: Ceremony* (1993), *Spenser: Pale Kings and Princes* (1993), *Spenser: The Judas Goat* (1994), and *Spenser: A Savage Place* (1995). Barbara Williams played Susan Silverman in the first two films; Wendy Crewson was Susan in the final two. On July 18, 1999, the A&E Network revised the concept with Joe Mantegna as Spenser; Shiek Mahmud-Bey as Hawk; and Marcia Gay Harden as Susan. The films (to December 31, 2002) are: *Spenser: Small Vices* (1999), *Spenser: Thin Air* (2000), and *Spenser: Walking Shadow* (2001). Ernie Hudson replaced Shiek Mahmud-Bey as Hawk in the second and third features.

115. Starsky and Hutch (ABC, 1975–1979)

Dave Starsky (Paul Michael Glaser) and Ken "Hutch" Hutchinson (David Soul) are dedicated plainclothes detectives with the Metropolitan Division of the L.A.P.D. Their car code is Zebra 3.

Starsky lives at 2000 Ridgeway Drive; Hutch resides by the beach at the Venice Place Apartments at 1027½ Ocean in Sea Point. Starsky drives a candy apple red car with a white stripe, plate 537 ONW; Hutch has a scratched, dented, gas-eating, muffler-smoking, gray car, plate 552 LQD, with a bumper sticker that reads "Cops Need Love Too." Starsky loves junk food. Hutch is a vitamin fanatic; his watch alarm rings to remind him to take his vitamins. Starsky also has a watch, a $360 time piece, that Hutch hates "because you keep telling me how much it costs." Vitamin E and wheat germ appear to be the most important supplements to Hutch's diet.

Hutch plays guitar, is a ladies man and takes his guns everywhere he goes — on a date, to the store, to visit his mother. While Starsky and Hutch most often ride in Starsky's car, Hutch refuses to let Dave drive it when he's eating — "You're dangerous." Starsky enjoys the holidays, especially Christmas; Hutch is just the opposite and says he is not going to let the Christmas spirit affect him. Each year he says it and each year something always happens to change his mind. Hutch also has a bad habit of aggravating their captain by slamming his office door. "I'm working on it," says Hutch when the captain complains.

When Dave was a child he imagined his backyard as a magical playland called Doodletown. As a kid, Ken bought toys at Uncle Elmo's Toy Shop; it's now Uncle Elmo's Adult Toy Shop. In high school Hutch was called "The Pauper"; he was best friends with "a filthy rich kid." He was also class valedictorian and voted "Most Likely to Succeed." He has a dream of quitting the force to live life at sea as the captain of a ship. Although Starsky and Hutch constantly argue about everything — from food to girls to how to proceed on a case — they are best friends and, as Starsky says, "Me and thee are the only two people we can trust."

Captain Harold Dobey (Bernie Hamilton) is the Captain of Detectives. He complains not only about the door slamming and their continual bickering, but also that Starsky and Hutch turn their daily reports in on a weekly basis. Dobie's phone extension is 2268, later 3056; 900-21 is Dave and Ken's mobile phone number to Dobie.

Huggy Bear (Antonio Fargas) is the snitch (information man) most often used by Dave and Ken. Huggy fancies himself as a magician (Huggy, the Houdini with Soul) but is actually a man of many unlawful pursuits who helps Starsky and Hutch put criminals behind bars. He hangs out at a girlie bar called the Jungle Club and owns Huggy Bear's Restaurant, also called Huggy's Restaurant. License plates seen hanging on the wall of the business are 237 308, 182 174, 504 EB5 and IE 2174. Richard Ward played Captain Dobie in the pilot episode.

Lalo Schifrin composed the theme "Starsky and Hutch."

116. Street Justice (Syndicated, 1991–1993)

Adam Beaudreaux (Carl Weathers) is a sergeant with the Metropolitan Police Department of a Pacific Northwest city identified as being in the beautiful Evergreen State. Adam has decided on the life of a police officer to meet people and keep the trash off the streets.

Adam wears badge number 2230 and lives at 2731 West Bond Street. He is independently wealthy and is partners with a woman known only as Molloy (Charlene Fernetz) in a business called Molloy's Bar. The bar is located at 843 Third Street and other than Molloy's license plate number, QXB 483, nothing else is known about her.

Before becoming a cop, Adam served with the Special Forces Unit in Vietnam. It was here that he met and befriended a young boy named Grady Jameson (Devon LaChance). Grady, the son of missionary parents, was born in the Chan Lo village in Vietnam. When the Vietcong invaded his village and killed his parents, Grady was rescued by Adam, who made it his responsibility to raise him. Now grown, Grady (Bryan Genesse) works as Molloy's bartender as well as a martial arts instructor at Chan's Dojo School. Although not an official member of the police force, Grady uses his skills to help Adam collar criminals.

The police department is located at 540 Remity Street. Adam has an office in room 107 and his car code is 2-Henry-17, also given as Unit 217. His car license plate reads ISV 508, later MZG 735. Grady lives in the back of the bar and drives a motorcycle with the license plate 83-7201.

Lawrence Shragge composed the theme "Street Justice."

117. Strike Force (ABC, 1981–1982)

Room 414 of the Los Angeles Police Department is the headquarters of Strike Force, a special unit that is designed to battle the violent crimes that are considered too dangerous for ordinary police officers to handle. Frank Murphy (Robert Stack) is its captain; his team: Detective Rosie Johnson (Trisha Noble), Lieutenant Charlie Gunzer (Richard Romanus), Detective Paul Strobber (Dorian Harewood) and Detective Mike Osborn (Michael Goodwin). Their superior is Herbert Klein (Herb Edelman), the deputy police commissioner.

The team goes undercover when necessary; they kill when they have to — "This is what we do." Code Green indicates to the police that a case has been resolved by Strike Force. When the police commissioner wants Strike Force, they're on it — "Do it, Frank, just do it." When there is no time to find a pattern and a strike has to be made, Strike Force is sent into action — the reason why it was formed.

Frank lives in a rather untidy house at 36 Crest Drive. He has two pink flamingo decorations on his front lawn and lives for his work. He is now divorced after being married eight years "to a tyrant named Donna"; in later episodes, she is called Eve. Frank also has a dog, Sam, and drives a car with the license plate 376 42F.

Rosie, the team's only female member, is a beautiful cop who lives in an apartment at 136 Shore Drive. Her car license plate reads 6413FF, and she can be reached by telephone at 555-6162. When the series first began, Rosie, who is rather "well built" (measurements not given), was part of the era of "jiggle TV" and dressed to accentuate her bosom. As the series progressed, Rosie did less running and dressed in less revealing blouses; even her running sequences from the opening theme were replaced. Rosie was only in love once—"with a Mr. Right. But he was lost in some dumb rice paddy [Vietnam War] I can't even pronounce."

Paul, the team's only black member, is married and has two kids. Charlie, who makes the office coffee, which Rosie dislikes, lives in Apartment 42 at 1908 Harbor View Drive; his license plate reads 183 HYE. Joanna Cassidy appeared as Frank's ex-wife, Eve Murphy.

Dominic Frontiere composed the theme "Strike Force."

118. The Strip (UPN, 1999–2000)

Elvis Ford (Sean Patrick Flanery) and Jesse Weir (Guy Torry) are former police officers turned private security consultants for Cameron Greene (Joe Viterelli), owner of Caesar's Palace Hotel and Gambling Casino in Las Vegas. Crime and corruption are a part of the Strip. "If a guest has a problem, I have a problem," says Greene. "All my guests are like family" and Elvis and Jesse have been hired to protect that family.

Elvis and Jesse were detectives with the Las Vegas Police Department who quit the force when corrupt federal agents tried to frame them for robbing slot machines. Elvis became a cop "because I liked to carry a gun." He was born in Las Vegas and lives on a boat called *Gonzo*, which he calls a big trailer with sails. He won the boat in a game of five card stud and it is dry docked at his ex-stripper grandmother's desert trailer park. Elvis is a junk food junkie and has a gambling problem. He usually has a burrito for breakfast and is hooked on Yoo Hoo Soda; he gets irritable if he has to go without one. He has a photographic mind and always looks mad. Cleo's is Elvis's favorite bar hangout, and he drives a car with the license plate DRL 320.

Jesse worked as a Federal Task Officer in his home town of Philadelphia before moving to Las Vegas. He is married to Vanessa (Stacy Dash), a real estate agent for Sand Dune Realty. Jesse is the stable partner, always calm and practical in each situation. Elvis is more of a renegade and plunges head first into situations. Elvis has a knack for getting into locked places by using whatever he can find. Jesse calls him "MacGyver," a resourceful character from the TV series *MacGyver*. Jesse is a gourmet but Elvis can't comprehend anything that doesn't come with French fries and a coke. Jesse prefers coffee at Starbucks; Elvis at "7-11 because I can pour my own." Jesse and Vanessa live in a home at 346 South Vista; 555-6613 is their phone number.

Cameron's real name is Carmine Quinelli "but it didn't fit my business purposes and I changed it." In his youth he was an Eagle Scout and won awards for cooking and marksmanship. He is now a billionaire — "three commas, three zeros" and is hooked on cigarettes — three packs a day. He is also distrustful of cell phones; "They rot your brain cells." He set up Elvis and Jesse as his personal security staff because he felt the cops are overworked and hotel security needs to stay indoors.

Mark Mancinia composed the theme "The Strip."

119. Sue Thomas, F.B.Eye (PAX, 2002)

Suzanne Thomas (real life deaf actress Deanne Bray) is a young woman who sees what she cannot hear. She is deaf and reads lips to understand the world around her. For Suzanne, called Sue, it began at an early age. One day, after playing outdoors, Sue turned her attention to watching cartoons on TV. During a "Sylvester and Tweety Pie" episode, she began to experience a hearing loss. Before the cartoon ended she was totally deaf. This became noticeable to her mother when Sue approached the TV and turned up the volume in an effort to hear it. Sue was taken to several doctors but each was unable to explain the reason for her sudden hearing loss. Despite her handicap, Sue's mother was determined to see that her daughter would lead a normal life. A special tutor was hired and Sue was taught how to speak and hear things by reading lips and eyes. Sue's mother rejected the notion that her daughter be enrolled in a special school. Sue was sent to a normal school and survived from kindergarten through graduation from college. She was made fun of (called "a retard" in early grammar school), but her strong will and determination to be normal helped her survive a challenging school career. "You can't ever let them see you're scared," Sue's mother would tell her. "They'll think you don't belong."

Keep moving forward; God will let you know if you're on the right track is a philosophy Sue's mother taught her and that she now lives by. To help her in her daily life, Sue decides to get a hearing aid dog trained to let her know when somebody is trying to get her attention, to let her know when the doorbell rings, when the phone rings, etc. An abused golden retriever she names Levi becomes her "ears." "Nobody wanted him," Sue says, "except me. I knew he would make a good hearing aid dog."

Sue lives in an unspecified Midwest city. While not babied because of her impairment, Sue feels she must take her place in the world. She applies for and receives a position with the FBI in Washington, D.C. ("Never in a million years did I think I'd be working for the FBI"). Sue's enthusiasm is shattered a bit when she arrives in D.C. to begin her job: Fingerprinting — examining fingerprints, identifying them and routing them for filing. "It's a fancy name for where they put people with disabilities," she says.

Sue does not consider herself disabled. She wants to show everyone she can survive on her own. With a hope of convincing personnel that she is suited for something better, Sue approaches Jack Hudson (Yannick Bisson), an FBI agent she mistakes for the personnel director. When Jack explains that personnel has moved to the fifth floor but discovers Sue is deaf and can look around a room and see what everybody is saying, he hits on an idea to use her skills in his surveillance unit. When Sue proves her ability during a test case, she is transferred. Levi, who is given his own FBI badge, also becomes part of the team. "We're going to make it, Levi," Sue said, "as long as we stick together."

Sue claims she is practical. Her car trip from the Midwest to D.C. took six hours; 4TG 750 is her car license plate number. She lives in a noisy (but not a matter of concern) apartment over a bowling alley about five minutes from headquarters. She has a special phone that allows her to speak and "hear" the other party via a message unit that displays the caller's words. One of Sue's greatest fears is ice skating due to a tragic event from her past. Although deaf, Sue attempted to become a figure skater while in grammar school. She was a regional champion and she and her girlfriend, Judy, were contenders in the Midwest finals. Even though she was unable to hear the music she was skating to, Sue had her routine timed to the length of the music. During her final performance she lost her timing and performed badly, losing the competition to Judy. Sue was not bitter, but proud that Judy had won. En route to the state championships, the bus on which Judy was traveling crashed. Judy was killed and Sue blamed herself—"I should have been on that bus, not Judy." She has kept the memory of Judy and the close friendship they had shared alive in her heart every day since.

Levi weighs 60 pounds and dislikes loud noises. He is extremely faithful to Sue and is constantly by her side. Sue is teaching him to read sign. Sue tries to be open and honest about everything. She plays music because she likes to feel the vibrations; she watches TV with the closed captioning on. Sue's official title is Special Investigative Assistant; NC2 5V2 is the license plate of her FBI issued car. To be sure of her facts, Sue always takes notes of the interviews she conducts with suspects.

Jack is from Wisconsin. He was always interested in law enforcement, but during high school he showed promise as a member of the hockey team. That career ended when he was injured and Jack pursued his goal of becoming an FBI agent. He believes an innocent person tries to get rid of him when he asks questions while a guilty person offers ways of finding a killer.

Lucy Dotson (Enuka Okuma) is the FBI office router (keeps things moving) who becomes Sue's best friend, beside Levi. It is Lucy who becomes her roommate in later episodes when she convinces Sue to move out of the loft over the Rock, Rattle and Roll Bowling Alley to a quieter, more respectable apartment at 11 Hayden Place.

Related Series

1. *Longstreet* (ABC, 1971–1972). James Franciscus as Michael Longstreet, a blind investigator for the Great Pacific Casualty Insurance Company in New Orleans. Michael was blinded in an explosion that killed his wife, Ingrid. The explosion was set up by jewel thieves who feared Michael was coming too close to catching them. Michael lives at 835 Charters Street and has a seeing eye dog named Pax. Duke Paige (Peter Mark Richman) is Michael's superior; Nikki Bell (Marlyn Mason) is Michael's braille teacher; and Li Tsung (Bruce Lee) is Michael's self-defense instructor. Judy Jones plays Ingrid in flashbacks; Bradford Dillman played Duke in the pilot and Martine Beswick was Nikki in the pilot.

2. *Reasonable Doubts* (NBC, 1991–1993). Tess Kaufman is a prosecuting attorney for the Chicago District Attorney's office. Tess, played by hearing-impaired actress Marlee Matlin, is deaf but can read lips; she is accompanied in the field by Richard Cobb (Mark Harmon), a tough detective with the Metropolitan Police Department, District 26. Richard is the only cop on the force who can read and speak in sign language which he learned from his deaf father. Through a special arrangement with the D.A.'s office and the police department, Cobb has been reassigned to assist Tess.

Tess lives at 1422 Barrington Avenue. Her phone number is 555-1311 and her car license plate reads F4R 526. Richard, called Dicky, lives at 703 Beckman Place, Apartment 2, and has a dog named John. His car license plate reads T5H 693. Tess and Cobb are members of the D.A.'s, a softball team, and play at Longwood Park.

Kay Lockman (Nancy Everhard) is Cobb's romantic interest and the owner of the Setup Bar. Maggie Zombro (Kay Lenz) is the expensive, private practice defense attorney who most often faces Tess in courtroom battles.

Related Projects (Unsold Pilots)

1. *Hear No Evil* (CBS, November 10, 1982). Gil Gerard as Bill Dragon, a deaf police inspector with the San Francisco P.D. Bill is aided by his special therapist, Meg (Mimi Rogers) and his hearing aid dog, Bozo. Bill lost his hearing as a result of a car explosion set by members of a motorcycle gang who feared he was coming too close to catching them and busting their illegal drug operations. The pilot story follows Bill as he attempts to readjust to life after the explosion and seek those responsible for his plight.

2. *The Dancing Bandit* (CBS, March 3, 1995). See *Picket Fences* for information.

120. SurfSide 6 (ABC, 1960–1962)

Dave Thorne (Lee Patterson), Ken Madison (Van Williams) and Sandor Winfield (Troy Donahue) are three handsome young bachelors who operate the SurfSide 6 Agency, a private detective organization that is located in a houseboat moored at SurfSide 6 on Indian Creek in Miami Beach, Florida.

Dave was born in New York City and began a law practice shortly after graduating from N.Y.U. He became a prosecutor but quit when he found legal loopholes prevented him from getting convictions. Ken was born in Texas and is a graduate of the Tulhane University Law School. Like Dave, Ken was disillusioned with his practice in criminal law and wanted to do more than just defend people. Sandor, called Sandy, was born in Miami Beach and is the son of a wealthy family. He lives the life of a jet setter but feels the need to help people in trouble. He helps Dave and Ken more for the excitement their cases bring him rather than for its monetary rewards. Although the three are from different backgrounds, they rarely argue and live well together on the houseboat. The character of Ken Madison first appeared on the series *Bourbon Street Beat* (see entry).

Daphne DeWitt Dutton (Diane McBaine), billed as "the girl in the yacht next door," is a beautiful jet setter and heir to the Dutton Farms and the Dutton Racing Stables. Daphne, called Daphe, is a friend of Sandy's and helps him, Ken and Dave when needed. She has a horse named Par-a-kee that she raised from a colt. Cha Cha O'Brien (Margaretta Sierra) is a singer and dancer who performs in the Boom Boom Room of the famed Fountainbleau Hotel, which is located directly opposite SurfSide 6 on Ocean Avenue. Cha Cha was born in Madrid, Spain, and has been singing and dancing since she was four years old.

Dave, Ken and Sandy first work with Ray Snedigar (Donald Barry) then Gene Plehan (Richard Crane), both lieutenants with the Miami Police Department, Homicide Division. Mousie (Mousie Garner) is the Boom Boom Room waiter who supplies information to Sandy, Dave and Ken.

Mack David and Jerry Livingston composed the theme "SurfSide 6."

121. Sweating Bullets (CBS, 1991–1993)

Nick Slaughter (Rob Stewart) is a former government agent turned private detective. Sylvie Girard (Carolyn Dunn) is a former travel consultant turned amateur sleuth and Nick's partner. Together they operate a company called Nick Slaughter—Private Investigator, the only detective agency on Key Mariah, a small coastal town in Florida.

Nick worked previously for the D.E.A. (Drug Enforcement Agency). Nick first says, "I was laid off because they ran out of bad guys." He next claims, "I got tired of seeing them railroad innocent people so some prosecutor could have an impressive record. When I tried to do something about it, I got fired." He finally says, "I believed the suspect was being set up for something she didn't do. So I helped her get out of the country and was fired." He became a private detective so he could help people he honestly felt were in trouble without repercussions.

Nick has offices in a building at 45 Lafayette Street. His fee is $250 a day plus expenses, and he drives a jeep with the license plate BZN N57, then NIR 548 and finally PZE 181. Nick was born in Florida, attended Lakeside High School and worked as a cop for the Miami P.D. for five years before joining the D.E.A.

Sylvie, born in Miami, is a graduate of State University. She worked as a consultant for travel agencies that catered to the rich and famous. At one such agency, a yacht was left in her care. When the yacht suddenly vanished, she hired Nick to find it. Although Nick found it with Sylvie's assistance, Sylvie was fired when her employer learned the yacht was being used by drug smugglers; "We don't want a yacht saboteur in our employ." Sylvie believes she and Nick work well as a team and feels that the disorganized Nick needs help. She appoints herself as Nick's partner "to organize and turn your pathetic life around." Nick is not the type to argue with a beautiful woman and hires her at a salary of 25 percent of what he makes each month.

Nick calls Sylvie the brains of the outfit. She was a beauty contestant in the 1985 Miss Brick and Mortar Pageant as a favor for her father, who owned a brick laying company and needed a contestant. Sylvie is a whiz at manipulating and reading people. She can sweet talk men into almost anything and uses this "gift" to help keep the agency afloat. Nick neglected to pay taxes for eight years and owes the IRS a great deal of money. Sylvie's biggest challenge is to pay off the IRS and keep Nick out of jail. Sylvie doesn't trust Nick with sharp weapons and beautiful women. Nick hates the "R" word [relationship] and tends to fall to pieces when he meets a woman and things don't work out. Sylvie's license plate reads J8E 731.

Ian Stewart (John David Bland) is a friend of Nick's, a former rock star who now runs the Tropical Heat Bar on Key Mariah. Nick and Sylvie often work with Sergeant Ollie Porter (Eugene Clark) and Lieutenant Carren (Pedro Armendariz) of the Miami Police Department.

Fred and Larry Mollin composed the theme "Anyway the Wind Blows."

122. Switch (CBS, 1975–1978)

Frank MacBride (Eddie Albert) and Peterson T. Ryan (Robert Wagner) are partners in a private detective agency called both MacBride-Ryan Investigations and The Ryan-MacBride Private Detective Organization located at 1019 Florida Street in Los Angeles. People say, "They're the last hope you have. If they can't prove your innocence, no one can." To achieve their goals, Frank, called Mac, and Peterson, called Pete, use cons to beat swindlers at their own game.

Mac was formerly a cop with the Central Division of the L.A.P.D. Twenty of his twenty-five years on the force were spent in the bunco division where he made an impressive number of arrests by posing as a mark and nabbing the country's most wanted felons.

Pete is a sophisticated con artist who pulls off scams that will make him a great deal of money. Pete's shortcoming is that he always underestimates the police; a flaw that enabled Mac to capture him. It was "a battle of wits for ten years," says Mac. "He's the best con man I ever tried to catch."

Mac retired from the force at about the same time Pete was being released from serving a two-year sentence at San Quentin. They became friends over the course of time and decided to pool their talents to help people by opening the agency.

"I don't know why I just don't quit this screwy job," exclaims Maggie Philbin (Sharon Gless), the agency's pretty but naive secretary. Maggie took the job with a hope of learning the business and starting her own detective agency. Mac and Pete see her as their girl Friday and use her any way they can to assist in a con.

Ali McGinnis (Jaclyn Smith), who Pete says can talk the curves off a hockey puck, is a stunning brunette Pete uses to run interference during a con. Ali, a con artist herself, uses her beauty to accomplish her goals.

Malcolm Argos (Charlie Callas) is a friend of Pete's who runs the Bouziki Bar, the hangout. He too has a genius for the con and helps Mac and Pete when necessary. Revel (Mindi Miller) is the sexy waitress at the bar.

Jails make Pete nervous. Pete's license plate is 191 OJB; Mac's car license plate reads 1409B; Maggie lives at 46710 Hillcrest Drive; and the agency's phone number is 213-555-1678. Glen A. Larson composed the theme.

123. Ten Speed and Brown Shoe (ABC, 1980)

The Lionel Whitney Agency, also called Whitney Investigations, is a Los Angeles-based private investigation organization owned by Lionel Whitney (Jeff Goldblum) and his partner, E.L. Turner (Ben Vereen).

Lionel previously worked as a stockbroker for a company called Grey, Johnson and Smith. He was all work and no play, had few pleasures in life but found adventure by reading private detective books called *A Mark Savage Mystery* by Stephen J. Cannell, the show's producer. Lionel is a graduate of Pomona College where he had the nickname "Bunky" and was a member of the Pistol Range Club. He drives a blue Datson and lives in an apartment on Melrose; 555-1131 is his phone number.

E.L. is an ingenious, streetwise con artist. E.L., nicknamed Tenspeed for his ability to move fast especially from endangering situations, claims the E.L. stands for Early LeRoy; he was born in the taxi cab that was taking his mother to the hospital. E.L. studied law at Yale but was expelled after two years for rigging student elections and skipping off to Tijuana with the funds. E.L. feels Lionel is too uptight and calls him Brown Shoe — a guy in a three piece suit with brown shoes; a square, a Dow Jones. It was a con by E.L. that brought him and Whitney together. At San Francisco International Airport, a plan by E.L. to heist gangland money backfires. He uses Lionel as a pawn to smuggle the money into Los Angeles. The ensuing adventure, as they try to elude mobsters and help the police collar a crime boss, instills Lionel with a sense of excitement that he thought he could only get from reading books. Although he was up for a promotion as head of institutional sales, Lionel quit to open the agency with E.L. The pilot episode shows Lionel reading *A Mark Savage Mystery* called *The Screaming Dead Man*.

Mike Post and Pete Carpenter composed "The Theme from Ten Speed and Brown Shoe."

124. Tequila and Bonetti (CBS, 1992)

Nico Bonetti (Jack Scalia) is a detective with the South Coast Police Department in California. He is partners with Angela Garcia (Mariska Hargitay), a very pretty rookie officer, and Officer Tequila (voice of Brad Sanders), a burrito-loving dog who comments on the actions of Nico and Angela as they investigate crimes (heard only by the viewing audience).

Nico is on loan to South Coast from the N.Y.P.D.'s 62nd Precinct in Brooklyn. During an assignment, Nico was faced with a life and death situation: kill or be killed by a 12-year-old girl wielding a gun. Although Nico was exonerated by the Firearms Control Board ("a justified shooting"), Nico was shattered by the incident. To help him overcome his ordeal, he became part of an exchange program.

Nico owns a 1957 dusty rose-colored classic Cadillac convertible, license plate BX2 100LB. He drove from New York to California in 37 hours and 14 minutes. In New York, Nico lived at 41445 Brooke Avenue in the Bay Parkway section of Bensonhurst; he now resides at 2291 Pacific Way, the address of a former dance studio. As part of his assignment, Nico must care for Tequila; departmental regulations also require that the dog live with him. Nico is divorced from Terry (Elena Stiteler), a former Rockette dancer.

Angela, described as "the best damned rookie that has come through here in years" by her captain, has been assigned to Nico to teach her the ropes. Angela is a widow (her husband, Officer Paulie Garcia, was killed in the line of duty) and the mother of a young daughter named Teresa (Noley Thornton). Angela and Teresa live at 36112 Parker Drive; IB 896 is Angela's license plate number. Teresa is unaware that her mother is a police officer; she believes Angela works in an art gallery. Angela gave up her job at the gallery to become a cop; she fears telling Teresa the truth at this time because of what happened to Paulie. Teresa attends the Briarwood School and on special occasions, she and Angela have backwards dinners — the dessert first then the meal. Angela orders pizza from a store called Tootsie's. Angela is a graduate of Long Beach State College where she met Paulie, and her and Nico's car code is K-1-9.

Tequila, a brown dog, is a graduate of the L.A. Canine Academy. He is not much on looks but he has more busts than most cops — "Tequila will cover your butt better than any cop." Tequila dreams of French poodles, calls Angela "Sweet Pea," Nico "B" and crooks "Dirt Bags." Tequila, a Leo, earned the nickname Wonder Dog when he rescued a baby from a burning building. He was also "spokesdog" for Gold Badge Security Systems. Tequila, played by Foster, is a French breed of dog called DeBordeaux.

Captain Midian Knight (Charles Rocket) is Nico's superior. He calls Nico Visiting Detective Bonetti and hates to be called Captain Midnight. As a child Midian had a dog, Scruffy, an imaginary girlfriend, Sophia, and a plush dog, Little Gino. He served with Bravo Company of the Fifth Marines in Vietnam. His license plate reads CAP MID and he frequents a restaurant called Finocci's. Mike Post composed the theme.

Related Projects (Pilots)

1. *Sam* (CBS, May 24, 1977). The pilot for *Sam*, a six-episode series (March 14 to April 18, 1978) about Mike Breen (Mark Harmon), a Los Angeles police officer who is teamed with Sam, a Labrador Retriever, in a man-and-dog patrol car unit designated Two-Henry-Six.

2. *Alex and the Doberman Gang* (NBC, April 11, 1980). Jack Stauffer as Alexander Parker, a private detective with five unusual assistants: Duke, Rocky, Harlow, Little Bogie and Gabel, Doberman pinchers he inherited from a carnival performer.

3. *Nick and the Dobermans* (NBC, April 25, 1980). A revised version of the prior pilot that teams New York-based private detective Nick Luchese (Michael Nouri) with Duke, Erskine and Pee Wee, three smart Doberman pinchers he inherited from a carnival performer and who now assist him in solving crimes.

4. *K-9 and Company* (Syndicated, 1985). A proposed spinoff from the series *Doctor Who* that teams newspaper reporter Sarah Jane Smith (Elisabeth Sladen) with K-9 (voice of John Leeson), a mechanical dog she uses to help her solve crimes.

5. *Sniff* (CBS, August 9, 1988). Robert Wuhl as Sid Barrows, a reporter for the *Herald*, who receives help in solving crimes from Sniff, a bloodhound with a sense of smell a million times more acute than a human's, who thinks he is a detective.

6. *K-9000* (Unaired, 1989). A battle against crime as seen through the cases of Eddie Monroe (Chris Mulkey), an L.A.P.D. detective who has been assigned to work with Aja (Catherine Oxenberg), a beautiful British scientist who has created Niner, a cloned German shepherd with a computer enhanced brain.

7. *Poochinski* (NBC, July 9, 1990). Robert McKay as George Newbern, a detective who solves crimes with the help of his former, late partner, Stanley Poochinski (Peter Boyle) who has been reincarnated as an English bulldog.

8. *Turner and Hooch* (NBC, July 9, 1990). A TV adaptation of the feature film about Scott Turner (Tom Wilson), a detective with the Cypress Police Department, and his mischievous canine partner, Hooch.

9. *Tequila and Boner* (Unaired, 1991). The original pilot film for *Tequila and Bonetti*. Here, Rick Rossovich played T.T. Boner, a hip, new wave cop, who is teamed with a police dog named Tequila (voice of Pat Corley).

10. *K-9* (ABC, July 6, 1991). Robert Carradine as Jack Bergen, an L.A.P.D. officer who receives help in solving crimes from Jerry Lee, a German shepherd and graduate of the department's Canine Academy.

Related Series

1. ***Sam.*** See number one under Related Projects.
2. ***Rin Tin Tin, K-9 Cop*** (CBN, 1988–1989). The famous German shepherd, Rin Tin Tin, is now a "police officer" with the canine division of the Bay City Police Department. Jesse Collins plays his human assistant, Officer Hank Katz. CBN is the now defunct cable channel, Christian Broadcasting Network.

125. The Thin Man (NBC, 1957–1959)

Nick and Nora Charles (Peter Lawford, Phyllis Kirk) are a happily married young couple who live in an apartment in New York's Greenwich Village; Regent 4-4598 is their phone number. Nick is a former private detective (owner of Nicholas Charles — Confidential Investigations) turned mystery editor for an unnamed publishing house in Manhattan. Nora, maiden name Nora Clairidon, was born in San Francisco. She is heir to the Clairidon family fortune and has a wirehaired terrier name Asta. On the twenty-eighth of each year (month not named), she and Nick celebrate "Asta Day," the day Asta brought them together. Nick bought the dog to impress Nora, a girl he was trying to date but ignored him — until Asta came along. Nick and Nora married in 1950 and honeymooned at the Ambassador Hotel; they stayed in room 3C.

Nora is beautiful, fashion conscious and a standout at society functions. She also possesses an uncanny knack for stumbling upon crimes — usually murders. Nora also believes she possesses the skills to solve crimes. Nick feels differently and returns to his private eye status to keep Nora from getting herself killed as she will attempt to solve crimes on her own.

Nick uses the "laundry list" method to solve crimes; Nick relates the facts, Nora writes them down. When someone takes a shot at Nick, he falls down so as not to disappoint the shooter — "It also prevents them from taking another shot." Nick calls Nora "Tiger"; Nora calls Nick "Nickie." Nick has an eye for the ladies although he tells Nora, "None are as beautiful as you." Nora becomes very jealous when girls start making goo goo eyes at Nick. It is at these times that Nora calls Nick "Nicholas!" Nora wears a size eight dress and is a member of both the Junior Matrons' Breakfast Club and a charity called the Junior Guild. Nora feels her intuition is better than Nick's experience when it comes to solving crimes. She also never thinks in emergencies — "I only have hunches."

Nick calls Asta their child because of the way Nora babies him. Even though the dog is a male, Nora gave him a girl's name based on her Uncle

Harry's theory that a sissy name will make a man out of a boy. When Asta wants to go for his walk, he brings his leash to either Nick or Nora although Nick believes he is Asta's choice more often. Nick reads the New York *Chronicle*, hates to have his sleep disturbed and drives a convertible with the license plate NICK I.

Beatrice Dean (Nita Talbot) is a beautiful con artist who goes by the alias of Blondie Collins. "Blondie has a knack for larceny," says Nick, who has arrested her on several occasions. She often serves time at the Elmsville Prison for Women. When Blondie is in trouble and needs refuge, she considers the Charleses' home a port of call and retreats to it for help and Nick's affections. Despite Nora's jealousy, Nick can't resist "a gorgeous doll" and always helps Blondie.

Blondie calls Nick "Nickie Lover" and "Nickie Darling" and Nora "That Woman" because she feels Nora "is trying to horn in on me and Nickie." Despite Blondie's dislike for Nora for being married to Nick, Blondie knows she needs Nora and uses sob stories about her life to get Nora on her side. Nora knows when Blondie and trouble are coming—"I can feel it in my bones." Blondie attributes her present lifestyle to being a victim of a broken home. "I had no mother to guide me."

Hazel (Patricia Donahue) is Nora's friend, an attractive single woman who has a crush on Nick and flirts with him at every opportunity. She lives in the brownstone next to Nick and Nora's. In second season episodes, Nick and Nora appear to live in a brownstone rather than an apartment as evidenced by outdoor scenes. Ralph Raine (Stafford Repp) and Harry Evans (Jack Albertson) are lieutenants with the Homicide Division of the N.Y.P.D. who assist Nick and Nora in solving crimes.

In the opening theme, Nick and Nora are seen driving on a deserted country road. Following a closeup of Nick's license plate and the series title, a sign post is seen that reads "Curves Ahead." This is followed by billboards reading "Peter Lawford as Nick," "Phyllis Kirk as Nora" and "Asta as Asta." In the final scene, the car is stopped and Nick attempts to kiss Nora. Asta whines, Nora looks to the camera, taps Nick on the shoulder. He and Nora smile and the scene fades to black.

Johnny Greene composed the original theme "The Thin Man." Pete Rugolo composed the second season "Thin Man Theme."

Note: The only other attempt at a *Thin Man* series was an unsold pilot that ABC broadcast on March 4, 1975 called "Nick and Nora." Nick Charles (Craig Stevens) and his wife Nora (Jo Ann Pflug) are a bit older here but just as much interested in solving crimes. In the story, based on characters created by Dashiell Hammett, Nick and Nora attempt to solve a murder in a luxurious Los Angeles hotel.

126. Thunder in Paradise (Syndicated, 1994–1995)

The Scuttlebutt Bar and Grill is a small eatery run by Kelly LaRue (Carol Alt) in Paradise Beach, Florida. Randolph Spencer (Terry "Hulk" Hogan) and Martin Brubaker (Chris Lemmon) are friends who hang out at the bar.

Spencer, called Hurricane and Spence, and Brubaker, called Bru, operate *Thunder*, a high tech boat for hire at $5,000 a day. Spence and Bru were Navy S.E.A.L.S. during the Vietnam War. They became friends after Spence saved Bru's life twenty years ago. It was during this time that Spence got the nickname Hurricane for flattening everything in his path and that Bru developed the plans for *Thunder*. When the Navy rejected the plans, Bru quit and built *Thunder* for himself. Bru graduated with top honors from M.I.T. and previously developed the RF15 navigational system for the Navy. He calls Kelly "Legs."

Thunder has hydro thrust for fast motion and it can only be started by a secret password (not said); if the password is not given, the intruder receives an electrical shock. *Thunder* and its portable speed boat, *Trigger*, are docked at the Suncoast in Florida. Spence and Bru use their skills as S.E.A.L.S., a special warfare team, to fight the crime and corruption they encounter. Bru and Spence, partners in *Thunder*, owe $93,000 in bank loans on the boat and Bru is hoping to advance *Thunder* to a sub-oceanatic status. Russ Wheeler provides "The Thunder Computer Voice."

Spence and Bru also care for Jessica "Jess" Whitaker (Robin Weisman, Ashley Gorrell), the nine-year-old daughter of Megan Whitaker (Felicity Waterman), the owner of the Paradise Beach Hotel. Although the hotel was owned by Megan, her uncle, Edward Whitaker (Patrick Macnee) threatened to take it away from her if she didn't follow the conditions of her late father's will which stipulated that she must be married to retain the hotel. Megan, a widow, makes a deal with Spence: she will pay off Thunder's debts if he will marry her. Spence agrees. All goes well until Megan is killed one foggy night in an auto accident. Now Spence, as Jess's legal guardian, must not only raise her, but fight Edward for Jess's legal right to become the hotel's owner when she comes of age. In the meantime, Edward, made a knight by the Queen of England for his heroic service with the Royal Navy during World War II, oversees the hotel's operations. As the series progressed, Spence and Edward became friends. Jessica attends St. Martin's Academy grammar school.

Adam McCall (Sting), also known as Hammerhead, is a former Navy buddy of Spence and Bru who is now their worst nightmare. When in the service they were sent on a mission to retrieve stolen weapons. Hammerhead thought the weapons would be worth a lot of money on the open market; Spence didn't. Hammerhead was captured and sent to Sea Quentin, a prototype underwater prison. He escaped and now seeks to ruin Spence.

127. Tightrope (CBS, 1959–1960)

Nick (Mike Connors) is a man who plays the underworld's most dangerous game — the double cross. His job is to infiltrate the mob. "When you work undercover, you have to do a lot of things you don't like to," he says. Nick is a man who walks the tightrope between good and evil, a vital part of his job as an undercover cop for an unspecified agency. Only his superior at headquarters knows Nick's full name. He was called Nick Stone, but he is also referred to as Nick, the Unnamed Agent and the Undercover Agent. Mike Connors is credited on the screen as "Nick" in the closing theme.

Nick is considered the best undercover cop there is; "I have to live like a hood to catch a hood." Nick's job takes him to any city where there is a crime. "One slip and you're through," he says, "because you're always walking a tightrope." Nick is an expert at cons and a real hot shot with the dames. He carries a gun on a belt that has its holster in the middle of his back. In the opening theme, Nick fires four shots. George Duning composed the theme "Tightrope."

Related Project (Unsold Pilot)

The Expendables (ABC, September 27, 1962). An attempt to revise the *Tightrope* series with Mike Connors as Mike, a police undercover agent who tackles dangerous assignments that involve infiltrating the underworld. The pilot story finds Mike attempting to rescue a kidnapped policeman from mobsters.

128. T.J. Hooker (ABC, 1982–1985; CBS, 1985–1987)

T.J. Hooker (William Shatner) is a sergeant with the Academy Precinct of the L.C. City, California, Police Department; what the L.C. and T.J. stand for is not mentioned. Hooker, as everyone calls him, is divorced from Fran (Leigh Christian, Lee Bryant) and the father of Chrissy (Nicole Eggert, Jenny Beck), Cathy (Susan McClung) and Tommy (Andre Gower). Fran is a nurse at Memorial Hospital; the children attend Lakeside Grammar School. Hooker is a third generation cop and is following in the steps of his father and grandfather. He wears badge 115, also seen as 14, and has the car code 4-Adam-30. He resides in a rather untidy room at the Safari Inn while his wife and children live in his former home at 1310 Forrest Drive. Hooker wears a Magnum Body Armour bullet proof vest and holds the department record for the most damaged or destroyed police cars.

While in charge of a squad of officers, Hooker works most closely with Stacey Sheridan (Heather Locklear), Jim Corrigan (James Darren) and Vince Romano (Adrian Zmed). Vince, Hooker's partner, was born in South Philadelphia and as a kid had a dog named Bear. Stacey and Jim work as a team; 4-Adam-16 is their car code. Stacey, the daughter of a police captain, was born in California and lives in an apartment at the Marina Club; 280 is her badge number. Jim, a former officer with the San Francisco Police Department (his home town), is a bit older than Stacey and Vince and has refused a promotion to remain in uniform to patrol and protect the streets. He lives in an apartment at 62 Foster Lane. While Vince hangs out with Hooker, Stacey and Jim at the Mid-City Bar, later Sherry's Bar, he prefers an afterhours hangout called Adrienne's Bar. Stacey's father, Captain Dennis Sheridan (Richard Herd) is their superior.

Mark Snow composed the theme "T.J. Hooker."

Proposed Spinoff (Unsold Pilot)

Hollywood Starr (February 23, 1985). Sharon Stone as Dani Starr, a beautiful female detective with the Vice Squad Division, Hollywood Station of the L.A.P.D. Dani's badge number is 322; Sky King 22 is her car code and she has a pet tortoise named Beauregard. The pilot story finds Dani seeking the killer of an adult film producer.

129. Total Security (ABC, 1997)

Total Security is a Culver City, California-based private detective organization whose main objective is to make their clients feel secure. Their true mandate is crime prevention. They provide personal home security, threat assessment, skip tracing, counter intelligence at the corporate level "and more." The company was founded by Frank Cisco (James Remar), a former L.A.P.D. homicide detective when he felt he could do more to help people by attacking crime from outside the system. "Law enforcement responds to the crimes committed; we do certain work after the fact to those who won't or can't turn to the police for help." Steve Waigman (James Belushi), Jodie Kiplinger (Debrah Farentino) and Ellie Jones (Tracey Needham) are Frank's operatives.

Frank is 40 years old and hates to celebrate birthdays as it reminds him he is getting a year older. He is totally honest and draws the line at things that are immoral, illegal and unprofessional — "I deal straight up with everyone." While Frank may be forthright and upstanding, he is rather cold and harsh; people say Frank needs people skills. Even though Frank is no longer a cop, he thinks like one and uses his prior experiences to help him nab criminals. He has feelings for his clients and does show remorse when a case turns bad; for example, "That lady would still be alive if we didn't take the case." Frank's favorite eatery is a restaurant called the Armory; his car license plate reads 3LJ 8284; and 555-0189 is his phone number.

Steve is a sleazy investigator who contradicts Frank's beliefs. It is hard to establish their relationship by the introduction given. Based on the pilot and several other episodes, Steve is a down-on-his-luck private detective who worked for Frank when the company first began. Frank's company provides security for a hotel called the Seven Palms. It appears that Steve's unethical approaches to providing that security upset hotel manager Luise Escobar (Tony Plana) who called him dangerous. Although Frank said he would no longer require Steve's services, Steve sweet talked Frank into rehiring him with a promise to curtail his ways. Steve tries but relies on underhanded methods — from lying to stealing — to satisfy a client and Frank. Steve cons clients into paying the money they owe (Frank appears to have a number of clients who do not pay their bills) and relishes setting up stings to apprehend criminals.

Steve was a Boy Scout and because of its motto — "Be Prepared" — he is prepared for anything on any assignment from "packing heat" to plastic explosives. He enjoys playing the harmonica and singing; Jerry Lee Lewis is his favorite singer. Steve has a weakness for beautiful women and drinking; the Blue Lion is his favorite bar; 789 is his phone code to his bookie. Steve drives a 1962 Cadillac with the license plate 3LYD 316 and enjoys smoking cigars.

Jodie is a recent widow whose husband, a cop, killed himself when the pressures of his job became overwhelming. By the third episode, she and Frank began a relationship. Jodie was born in Los Angeles and is a graduate of UCLA. She carries a .38 for backup and is too sure of herself. She feels she can handle any case alone; Frank fears her overconfidence will eventually cost Jodie her life.

Ellie, like Jodie, has little background information. She is called Jonesy by everyone and often goes undercover when a sexy or ditzy blonde is required for a sting. She is a native Californian and attended Berkeley. She often complains about the equipment she has to sometimes wear to record evidence. She most objects to wearing a micro camera she calls a cleavage cam in her bra because she has to get suspects to look at her breasts in order to record their faces. Like Jodie, she appears to be a vegetarian.

Also working for Frank are Nevil (Flex Alexander), Geneva (Kristin Bauer) and George (Bill Brochtrup). Other than keeping the books and complaining about overdue bills and Frank's habit of taking cases for free, no other information is given about George. Nevil is Frank's electronics expert and inventor of "The Cleavage Cam." He is an expert at phone tapping, computer hacking, satellite surveillance and responsible for installing the company's rather costly security systems—$50,000 and up. Geneva is the firm's receptionist. While she does have skills taking messages and dictation, she was hired principally because she said she would not be interested in an acting career. Frank's prior receptionists were apparently bitten by the acting bug and quit. Geneva possesses a degree in secretarial services from El Camino College and is terrified of birthday parties. "When I was a kid we use to break open pinyatas but my brother told me that pinyatas had once been real animals that were force fed candy and small toys by pinyata ranchers."

Mike Post composed the theme "Total Security."

130. 21 Beacon Street (NBC, 1959–1960)

The David Chase Detective Agency is a sophisticated organization located at 21 Beacon Street in Boston. It is run by David Chase (Dennis Morgan); he is assisted by Lola (Joanna Barnes), Brian (Brian Kelly) and Jim (James Maloney).

David is a former World War II intelligence officer for the O.S.S. (Office of Strategic Services) who now uses his skills in the private sector to help people in trouble. He tackles each case as if it were a military operation. Elaborate cons are established to outwit confidence men; complex stings are set up to bring criminals to justice; and well-calculated maneuvers are used to help the police nab killers. While David actively participates in each caper, he also oversees its operations and demands that each of his operatives follow strict protocol. Once a case has been established, the program becomes a "Mission: Impossible"-type of series with the team executing complex maneuvers to accomplish their goal. Viewing requires strict attention to follow the plot. While the Chase team works for the public, the police and the Gravestake Insurance Company, it appears they are only hired because they are the last hope anyone has. Once a case has been accepted, the program details the step-by-step planning, its execution and the apprehension of the sought culprit.

Lola, also called Jo, is a former chorus girl—Broadway and Las Vegas—who uses her skills (her beauty) for distraction. Brian and Jim are experts at disguises and knowledgeable in the art of cons. Dave Kahn composed the theme "21 Beacon Street."

131. **21 Jump Street** (Fox, 1987–1990; Syndicated, 1990–1991)

An abandoned chapel at 21 Jump Street and 6th Avenue in Los Angeles is the secret headquarters for Jump Street Chapel, a special squad of undercover detectives assigned to curtail the rising crime rate in high schools. The unit, a division of the Metropolitan Police Department, recruits young looking cops and teaches them to be teenagers. Tom Hanson (Johnny Depp), Judy Hoffs (Holly Robinson), H.T. Ioki (Dustin Nguyen) and Doug Penhall (Peter DeLuise) are the officers assigned to infiltrate high schools to battle juvenile crime. Richard Jenko (Frederic Forrest) was the first captain. He was replaced by Adam Fuller (Steven Williams) when Jenko was killed in a hit and run accident.

Tom is 21 years old and the son of a cop. After graduating with top honors from the Academy, he became a patrol car officer with the Metro Police Department. He rode in Car 25 and 1-Zebra-6 was his mobile code; his car license plate reads LCH 937. He enjoys bowling; he is on a team called the King Pins. His first assignment occurred at Amhurst High School. Tom lives in an apartment at 609 West Lindsey Avenue. Jeff Yagher played Hanson in the original, unaired pilot version.

Judith Marie Hoffs, called Judy, is a strikingly beautiful black cop who worked undercover as a hooker for the Vice Squad before being transferred to Jump Street Chapel. Judy was born in Chicago and in high school was a three time all city guard on her basketball team. Judy, a victim of rape, spends Wednesday evenings as a counselor at the West Side Rape Clinic. Judy has an account at the First City State Savings and Loan and her car license plate reads DVL 737. She enjoys Ocean Spray Cranberry Juice (bick packs) and was assigned to show newcomer Hanson the ropes. On his first time out, Tom paid $200 for a pair of socks he thought were filled with drugs. Judy's telephone number is 555-3436; she lives in an apartment at 703 East Varona Drive.

H.T. Ioki is a Vietnamese refugee. His real name is Vinh Von Tran and he was born in Saigon; he lived on Kanot Street. In April of 1975, when he was 14 years old, the Vietcong invaded his city. He fled Saigon and found himself in St. Louis, where he was raised by a woman named Bessy Mason. He became the first Vietnamese refugee in St. Louis. He learned to speak English by watching *Sesame Street* and loved cop shows; *S.W.A.T.* was his favorite. They instilled in him a desire to become a law enforcement officer.

After high school graduation, he went to San Francisco and posed as a reporter to gain access to death records. He took the name H.T. (Harry Truman) Ioki, enrolled in the police academy and finished fifth in his class. He was assigned to Jump Street Chapel by Captain Jenko. He lives in a small apartment at 11 Newline Place and is well versed in the martial arts.

Doug Penhall stands five feet ten inches tall and weighs 165 pounds. He was born on March 1, 1964, and lives at 8137 Juniper Street. His car license plate reads 71 6583, and he often plunges into dangerous situations without thinking first. He was joined by his brother, Joey Penhall (Michael DeLuise) in later episodes. Joey's first assignment was infiltrating the religious cult Heaven's Gate. Kati Rocky (Alexandra Powers) was a federal agent who worked briefly as a Jump Street cop; she had a cat named Bugsy. Sal Banducci (Sal Jenco), called Blowfish, is the Chapel's jovial maintenance man. Captain Jenko called Tom "Sport" and played lead guitar in a band called the Bunco Dudes on Saturday nights. Jimi Hendrix was Jenko's idol and 9486 EO was his license plate number. Captain Fuller was a graduate of the University of Toronto and often went undercover as a teacher in troubled schools.

The soda machine at Jump Street Chapel is contained in a device that resembles a gas station pump. "Roar with Gilmore Gasoline" is the slogan on the pump. In the opening theme, when "21 Jump Street" is sprayed on, the paint runs on the letters *J* and *S*. Holly Robinson sings the theme "21 Jump Street."

Spinoff Series

Booker (Fox, 1989–1990). Fed up with his life as a cop for having to obey the rules, Dennis Booker (Richard Grieco) leaves Jump Street Chapel to become the head investigator for the Teshima Corporation, a Los Angeles-based, Japanese-owned insurance company located in the Teshima Tower Building. Alicia Rudd (Marcia Strassman) is Booker's supervisor, the vice president in charge of corporate acquisitions. Suzanne Dunne (Lori Petty) is Booker's assistant. Booker's license plate read DVP 762; Suzanne's license plate is PX 29190. The song "Hot in the City" by Billy Idol is used as the theme.

132. Unsub (NBC, 1989)

Before there were such forensic-oriented series like *C.S.I.: Crime Scene Investigation* and *Crossing Jordan* (see entries), there was *Unsub*, a little known, short-lived series (February 3 to April 14, 1989) that, by today's television standards, was ahead of its time. The setting was the fictional Behavioral Sciences Unit of the U.S. Department of Justice where a special team of forensic investigators incorporate the latest scientific technology to help various police departments solve baffling crimes. When a culprit cannot be determined, they refer to him or her as "Unsub" (unknown subject). The team prefers to investigate a crime scene that is "sealed up tight — no one touching it before we do." They approach each crime scene wearing hospital gloves, gowns and slippers so nothing gets disturbed. Team director Wes Grayson (David Soul) explains: "We had a case last year. We found a hair, one red hair. Special analysis told us that the host body hadn't eaten for a couple of days and we discovered that the follicle had been washed with a chemical compound we later identified as a rare French shampoo. We traced the store that sold the shampoo, put out 30 feds on the street with a criminal profile, all looking for a thin red haired killer. It was my wife! The hair had come from my coat. She had been dieting and using a French shampoo that her sister sent her for Christmas. That's why we're careful."

In addition to Wes, the team consists of Ann Madison (Jennifer Hetrick), a RNDSC (a registered nurse who is also a doctor of psychology) who gives them their psychological killer profiles. Ned Platt (M. Emmet Walsh) "is one of the best old time feds who ever walked. Ned knows more tricks about solving cases than you and I put together," says Wes.

Allen McWhirter (Kent McCord) is a forensic scientist. He can make a crime scene talk. Jimmy Bello (Richard Kind) has a degree in advanced hypnotic therapy and uses hypnosis to make witnesses recall something they never remember seeing. Wes keeps Jimmy around "because he is so uncomplicated; he helps the rest of the team when they become eaten by crimes."

Tony D'Agostino (Joe Maruzzo) is the rebellious member of the team and is constantly at odds with Wes. Wes is opposed to Tony's tardiness but needs his unique ability to approach a crime scene and psychologically become the Unsub. Through Tony, the team learns the sometimes elusive motive behind a crime.

Jimmy calls Wes "Skipper." Wes was born in Key Largo, Florida. Ned likes to talk to people around the crime scene to feel them out. When they are at their base in Washington, D.C., the team rides in a sedan with the license plate 37242.

Mike Post composed the theme "Unsub."

133. The Untouchables (ABC, 1959–1963; Syndicated, 1993–1994)

ABC Version: The program is set in Chicago during its turbulent years of mobster rule during the late 1920s and '30s. Walter Winchell, the program's narrator, tells us that in 1929 the country was dry—bootlegged beer had been outlawed—but through conveyance with Al Capone, Chicago was wet—helped by corrupt officials and a public that was indifferent. To battle Capone and stop his illegal activities, the U.S. District Attorney assigns their top Prohibition Agent, 26-year-old Eliot Ness (Robert Stack) the task. There are 300 federal agents in Chicago. "Some can be bought," says Ness, "but what if you have a special squad, small, operating on its own; every man thoroughly investigated; brought in from all parts of the country. Men who will spit on Capone's graft; just a few he can't buy."

On June 28, 1929, Ness is given full access to all federal agents' files. His task: to find six or seven men who are reliable, courageous, dedicated and honest. "Six or seven of the most honest men."

Several days later, on July 5, 1929, in office 208 of the Federal Building in Washington, D.C., Ness meets with the men he has chosen to become the Federal Special Squad, dubbed "The Untouchables" by the press, as they cannot be touched by the mob: Martin Flaherty (Jerry Paris), a former Boston police officer with an outstanding arrest record; William Longfellow (Abel Fernandez), a full-blooded Cherokee Indian, responsible for the breakup of the Oklahoma booze ring; Jack Rossman (Steve London), a former New York telephone company lineman, now a wiretap expert; Lamar Kane (Peter Leeds), an agent with the Richmond, Virginia, bureau, a law school graduate, married and the father of two children; Eric Hanson (Eddie Firestone) of the San Francisco bureau, a former guard at San Quentin's Death Row Prison; and Enrico Rossi (Nicholas Georgiade), a former barber who became an agent after he testified as a witness against mobster Frank Nitti. He witnessed a mob hit that claimed the life of an innocent 17-year-old girl.

The pilot episode, broadcast as two segments of *Desilu Playhouse* (April 20 and 27, 1959) also featured agents Tom Kopka (Robert Osterloh) of the Sacramento Bureau, a former Pennsylvania State Trooper and World War I hero, and Joe Fuscelli (Keenan Wynn), a man who speaks the Sicilian and Neopolitan dialects, who spent five years in prison for robbery and knows every street and alley in the city—the best driving hands in Chicago. Joe was killed off and Tom was dropped. They were replaced by agents Lee Hobson (Paul Picerni) and Cam Allison (Anthony George).

At the age of 26, Eliot Ness headed the most elite crime fighting unit in the country. While it took him 18 months to bring Capone to justice (nailing him on an income tax evasion charge), Ness fought corruption until his death in 1957.

The team was first dubbed "The Untouchables" by the Chicago *Bulletin* when it ran the headline "Untouchables Defy Capone." Al Capone

(Neville Brand) had his headquarters in a room above the Montmartre Cafe in Chicago. When caught by Ness, he was sentenced to 11 years in the Atlanta State Penitentiary, Cell 39, Block D. His prison I.D. number was 40886. In the show's opening theme, the book, *The Untouchables* by Eliot Ness and Oscar Fraley is seen in the center of the screen. Two guns are on the left side of the book; a box of bullets with 13 visible shells is on the right side. Eliot's office phone number is Superior 7-599. Eliot dated Betty Anderson (Patricia Crowley) and married her in November of 1929. Superior 2-198 was her phone number. In the pilot episode, Bill Williams played Martin Flaherty; Paul Dubov was Jack Rossman; and Paul Picerni was Tom Lugari. Nelson Riddle composed the theme "The Untouchables."

Syndicated Version: An update of the prior series that chronicles the battle for control of prohibition-era Chicago between law enforcement officials and the mob. The series begins with some background information that was not given in the original series. Eliot was born in Chicago in 1900. His sister was married to a federal agent and Eliot grew up admiring his uncle, who would tell him exciting stories about his work. At the age of 15, Eliot was given a bee bee gun by his uncle. At this same time in Brooklyn, New York, a kid named Alfonse "Al" Capone was growing up on the streets and eventually found his way into the mob.

Eliot attended Fenger High School, where he was a member of the debate team. During a debate with a rival school (Jefferson High), Eliot met a girl named Catherine Staley. She vowed to one day marry Eliot. Several years later they met at the University of Chicago and dated. Meanwhile, Capone has made a name for himself in the New York mob but kills a cop on the take who tried to steal from him. He flees to Chicago, where he sets up his illegal alcohol operations. Eliot, who has been studying law in college, and Catherine wed when Eliot acquires a job as a junior partner with the Perenniel Life Insurance Company. Eliot hadn't thought about a career in law enforcement until fate steps in. A short time later, Eliot (Tom Amandes) and Catherine (Nancy Everhard) witness a gangland hit that goes wrong when the son of a friend of theirs is killed in the crossfire. Bitter and angered, Eliot quits his job and approaches his uncle for a job in law enforcement.

In 1929 President Hoover vows to end organized crime and creates the Federal Task Force. Although many federal agents are believed to be mob connected, the force will be comprised of seven men the mob cannot touch — "The Untouchables." Eliot Ness is chosen to head the team. Ness chooses the following men as his agents: Tony Pagano (John Haymes Newton), a Harvard graduate, is from the Detroit Bureau. He possesses degrees in English and engineering and drives midget race cars as a hobby. Paul Robbins (David Elliott) is from the St. Louis Bureau. He is an ex–fighter pilot for the Army Air Corps and worked as a district attorney before joining the Treasury Department. George Steelman (Michael Horse) is a full-blooded Cherokee Indian. He was based at the Omaha office and is a former Carlyle University football star and expert wire tapper. Mike Malone (John Rhys Davies) is the last of Ness's squad, a tough ex-cop and explosives expert. Eliot and his team are based at 4478 Racine in a brewery once occupied by Al Capone (William Forsythe); Ness fears the Federal Building "may have ears." Joel Goldsmith composed the new "Untouchables" theme.

Note: NBC aired *The Return of Eliot Ness*, a two-hour TV movie on November 10, 1991, wherein Robert Stack reprised his role as Eliot Ness. The story is set in Chicago in 1947. Eliot has been living in Omaha but returns to Chicago when former Untouchable, Marty Labine, is killed in what appears to be a cop-on-the-take situation. Ness teams with Marty's son, police sergeant Gil Labine (Jack Coleman) and proves that Marty was framed by a mobster who wanted to further his position in the organization. The movie was actually a pilot that failed to produce an update of the original ABC series.

Proposed Spinoffs (Unsold Pilots)

1. *The Seekers* (ABC, November 20, 1962). Barbara Stanwyck as Agatha Stewart, a lieutenant with the Chicago Police Department's Bureau of Missing Persons during the 1930s. The story, titled "Elegy," finds Agatha seeking the missing daughter of a dying mobster.

2. *The Floyd Gibbons Story* (ABC, December 11, 1962). Scott Brady as Floyd Gibbons, a World War I combat photographer turned investigative reporter battling corruption in 1930s Chicago. The pilot finds Gibbons investigating the suspicious death of an old friend. "Floyd Gibbons, Reporter" was the proposed series title.

3. *The Seekers* (ABC, January 1, 1963). A second pilot for Barbara Stanwyck as Lieutenant Agatha Stewart of Chicago's Bureau of Missing Persons. The story, titled "Search for a Dead Man," finds Agatha seeking the identity of a body found in Lake Michigan.

134. Walker, Texas Ranger (CBS, 1993–2001)

C.D.'s Bar and Grill in Fort Worth, Texas, is the gathering place for three close friends: Cordell Walker (Chuck Norris), Jimmy Trevette (Clarence Gilyard, Jr.) and Alexandra Cahill (Sheree J. Wilson). Cordell and Jimmy are Texas Rangers; Alexandra is the prosecuting assistant district attorney.

Cordell exceeds authority to get the job done. He is skilled in the use of martial arts and uses his upbringing as a Cherokee Indian to help him outwit and capture criminals. Walker's father, John Firewalker (Dan Brook), was a full-blooded Cherokee; his mother, Elizabeth (Kathleen Steele), was a white woman John met at a rodeo. They dated and married and had only one child — Cordell. Tragedy struck when Cordell was ten years old. Cordell and his family were leaving a county fair when three drunken thugs approached them. A fight began when the thugs insulted Elizabeth "for marrying a red skin." John and Elizabeth were killed and Cordell was raised by his uncle, Ray (Floyd "Red Crow" Westerman, then American Indian actor Apesanahkwat) on the reservation. No mention is made of what happened to the thugs. Cordell was given the Indian name Warshaw (Lone Eagle) and raised in the ways of both the Cherokee and the white man. When the series begins, Cordell is living with his Uncle Ray on his parents ranch on South Road 8 in Springfield, Texas; 555-4928 is his phone number. The above story line was detailed in a flashback. Dialogue from prior episodes changed Cordell's upbringing. It was first said that his parents were killed in a car crash and he was sent to the Cherokee Reservation in Oklahoma to be raised. It was next said that after his parents death, Cordell was raised at the Santa Rosa Orphanage.

Cordell served in the Vietnam War (he was a captain and called "The Nighthawk") and was a kick boxing champion in 1978. He also teaches karate and began a drug free program for kids called Kick Drugs Out of America. Turkey meatloaf is Cordell's favorite meal. He drives a Dodge 4X4 with the license plate AUQ 075, originally DV4 708 then 495 3XA. He had three horses throughout the series run: Cookie, Amigo and Ranger. Walker's car code is 8157 and he bears an uncanny resemblance to Hayes Cooper, a former Old West Texas Ranger, played by Chuck Norris in flashback episodes.

Jimmy was born in Baltimore on the wrong side of the tracks. He attended Penn State College and was first said to be a member of the wrestling team. This changed to a member of the football team where he showed potential for becoming a pro. A shoulder injury ended that career. Somehow he found his way to Texas and joined the highway patrol. Shortly after, he worked with the narcotics division of the Texas P.D. He then became a Texas Ranger. Another episode finds Jimmy as a pro football player for the Dallas Cowboys where he suffered a serious shoulder injury that ended his career. It was at this time that he met C.D., a former Ranger who helped him get his life back together and paved the way for his becoming a Texas Ranger. Later, Jimmy was said to be a Texas police officer on a riot assignment when he was attacked by several hoods. From out of the shadows a Texas Ranger appeared and saved him. Trevette saw the Ranger's badge and knew what he had to become — a Texas Ranger. It was not until he and

Walker were partners years later that Jimmy learned it was Walker who saved his life. *The Lone Ranger* is Jimmy's favorite television show; he drives a car with the license plate 595 NYD, also seen as FY4 161, 278 556 and 853 4FP. Jimmy and Walker are members of the Brown's basketball team.

In addition to being the Assistant D.A. of Fort Worth, Alexandra, called Alex, teaches evening classes in law enforcement at the Irving Campus of Mid-Texas University. Alex had to fight for everything she got and Walker believes she is too stubborn for her own good. She believes there is a special place in Heaven for a man like Walker. Alex often helps Walker so cases will not fall through the cracks in the system. Alex has a horse named Amber and a car with the license plate 364 H2R, also seen as TEH 2R9; 555-3165 is her phone number. Alex, like Walker, cares for people. She conducts a Victims of Crime women's support group at the South Shore of Stuart Lake that she calls Camp Cahill. She later opens a help center called H.O.P.E. (Help Our People). Alex's favorite month is May and, as the series progressed, a romance developed between her and Walker. They married in May of 2000 and in the series finale, May 19, 2001, Alex gives birth to a girl she and Cordell name Angela Walker. Alex mentioned that *Sparticus* was her favorite movie.

C.D. Parker (Noble Willingham) is a retired Texas Ranger turned bar owner. He was a Ranger for 15 years but received a medical discharge five years ago when he was shot in the knee. He writes an advice column for the *Gazette* under the pen name Trail Buddy. C.D. has a 1964 Cadillac he calls Old Goldie, license plate 519 FUL, and a boat he calls *Winky Dink*.

Sydney Cook (Nia Peeples) and Francis Gage (Judson Mills) are other members of Walker's unit at the Department of Public Safety, Texas Ranger Unit. Other than adding action to the series, little information is given about these characters. Both Sydney and Gage are well versed in the martial arts. Sydney caught the bouquet at Alex's wedding and often goes undercover on assignments with Gage while Walker and Trevette direct operations. Gage is never called by his first name; "I use my last name because of my first name." His car license plate reads 364 H24; Sydney's license plate is 777 J9H. Both she and Gage do volunteer work for kids at the Christian Community Center.

Chuck Norris sings the theme "The Eyes of the Ranger." See also *Sons of Thunder*, the spinoff series.

Appendix A: Television's Experimental Crime Fighters

Four detective-based experimental programs broadcast between 1937 and 1946

135. ***The Three Garridebs*** (NBC, November 27, 1937). The first television adaptation of the Sherlock Holmes stories by Sir Arthur Conan Doyle. The story, set in London, finds the famous consulting detective, Sherlock Holmes (Louis Hector) and his biographer, Dr. John H. Watson (William Podmore) attempting to find a man with the odd name of Garrideb to fill the conditions of an eccentric's will and allow a lonely old man to collect an inheritance. Violet Bosson played Mrs. Hudson, Holmes' landlady at 221-B Baker Street, and Eustace Wyatt was Inspector Lestrade of Scotland Yard. Also in the cast were Arthur Maitland as John Garrideb and Harold DeBecker as Nathan Garrideb. See also *Sherlock Holmes* in Appendix B.
136. ***The Mysterious Mummy Case*** (NBC, May 17, 1938). The story of a man (Tom Terris as himself) as he attempts to uncover the source of several mysterious deaths. *Also in the cast:* Dorothy McGuire (Miss Clark), Ned Wever (Curt), William David (Edward Lawson) and Arthur Maitland (Dr. Harvey). The mystery was broadcast live and was the first program to incorporate film inserts, slides and fades to black for transitions (costume and set changes).
137. ***The Item of the Scarlet Ace*** (NBC, November 29, 1941). A television adaptation of the radio series *The Bishop and the Gargoyle*. The Bishop (Richard Gordon) is a crime fighter who once served on the parole board of Sing Sing Prison. The Gargoyle (Ken Lynch) is a convict the Bishop befriended. Upon his release, the Gargoyle became the Bishop's aide, the man who provides the physical force when it comes to fighting criminals. The story finds the Bishop and Gargoyle seeking an elusive criminal known as the Scarlet Ace. *Also in the cast:* Peggy Allenby, Parker Fennelly, Jane Lauren, Ernie Owen and Howard Petrie.

Appendix A: Experimental

138. ***Diary of Death*** (CBS, September 20, 1945). A television adaptation of an episode, "Diary of Death," of the radio series *Casey, Crime Photographer* with Oliver Thorndike as Casey, a photographer for the *Morning Express*, a crusading New York newspaper. He is assisted by reporter Ann Williams (Ruth Ford) and hangs out at the Blue Note Cafe, a bar owned by Ethelbert (John Gibson). The story finds Casey attempting to clear Ann of a false murder charge. See also *Crime Photographer*, program number 20.

Mr. and Mrs. North (NBC, May 16, 1946) see *Mr. and Mrs. North*

Appendix B:
Pilot Films

An alphabetical listing, with brief descriptions, of unsold pilot films featuring cops, detectives, sheriffs and amateur sleuths

139. **Ace** (ABC, July 26, 1976). Bob Dishy as Edward R. Ace, an eccentric private detective.
140. **Acting Sheriff** (CBS, August 17, 1991). Former movie and television star Brent McCord (Robert Goulet), star of the ill-fated series "Scuba Sleuth," as the real life sheriff of LoMiceda County, California.
    Adams Apple (CBS, August 23, 1986) see *Leg Work*
141. **Adams of Eagle Lake** (ABC, November 10, 1975). Andy Griffith as Sam Adams, the sheriff of Eagle Lake, a small California resort town. Abby Dalton co-stars as Margaret Kelly, his girl Friday.
142. **Adams of Eagle Lake: The Treasure Chest Murders** (ABC, February 26, 1975). A second attempt at a series starring Andy Griffith as Sheriff Sam Adams of Eagle Lake, California. Sam lives at 500 North Shore Road; Margaret Kelly (Abby Dalton) at 637 Pine Valley Road.
143. **The Adventures of Mary Kate and Ashley** (ABC, April 22, 1995). Eight-year-old twins Mary Kate and Ashley Olsen as themselves, the operators of Mary Kate and Ashley Detective Services. Tracy Nelson and William R. Moses play their parents, Terry and Jack Olsen.
144. **The Adventures of Nick Carter** (ABC, February 20, 1972). Robert Conrad as Nick Carter, a master detective operating out of New York City during the early 1900s.
145. **Adventuring with the Chopper** (NBC, August 7, 1976). Comical crime solving with black detectives Arnold "The Chopper" Jackson (Harrison Page) and Leonard Jones (Antonio Fargas).
    Alex and the Doberman Gang (NBC, April 11, 1980) see *Tequila and Bonetti*
146. **Alias Mike Hercules** (ABC, July 31, 1956). Hugh Beaumont as Mike Hercules, a private detective working out of San Francisco. Filmed in 1954.
147. **Allison Sidney Harrison** (NBC, August 19, 1983). High school girl and ama-

Appendix B: Pilot Films   190

teur sleuth Allison Sidney Harrison (Katy Kurtzman) teams with her father, San Francisco private detective David Harrison (Ted Danson) to solve crimes.

148. **Almost Partners** (PBS, May 16, 1987). An unlikely crime fighting duo: Jack Wilder (Paul Sorvino) and his unofficial partner, Molly McCue (Royana Black), a very pretty 14-year-old girl with the mind of Sherlock Holmes.

149. **Along the Barbary Coast** (NBC, February 27, 1961). Jerome Thor as Pete Bishop, a private eye based on San Francisco's Barbary Coast.

Angie, the Lieutenant (ABC, February 1, 1992) see *Police Woman*

150. **Ann in Blue** (ABC, August 8, 1974). Penny Fuller as Ann Neal, a sergeant with the 27th Precinct of the N.Y.P.D.

151. **Arly Hanks Mysteries** (CBS, August 20, 1994). Kate Jackson as Arly Hanks, a former New York private detective turned police chief of Maggody, an Arkansas community of 755 people.

152. **The Art of Crime** (NBC, December 3, 1975). Ron Leibman as Roman Grey, a Gypsy antique dealer and amateur sleuth working out of New York City.

153. **The Asphalt Cowboy** (NBC, December 7, 1980). Max Baer as Max Caulpepper, a private detective who owns the Los Angeles-based Caulpepper Security Service.

154. **The Bait** (ABC, March 13, 1973). Donna Mills as Tracy Fleming, an undercover police woman who poses as the bait to nab criminals.

155. **Battles** (NBC, March 9, 1980). William Conrad as William F. Battles, a former Los Angeles policeman turned football coach and security guard for Hawaii State University who helps the police solve baffling crimes.

156. **Beach Patrol** (ABC, April 30, 1979). The work of Jan Plummer (Christine DeLisle), Marty Green (Jonathan Frakes), Earl Hackman (Richard Hill) and Russ Patrick (Robin Strand), members of the Beach Patrol Unit of the San Gabriel P.D.

157. **Bender** (CBS, September 12, 1979). Harry Guardino as Bender (no first name), a former N.Y.P.D. detective turned sheriff of Tamarisk Wells, a rich California resort community.

158. **Benny and Barney: Las Vegas Undercover** (NBC, January 19, 1977). Terry Kiser and Tim Thomerson as Benny Kowalski and Barney Tuscom, Las Vegas P.D. officers who moonlight as nightclub singer-musicians.

159. **The Big Easy** (NBC, August 15, 1982). William Devane as Jake Rubidoux, a detective who occasionally plays clarinet at The Big Easy, a nightclub in the French Quarter of New Orleans.

160. **Big John** (NBC, December 3, 1983). Dale Robertson as "Big" John Corbin, a Conway County, Georgia, sheriff who is studying crime detection methods with the N.Y.P.D.

161. **Big Rose** (CBS, March 26, 1974). Shelley Winters as Rose Winters, a middle-aged private detective working out of Los Angeles.

162. **The Boston Terrier** (NBC, April 10, 1962). Robert Vaughn as A. Dunster Lowell, a Harvard-educated private detective based in Boston. A second pilot with Robert Vaughn repeating his role aired on ABC on June 11, 1963.

163. **The Boys in Blue** (CBS, September 9, 1984). Grace Carpenter (Maggie Cooper), Danny Harris (Dean Paul Martin) and Jeff Martin (Gregg Henry) as patrol car officers with the Prospect Division of the L.A.P.D.

164. **Braddock** (CBS, July 22, 1968). Tom Simcox as Braddock, a private detective with the firm of Braddock and Tratner Investigations in Los Angeles in the future—1977.
165. **Braker** (CBS, April 28, 1985). Carl Weathers as Harry Braker, a no-nonsense lieutenant with the L.A.P.D.
166. **Brock Callahan** (CBS, August 11, 1959). Ken Clark as Brock Callahan, a retired L.A. Rams football guard turned Beverly Hills private detective.
167. **Bulldog Drummond** (NBC, January 28, 1957). Robert Beatty as New Scotland Yard's intrepid investigator, Hugh "Bulldog" Drummond.
168. **Bunco** (NBC, January 13, 1977). The undercover work of L.A.P.D. Bunco Squad officers Ben Gordean (Tom Selleck), Ed Walker (Robert Urich) and Frankie Dawson (Donna Mills).
169. **Call Holme** (NBC, April 24, 1972). Artie Johnson as Fabian Holme, a private detective known as "The master of 1,000 disguises."
170. **The Casebusters** (ABC, May 25, 1986). Retired police officer Sam Donahue (Pat Hingle) finds help in solving crimes from his teenage grandchildren, Allie and Jamie Donahue (Virginia Keehne, Noah Hathaway).
  Cass Malloy (CBS, July 21, 1982) see *She's the Sheriff*
171. **Charley Hannah** (ABC, April 5, 1986). Robert Conrad as Charley Hannah, a tough but compassionate police captain with the Fort Lauderdale, Florida, P.D.
172. **The Cheap Detective** (NBC, June 3, 1980). Flip Wilson as Eddie Krowder, an L.A.-based private detective who charges $19.95 a day plus expenses.
173. **The City** (NBC, January 12, 1977). The work of L.A.P.D. detectives Matt Lewis (Robert Forster) and Brian Scott (Don Johnson).
174. **Clue You In** (Syndicated, July 1985). Adventures of pre-teen sleuths Paula and Tripper (Paula Hoffman, Tripper McCarthy), owners of an agency called Clue You In, Inc.
175. **Colorado, C.I.** (CBS, May 26, 1978). Cases that cross city and county lines are the work of Mark and Peter Gunnison (John Elerick, L.Q. Jones), brothers and members of the Criminal Investigation Unit of the Colorado P.D.
176. **Cool and Lam** (Unaired, 1957). Beany Venuta as Bertha Cool, the penny-pinching owner of the Cool and Lam Private Detective Company in Los Angeles. Billy Pearson is her partner, shrewd investigator Donald Lam. Based on the stories by Erle Stanley Gardner, who appears to introduce his characters.
  Crazy Dan (NBC, July 19, 1986) see *Sledge Hammer*
177. **The Crime Club** (CBS, March 6, 1973). Retired judge Roger Knight (Victor Buono) and L.A. private detective Paul Cord (Lloyd Bridges) team up.
178. **The Crime Club** (CBS, April 3, 1975). Newspaper reporter Daniel Lawrence (Eugene Roche), private detective Jake Keesey (Scott Thomas) and criminal lawyer Alex Norton (Robert Lansing) battle injustice.
179. **Crowfoot** (CBS, June 7, 1995). Jim Davidson as Nick Crowfoot, a Cheyenne Indian attached to the Maui, Hawaii, P.D.
180. **Dakota's Way** (ABC, August 20, 1988). Patricia Charbonneau as Dakota Goldstein, a former National Security Agency operative turned L.A.P.D. detective.
181. **Dan Turner, Hollywood Detective** (Syndicated, August 14, 1990). Marc Singer as Dan Turner, a smooth-talking private eye working out of Los Angeles in 1947.

Appendix B: Pilot Films

182. **Dana Hill** (NBC, April 29, 1975). Rookie police woman Dana Hill (Jo Ann Pflug) is teamed with seasoned officer Ed Wells (Gary Crosby) to solve crimes.
183. **The Danger Team** (ABC, July 3, 1991). Cheryl Singer (Kathleen Beller) is a detective who heads the Danger Team — Spex (voice of John Wesley Shipp), Nit (June Foray) and Truk (Christopher Collins), three miniature clay figures with sleuthing abilities who help her solve crimes. The figures came to life and were saved by Cheryl when a meteor crashed through a lab window and splashed them with rusty water.
184. **Dark Eyes** (ABC, June 8, 1995). Kelly McGillis as Mila McGann, a lieutenant with the Cleveland P.D.
185. **D.C. Cop** (CBS, August 27, 1986). Cotter Smith as Michael Halsey, a newspaper reporter turned detective for the Washington, D.C., P.D.
186. **The Detective** (NBC, October 12, 1975). Larry Hagman as Dennis O'Finn, a not-too-bright private detective.
Detective Finger, I Presume (NBC, May 2, 1981) see *B.J. and the Bear*
Dick Tracy (Unaired, 1967) see *Dick Tracy*
187. **Dirty Work** (CBS, June 6, 1985). Keerie Keane as Nadine Leevanhoek, a file clerk for the Wylie Detective Agency who solves crimes for her boss, George Wylie (Louis Giambalvo), who is on the run from the mob and police.
188. **Donato and Daughter** (CBS, September 21, 1993). Charles Bronson and Dana Delany as Mike and Dina Donato, a father and daughter team of crime fighters with the Central Division of the L.A.P.D.
189. **Dusty** (NBC, July 24, 1983). Saul Rubinek as Dusty, a cab driver with sleuthing abilities who helps detective Tim Halloran (Gerald S. O'Loughlin) solve crimes.
190. **Egan** (ABC, September 18, 1973). Eugene Roche as Eddie Egan, a former New York private detective working for the L.A.P.D.
Ellery Queen: Don't Look Behind You (NBC, November 14, 1971) see *Ellery Queen*.
191. **Empire City** (Unaired, 1991). Michael Pare and Mary Mara as Joe Andre and Nancy Kraus, N.Y.P.D. homicide detectives who investigate crimes involving the rich and famous. See also *Silk Stalkings*.
192. **Encyclopedia Brown — The Boy Detective** (HBO, March 3, 1989). Scott Bremner as Leroy Brown, a brainy kid and amateur sleuth who runs the Brown Detective Agency. Leroy, called "Encyclopedia," is assisted by his friend, Sally Kimball (Laura Bridge).
The Expendables (ABC, September 27, 1962) see *Tightrope*
The Eyes of Texas (NBC, November 10, 1979) see *B.J. and the Bear*
193. **Family in Blue** (CBS, June 10, 1982). Events in the lives of a family of law enforcers: Matty Malone (Efrem Zimbalist, Jr.), a former police chief turned private detective; Matt Malone, Jr. (Dirk Benedict), a police sergeant; Julie Malone (Nancy Dolman), Matty's daughter, a police lab technician; and Chester Malone (Dick O'Neill), Matty's brother, a police chief.
194. **Feel the Heat** (ABC, August 5, 1983). Nick Mancuso as Andy Thorne, an ex-cop turned private detective working out of Key Blanco, Florida.
195. **Flatfoots** (NBC, July 3, 1982). Comical crime solving with L.A.P.D. officers Frank Shackelford (John Reilly) and Gabe Fortunato (Todd Susman).

193 Appendix B: Pilot Films

   Force Seven (NBC, May 23, 1982) see *CHiPs*
196. **Four Eyes** (NBC, March 6, 1984). Stepfanie Kramer and D.D. Howard as Tracy and Jean, gorgeous private eyes based in Southern California.
197. **Fraud Squad** (ABC, May 17, 1985). Ann Dusenberry and Nana Visitor are Kelly Myerson and Bonnie Dalton, undercover agents for the Fraud Squad Division of the L.A.P.D.
198. **The Fuzz Brothers** (ABC, March 5, 1973). Louis Gossett, Jr. and Felton Perry as Francis Buchanan and Luther Prince, L.A.P.D. detectives plagued by endless problems.
199. **Green Dolphin Beat** (Fox, June 27, 1994). John Wesley Shipp as Terry Latner, a detective with Green Dolphin, a precinct in a crime-ridden Los Angeles neighborhood.
200. **Greyhounds** (CBS, June 24, 1994). Four old timers join forces to battle crime: Chance Wayne (Dennis Weaver), a former San Diego County sheriff; Robert Smith (Robert Guillaume), a retired judge; Akiro Mochizuka (Pat Morita), a former police coroner; and John Dolan (James Coburn), a reformed con artist.
201. **Hammer, Slammer and Slade** (ABC, December 15, 1990). Three friends join forces to battle crime: John Slade (Bernie Casey), an ex-cop; Hammer Wilson (Isaac Hayes), a former playboy; and Slammer Jenkins (Jim Brown), an ex-football player.
202. **Hanna** (Unaired, 1989). Scott Plank as Victor Hanna, a tough L.A.P.D. detective.
203. **Hardcase** (NBC, December 6, 1981). Beau Kayzer as Grover Harding Case, an unorthodox detective with the New Orleans P.D.
   The Hardy Boys (NBC, Semptember 8, 1967) see *The Hardy Boys*
   Harry (CBS, May 13, 1981) see *Mike Hammer*
204. **Hercule Poirot** (CBS, April 1, 1962). Martin Gabel as Hercule Poirot, Agatha Christie's famous Belgian detective who uses sheer wit to solve crimes.
205. **Hernandez, Houston P.D.** (NBC, January 16, 1973). Henry Darrow as Juan Hernandez, a detective with the Houston, Texas, P.D.
206. **Hide and Seek** (NBC, May 22, 1958). Everett Sloane as Dan Wilder, a detective who uses scientific methods to solve crimes.
   Hollywood Starr (ABC, February 23, 1985) see *T.J. Hooker*
207. **Hope Division** (ABC, August 17, 1987). Mimi Kuzak and Dorian Harewood as Anne Russell and James Reynolds, homicide detectives with the Hope Division of the L.A.P.D.
208. **I Love a Mystery** (NBC, February 27, 1973). Adaptation of the radio series about Doc Long (David Hartman), Jack Packard (Les Crane) and Reggie York (Hagan Beggs), private detectives who roam the world solving crimes. Filmed in 1966.
209. **I Was a Bloodhound** (CBS, February 15, 1959). Ernie Kovacs as Barney Colby, a detective who uses his uncanny sense of smell to solve crimes.
210. **Inspector Perez** (NBC, January 8, 1983). Jose Perez as Antonio Perez, an inspector with the San Francisco P.D.
211. **Jackie and Darlene** (ABC, July 8, 1978). Sarina Grant and Anna L. Pagan as Jackie Clifton and Darlene Shilton, police officers with the West Valley Precinct in California.

Appendix B: Pilot Films

212. **Jake's Way** (CBS, June 28, 1980). Robert Fuller as Jake Rudd, sheriff of Fox County, a rural town in San Antonio, Texas.
213. **Jarrett** (NBC, August 11, 1973). Glenn Ford as Sam Jarrett, an ex-prize fighter turned private detective who solves crimes associated with the fine arts.
214. **Joe Dancer** (NBC). Robert Blake as tough Los Angeles private detective Joe Dancer. Three pilots were made: "The Big Black Pill" (January 29, 1981), "The Monkey Mission" (March 23, 1981) and "Murder One, Dancer 0" (June 5, 1983).
215. **Johnny Blue** (CBS, September 4, 1983). Gil Gerard as Johnny Blue, a New Orleans private detective who also owns Johnny Blue's Restaurant.
216. **Juarez** (ABC, May 28, 1988). Benjamin Bratt as Rosendo Juarez, a Mexican-American sergeant with the El Paso, Texas, Sheriff's Office.
    Justin Case (ABC, May 15, 1988) see *Haunted*
    K-9 (ABC, July 1, 1991) see *Tequila and Bonetti*
    K-9 and Company (Syndicated, August 1985) see *Tequila and Bonetti*
    K-9000 (Unaired, 1989) see *Tequila and Bonetti*
217. **Ladies in Blue** (ABC, March 19, 1980). Michelle Phillips and Tanya Roberts as Casey Hunt and Britt Blackwell, police women with the San Francisco P.D.
218. **Ladies on Sweet Street** (ABC, August 16, 1990). Retired school teacher Ruth Egan (Gloria DeHaven) and former butcher Bea Morina (Doris Roberts) live in a retirement home on Sweet Street. They each consider themselves amateur sleuths and help the police solve crimes.
219. **Las Vegas Beat** (Unaired, 1964). Peter Graves as Bill Ballin, a former police officer turned detective who works for the Las Vegas Casino Owners Association.
220. **Last of the Private Eyes** (NBC, April 30, 1963). Bob Cummings as J.F. Kelly, a 1960s private eye who operates as a 1940s detective putting his nose to the grindstone to solve crimes.
    Lester (ABC, January 8, 1976) see *Harry O*
221. **Lone Star** (NBC, July 31, 1983). Crime solving in the Lone Star state with Ben and George McCollum (Lewis Smith, Alan Autry), brothers who are also Texas Rangers.
222. **The Loner** (ABC, August 18, 1988). John Terry as Michael Shane, an L.A.P.D. detective who finds true peace only when he is by himself.
223. **Lookwell** (NBC, July 28, 1991). Adam West as Ty Lookwell, former star of the TV series "Bannigan" about a homicide detective, who uses his television experience and honorary L.A.P.D. badge to solve real life crimes.
224. **Meet McGraw** (CBS, February 25, 1954). Frank Lovejoy as McGraw, a private detective who helps people unable to turn to the police for help.
225. **Mickey Datona** (Unaired, 1992). Ray Sharkey as Mickey Datona, a private detective based in Southern California.
226. **Mimi and Me** (CBS, September 7, 1991). Terry Farrell and Howard McGillin as Mimi Molloy and Howard Raney, a Los Angeles-based team of private detectives.
227. **Mr. and Mrs. Cop** (CBS, May 3, 1974). Crime solving with husband and wife police officers Paul and Nancy Roscommon (Anthony Costello, Marianne McAndrew).

Mr. and Mrs. North (NBC, July 4, 1949) see *Mr. and Mrs. North*

228. **Mr. and Mrs. Ryan** (ABC, April 12, 1986). L.A.P.D. detective lieutenant Michael Ryan (Robert Desiderio) finds help in solving crimes from his wife Ashley (Sharon Stone), a socialite with sleuthing abilities.
229. **Mr. and Ms.** (ABC). Two pilots were produced for a series about husband and wife private detectives David and Mandy Robbins (John Rubinstein, Lee Kroeger): "The Magic Studio Mystery" (December 16, 1975) and "The Bandstand Murders" (December 23, 1975).
230. **Mr. Inside/Mr. Outside** (CBS, March 4, 1973). Lou Isaacs and Rick Massi (Hal Linden, Tony LoBianco) are detectives with the N.Y.P.D. When Rick is shot and forced to retire, he becomes "Mr. Outside" and helps Lou, "Mr. Inside," solve crimes.
231. **Mitchell and Woods** (NBC, December 18, 1981). Jayne Kennedy and Cindy Morgan as Paula Woods and Melanie Mitchell, detectives with the Ocean City, California, P.D.
232. **Momma the Detective** (NBC, January 19, 1981). Ester Rolle as Momma Sykes, a housekeeper with sleuthing abilities who solves crimes.
233. **The Monk** (ABC, October 21, 1969). George Maharis as Gus Monk, a tough private detective with few friends, who wanders from state to state with his cat Aristotle.
234. **Mrs. R.** (NBC, May 20, 1975). Kate Reid as Shirley Ridgeway, a homicide detective with the L.A.P.D. who is called Mrs. R.
235. **Murder Ink** (CBS, September 6, 1983). Tovah Feldshuh as Laura Ireland, amateur sleuth and owner of a bookstore called Murder Ink, who helps her husband, Lou Ireland (Daniel Hugh-Kelly), a sergeant with the N.Y.P.D., solve crimes.
236. **Mystery and Mrs.** (ABC, September 27, 1950). Gale Storm and Don DeFore as Sally and George Fame, husband and wife private detectives.
237. **Mystery Dance** (ABC, June 29, 1995). Jane Curtin as Susan Baker, an amateur sleuth who solves crimes as a sideline to her job as community reporter to the Los Angeles *Paid Reader*.
238. **Nash's Vision** (Unaired, 1991). David Nash (Robert Taylor) is a detective with telepathic powers who receives help in fighting crime from his deceased son's little toy dinosaur, which is capable of transforming itself into a real, 50-foot tall beast.

Nero Wolfe (ABC, December 18, 1979) see *Nero Wolfe*

Nice Guys Finish Dead (NBC, November 16, 1979) see *The Rockford Files*

239. **Nichols and Dymes** (NBC, October 7, 1981). Rocky Bauer and Robin Strand as Buck Nichols and Willy Dymes, federal agents who help local law enforcement agencies solve complex crimes.

Nick and Nora (ABC, March 4, 1975) see *The Thin Man*

Nick and the Dobermans (NBC, April 25, 1980) see *Tequila and Bonetti*

240. **Nick Derringer, P.I.** (ABC, May 4, 1988). David Rappaport as Nick Derringer, a diminutive private eye whose motto is "No Case Too Small."
241. **Night Partners** (CBS, October 11, 1983). Yvette Mimieux and Diana Canova as Elizabeth McGuire and Lauren Hensley, auxiliary police women who help the victims of violent crimes.

Appendix B: Pilot Films 196

242. **The Nightengales** (NBC, May 19, 1979). Marcia Strassman and Colette Blonigan as Jenny Palmero and Cotton Gardner, L.A.P.D. officers who patrol the Hollywood beat at night as part of an experimental two woman unit called the Nightengales.
243. **Nightside** (ABC, June 8, 1980). Doug McClure and Michael Corneilison as Danny Dandoy and Ed Macey, L.A.P.D. officers who patrol the city at night.
    Off Broadway (ABC, May 13, 1995) see *The Commish*
244. **Old Dogs** (ABC, August 10, 1987). Jimmy Bryce (Robert Loggia) is a veteran cop who was suspended for breaking the rules. Mayo Dunlap (Robert Dunlap) is a retired police captain. Together they work as consultants to help the police solve crimes.
245. **O'Malley** (NBC, January 8, 1983). Mickey Rooney as Mike O'Malley, a 1940s-style, New York-based detective working in the 1980s.
246. **Palms Precinct** (NBC, January 8, 1982). Sharon Gless and Steve Ryan as Alexandra Brewster and Carmine Monaco, inspectors with the Palms City, California, P.D.
247. **Parker Kane** (Unaired, 1990). Jeff Fahey as Parker Kane, a former cop with the Long Beach, California, P.D. turned private detective.
248. **Partners in Crime** (NBC, March 24, 1973). Lee Grant as Meredith Leland, a judge turned private detective, and Lou Antonio as Sam Hatch, her investigator, a reformed ex-con.
249. **Patrick Stone** (CBS, July 16, 1965). Jeff Davis as Patrick Stone, a fumbling private detective who solves crimes quite by accident.
250. **Peter Hunter** (Syndicated, 1948). Frank Albertson as Peter Hunter, a tough New York-based private detective.
251. **The P.I.** (CBS, March 28, 1976). Vic Morrow as Frank Carey, a former gun-shy secret service agent turned roughneck private investigator.
    The P.I. (ABC, March 3, 1994; with George Peppard) see *Matlock*
252. **The Pigeon** (ABC, November 4, 1969). Sammy Davis, Jr., as Larry Miller, an easy-going private detective working out of Los Angeles.
253. **Police File** (ABC, June 25, 1994). Jacqueline Samuda and Sean McCann as Isabella Vargas and Jack O'Leary, detectives with a police precinct called the Two-Five (representative of any precinct in any city).
254. **Police Story** (NBC, September 8, 1967). Police work in action as seen through the eyes of James Paige (Steve Ihnat), the captain of a metropolitan police force.
    Ponch's Angels (NBC, February 28, 1981) see *CHiPs*
    Poochinski (NBC, July 9, 1990)) see *Tequila and Bonetti*
255. **Popeye Doyle** (NBC, September 7, 1986). Ed O'Neill as Popeye Doyle, a rough and rumpled detective with the N.Y.P.D. Based on the film *The French Connection*.
256. **Pros and Cons** (ABC, January 26, 1986). Bernie Casey and Carol Potter as Bernie Rollins and Patty Finley, members of the Fraud and Bunco Division of the L.A.P.D.
257. **Protect and Surf** (ABC, August 6, 1989). The work of Jodi Lampert (Tasia Valenza), Mike Deegan (David Oliver) and Randy Vasquez (Jesse Gomez), officers with the Santa Monica P.D. who share a beach residence called Surf House.
    Quick and Quiet (CBS, August 18, 1981) see *Haunted*

258. **Ray Alexander** (NBC). Louis Gossett, Jr., as Ray Alexander, a private detective and owner of a restaurant called Ray's Backyard Cafe. Two pilots were produced: "A Taste for Justice" (May 13, 1994) and "Menu for Murder" (March 20, 1995).
259. **The Return of Charlie Chan** (ABC, July 17, 1979). Ross Martin as the famous Oriental sleuth, Charlie Chan. Filmed in 1971 as "Happiness Is a Warm Clue."
260. **Rewrite for Murder** (CBS, September 14, 1991). Carolyn Hudson (Pam Dawber) is the creator-writer of the TV series "Miss Markham Mysteries." Nick Bianco (George Clooney) is an ex-con turned novelist and creator of Biff Brannigan detective stories. Nick is hired to assist Carolyn and together they solve real-life mysteries for story material.
261. **Rooster** (ABC, August 19, 1982). Brewster "Rooster" Steele (Paul Williams) is an L.A.P.D. psychologist who teams with William "Sweets" McBride (Pat McCormick), an ex-cop turned insurance investigator, to solve crimes.
The Rubber Gun Squad (NBC, September 1, 1977) see *Broken Badges*
Salathiel Harms, Bounty Hunter (CBS, January 25, 1976) see *Kojak*
262. **Sam Penny and Associate** (CBS, November 14, 1985). Robert Lansing as Sam Penny, a hard boiled detective one step away from bankruptcy. Caren Kaye plays his associate, Elizabeth Clarke.
263. **San Berdoo** (ABC, August 12, 1989). John Terry as Max Jericho, a private detective working out of San Bernadino, a community of Palm Springs, California, that is nicknamed San Berdoo.
Sanctuary of Fear (NBC, April 23, 1979; pilot for "Father Brown") see *Father Dowling Mysteries*
264. **Savage in the Orient** (CBS, June 21, 1983). Joe Penny as Peter Savage, a private detective who also operates the Peter Savage Antique Shop in Manila.
265. **The Search** (CBS, July 29, 1968). Mark Miller as Paul Cannon, a London-based American private detective who helps troubled U.S. travelers.
The Seekers (ABC, November 20, 1962) see *The Untouchables*
266. **Sergeant T.K. Yu** (NBC, April 19, 1979). Johnny Yune as T.K. Yu, a Korean police sergeant studying crime detection methods with the L.A.P.D.
267. **Shadow of Sam Penny** (CBS, November 3, 1983). Robert Lansing as Sam Penny, an aging detective working out of San Francisco.
268. **The Sheriff and the Astronaut** (CBS, May 24, 1984). Alec Baldwin as Ed Cassaday, sheriff of Carrow County; Ann Gillespie as Ellen Vale, his girlfriend, an astronaut at the Dwight D. Eisenhower Space Center.
269. **Sherlock Holmes** (Unaired, 1951). John Longden as Sherlock Holmes, the brilliant London-based consulting detective created by Sir Arthur Conan Doyle. Campbell Singer played his friend, Dr. John H. Watson. A syndicated series appeared in 1954 with Ronald Howard as Sherlock Holmes; H. Marion Crawford as Dr. Watson; and Archie Duncan as Inspector Lestrade. See also "The Three Garridebs" for an experimental version of the series.
270. **Sherlock Holmes** (ABC, February 12, 1972). Stewart Granger as consulting detective Sherlock Holmes; Bernard Fox as Dr. John H. Watson; and Alan Caillou as Inspector Lestrade.
271. **Silent Whisper** (CBS, July 26, 1988). Eric Bolan (David Beecroft) is a detective with the San Francisco P.D. During a case he is stabbed in the throat and left

with only a whisper of a voice. The series was to relate his relentless, silent pursuit of criminals.
272. **Simon Lash** (Unaired, 1960). Jock Mahoney as Simon Lash, a rugged, two-fisted private detective.
273. **Sirens** (CBS, September 4, 1987). Comical crime solving with Franny Aronson (Dinah Manoff) and Cheryl Kelly (Loretta DeVine), officers with the Metropolitan P.D.
274. **Sirens** (ABC, March 10, 1993). The daily activities of police officers Sarah Berkezchuk (Jayne Brook), Molly Whelan (Liza Snyder) and Lynn Stanton (Adrienne-Joi Johnson).

Sister Michael Wants You (CBS, May 13, 1994) see *Father Dowling Mysteries*
275. **Skip Taylor** (Syndicated, 1953). Mark Andrews as Skip Taylor, a rugged private detective.
276. **Slickers** (NBC, August 12, 1987). Michael Richards as Mike Blade, a disaster-prone N.Y.P.D. officer working in a small town (Littlefield, N.Y.) to teach law enforcement procedures to its sheriff, Elliott Clinton (Dana Carvey).

Sniff (CBS, August 9, 1988) see *Tequila and Bonetti*
277. **Sonny and Sam** (NBC, August 29, 1981). Sonny Bono and Lee Purcell as Sonny and Samantha Hunt, a Nashville-based, husband and wife team of private detectives.
278. **South of Sunset** (CBS, October 27, 1993). Glenn Fry as Cody McMahon, a former Paramount Pictures security guard turned owner of the Beverly Hills Detective Agency ("Located just a bit south of Sunset").
279. **Sparrow** (CBS). Randy Herman as Jerry Sparrow, an insurance company mailroom clerk turned private detective. Two pilots were produced and aired on January 2, 1978 and August 11, 1978.
280. **The Spirit** (ABC, July 31, 1987). Denny Colt (Sam Jones) is a police officer and famous mystery story writer. During a case, Colt is shot and falls off a pier and into the water below. He is found by a young hustler named Eubie (Bumper Robinson) and nursed back to health. Colt is believed to be dead and he decides to remain as such to fight crime as the mysterious Spirit.
281. **Spraggue** (ABC, June 29, 1984). Michael Nouri as Michael Spraggue, a college biology teacher and amateur crime sleuth who helps the police solve baffling crimes.
282. **Stark** (CBS). Two pilots were produced about Patrick Evan Stark (Nick Surovy), a tough, hard-drinking Kansas police detective: "Stark" (April 10, 1985) and "Stark: Mirror Image" (May 14, 1986).
283. **Stonestreet** (NBC, January 16, 1977). Barbara Eden as Liz Stonestreet, a former police officer turned private detective.
284. **Stormy Weathers** (ABC, May 4, 1992). Cybill Shepherd as Samantha "Stormy" Weathers, a gorgeous, L.A.-based private detective who charges $300 a day plus expenses.
285. **The Streets** (NBC, September 2, 1984). Michael Beck as Danny Wreade, an N.Y.P.D. officer who works undercover as a cab driver.
286. **The Streets of Beverly Hills** (ABC, July 13, 1992). Brian Keith as Charlie Street, a hard-nosed L.A.P.D. cop who transfers to the Beverly Hills P.D. to give his son, Kenny (Stan Kirsch) a better life.

Appendix B: Pilot Films

287. **Suburban Beat** (NBC, August 17, 1985). Dee Wallace (Joanne), Shelley Fabares (Mimi), Heather Langenkamp (Hope) and Patti Austin (Rosemary) as suburban housewives who ban together to help keep their community free of crime.
288. **Supercops** (CBS, March 21, 1975). Steven Keats and Alan Feinstein as Dave Greenberg and Bobby Hantz, N.Y.P.D. officers known as Batman and Robin for their daring tactics and arrest record.
    Task Force (NBC, March 2, 1976) see *Police Woman*
289. **The Texas Rangers** (NBC, May 16, 1981). Jeff Osterhage and Larry Gelman as Andy Bennett and Bill Cavanaugh, members of the Houston Division of the Texas Rangers.
290. **This Girl for Hire** (CBS, November 1, 1983). Bess Armstrong as Barbara Brady, a beautiful Los Angeles-based private detective who charges $200 a day plus expenses.
291. **Three Eyes** (NBC, June 27, 1982). Ed Marinaro, Michael Horton and Robin Strand as Tony, Buzz and Cowboy, private detectives who run Three Eyes, a combination nightclub and detective agency at 3645 Marina Del Rey in Los Angeles.
    The Tom Swift and Linda Craig Mystery Hour (ABC, July 3, 1983) see *The Hardy Boys*
    Toni's Boys (ABC, April 2, 1980) see *Charlie's Angels*
292. **Trouble, Inc.** (DuMont, July 27, 1949). Earl Hammond and Carol Hill as Jason and Jayne Meadows, marrieds who operate a detective agency called Trouble, Inc.
    Turner and Hooch (NBC, July 9, 1990) see *Tequila and Bonetti*
293. **Turnover Smith** (ABC, June 8, 1980). William Conrad as Thaddeus Smith, a criminology professor at San Francisco's Wellington University who helps the police solve crimes by taking evidence others have overlooked and turning it into a conviction.
294. **The 25th Man (Ms.)** (NBC, August 15, 1982). Ellen Regan as Lynn Taylor, the only female recruit in a group of 25 new rookies for the L.A.P.D.
295. **Twin Detectives** (ABC, May 1, 1976). Jim and Jon Hager as Tony and Shep Thomas, twins who are also police detectives.
296. **The Two-Five** (ABC, April 14, 1978). Don Johnson as Joe Bennett and Charlie Morgan as Frank Sarno, unorthodox police officers attached to a precinct nicknamed the Two-Five (for the 25th).
297. **Two for the Money** (ABC, February 26, 1972). Robert Hooks and Stephen Brooks as Larry Dean and Chip Bronx, cops who quit the force to earn more money as private detectives.
298. **A Very Missing Person** (ABC, March 4, 1972). A proposed series, to be called "Hildegarde Withers" with Eve Arden as Hildegarde, a retired New York City school teacher turned amateur sleuth who helps the police solve crimes.
299. **Waikiki** (ABC, April 21, 1980). Dack Rambo and David King as Ronnie Browning and Steve Marachuk, private detectives based in Waikiki, Hawaii, who help Cassie Howard (Donna Mills) of the Oahu P.D. solve crimes.
300. **Weapons Man** (ABC, April 6, 1963). J.D. Cannon as Mark Vickers, a weapons expert who assists the police in unusual cases involving the use of a weapon to commit a crime.

301. **Wheeler and Murdoch** (ABC, May 9, 1973). Jack Warden and Christopher Stone as Sam Wheeler and Terry Murdoch, Seattle-based private eyes.

Zoey (ABC, February 1, 1985) see *Matt Houston*

Index

References are to entry numbers.

Aames, Willie 45
Abbott, Dorothy 32
Adair, Deborah 73
Addison, John 33, 84
Aiello, Danny 25, 64
Aiello, Rick 25
Akins, Calude 4
Albert, Eddie 122
Albertson, Jack 125, 250
Albright, Lola 93
Alexander, Ben 32
Alexander, Flex 129
Alexander, Khandi 22
Allen, Joseph, Jr. 79
Allen, Philip R. 45
Allenby, Peggy 137
Alt, Carol 126
Amandes, Tom 133
Ames, Florenz 34
Amos, John 54
Anders, Merry 77
Anderson, Loni 46, 91
Anderson, Melody 16, 57
Anderson, Pamela 78
Anderson, Richard 45
Andre, Annette 49
Andrews, Mark 275
Andrews, Tige 80
Antonio, Lou 30, 248
Apesanahkwat 134
Applegate, Christina 51
Aprea, John 73
Arden, Eve 4, 298
Arlen, Roxanne 103

Armendariz, Pedro 121
Armstrong, Bess 290
Armstrong, Curtis 83
Arnole, Monroe 28
Ashton, John 43
Asner, Edward 93
Astley, Edwin 26
Atkins, Tom 106
Atwater, Edith 45
Austin, Patti 287
Autry, Alan 56, 113, 221

Babcock, Barbara 66
Bader, Diedrich 23
Baer, Max 153
Baggetta, Vincent 33
Bailey, Pearl 93
Bain, Barbara 102
Baio, Scott 27
Baker, Diane 63
Baker, Joe Don 56
Baker, Kathy 94
Baker, Lenny 8
Baldwin, Alex 268
Banfield, Bever-Leigh 11
Barilla, Courtney 54
Barnes, Joanna 130
Barnes, Priscilla 109
Barry, Donald 120
Barry, Gene 11
Barrymore, Drew 14
Barton, Peter 11
Barty, Billy 93
Basinger, Kim 14, 30

Index (to entry numbers)

Bassey, Jennifer 53
Batanides, Arthur 60
Bauer, Bruce 14
Bauer, Kristin 129
Bauer, Rocky 239
Baumann, Katherine 46
Beal, Jeff 81
Beasley, Allyce 83
Beatty, Robert 167
Beaumont, Hugh 146
Beck, Jenny 128
Beck, John 111
Beck, Michael 285
Beer, Jacqueline 107
Beery, Noah, Jr. 105
Beggs, Hagan 208
Bellamy, Bill 36
Bellaver, Harry 86
Beller, Kathleen 183
Belushi, James 129
Benedick, Dirk 193
Benz, Donna Kei 16
Bernard, Ed 96
Bernardi, Herschel 93
Bernstein, Elmer 106
Besch, Bebe 96
Beswick, Martine 119
Birkell, Lauren 87
Birney, David 106
Bisson, Yannick 119
Black, David 19
Black, Royana 148
Blake, Robert 37, 214
Blanc, Mel 28
Bland, John David 121
Blande, Christopher 45
Bleeth, Yasmine 88
Blonigan, Colette 242
Blood, Jay 28
Bloom, Lindsay 78
Bolan, Eric 271
Bono, Sonny 98, 277
Borish, Matthew 42
Bosley, Tom 37, 84
Bosson, Barbara 105
Bosson, Violet 135
Boswell, Connee 92
Bowman, Lee 34
Boyle, Peter 124
Brady, Scott 133
Brand, Neville 133

Bratt, Benjamin 216
Braugher, Andre 42
Brauner, Asher 2
Bray, Deanne 119
Bremner, Scott 192
Bridge, Laura 192
Bridges, Lloyd 177
Bridges, Todd 80
Brill, Charlie 110
Britton, Barbara 79
Broadhead, James E. 14
Brochtrup, Bill 129
Bronson, Charles 188
Brook, Jayne 29, 59, 274
Brooks, Avery 114
Brooks, Randi 65
Brooks, Roxanne 102
Brooks, Stephen 297
Brosnan, Pierce 101
Brough, Candi 4
Brough, Randi 4
Brown, Georg Stanford 95
Brown, Jim 201
Brown, Roger Aaron 29
Brown, Wally 103
Brubaker, Robert 77
Bryant, Lee 128
Buckner, Susan 87
Bunch, Ray 88
Buono, Victor 28, 177
Burgi, Richard 21
Burke, Delta 37
Burke, Paul 86
Burns, Bart 78
Bushkin, Joe 60
Butkus, Dick 109
Byrnes, Edd 107
Byrd, Ralph 28

Cacavas, John 62
Caicedo, Magali 14
Caillou, Alan 270
Cain, Marie 12
Campbell, Bill 82
Campbell, Carole Ann 45
Caffrey, Stephen 27
Calder, King 70
Callas, Charlie 122
Campbell, Jennifer 104
Canning, Sandra 14
Cannon, J.D. 300

Index (to entry numbers)

Canova, Diana 241
Capers, Virginia 31
Carlin, George 49
Carlyle, Richard 20
Carmel, Roger C. 4
Carney, Art 37
Carradine, Robert 124
Carroll, Janet 48
Carroll, Pat 109
Carpenter, Pete 17, 41, 54, 65, 69, 105, 123
Carter, Lynda 91
Caruso, David 22
Carvey, Dana 276
Casey, Bernie 201, 256
Cassidy, Shaun 45
Cathcart, Dick 92
Cavanaugh, Michael 54
Chadney, Bill 93
Champlin, Bill 56
Chaney, Rebecca 78
Charbonneau, Patricia 180
Charles, Ray 112
Chaykin, Maury 89
Chihara, Paul 68
Chiklis, Michael 18
Christian, Claudia 108
Christian, Leigh 128
Cibrian, Eddie 3
Clark, Eugene 121
Clark, Ken 166
Clark, Matt 30
Clarke, Lenny 58
Clarke, Patrick James 67
Clooney, George 260
Cmiral, Elia 88
Coburn, James 94, 200
Cochrane, Rory 22
Cole, Eddie 7
Cole, Michael 80
Cole, Tina 50
Coleman, Jack 133
Coleman, Lisa 21
Colin, Margaret 67
Collier, Lois 6
Collins, Christopher 183
Collins, Jesse 124
Collins, Lynn 49
Combs, Holly Marie 94
Connell, Kelly 94
Connors, Mike 127

Conrad, Robert 50, 144, 171
Conrad, William 57, 71, 89, 95, 155, 293
Considine, Tim 45
Constantine, Michael 101
Conti, Bill 12, 55
Conti, Vince 63
Convy, Bert 96
Conway, Gary 11
Conway, Russ 45
Cook, Elisha, Jr. 69
Cooper, Maggie 55, 163
Coote, Robert 89
Cope, Kenneth 49
Copley, Teri 55
Corbett, Gretchen 105
Core, Natalie 37
Corley, Pat 124
Corneilison, Michael 243
Cornell, Lydia 43
Cosby, Bill 19
Costello, Anthony 227
Courage, Alexander 9
Crane, Les 208
Crane, Richard 120
Crawford, H. Marion 269
Crenna, Richard 97
Crewson, Wendy 114
Cromwell, James 65
Crosby, Gary 15, 182
Crosby, Mary 111
Crowley, Patricia 133
Cullen, Brett 87
Cummings, Bob 220
Curtin, Jane 237

Dabson, Jesse 96
Dalton, Abby 1541, 142
Daly, Tyne 12
Danson, Ted 147
Danza, Tony 53
Darren, James 128
Darrow, Henry 46, 205
Dash, Stacy 118
Davalos, Elyssa 71
David, Mack 7, 50, 103, 107, 120
David, Thayer 89
David, William 136
Davidson, Eileen 8
Davidson, Jim 179
Davies, John Rhys 133

Index (to entry numbers)

Davis, Don 8
Davis, Jeff 249
Davis, John E. 11
Davis, Ossie 5
Davis, Sammy, Jr. 252
Davison, Bruce 54
Davison, Davey 28
Dawber, Pam 260
Dean, Ron 1
DeBecker, Harold 135
DeBenedictis, Dick 27, 37, 57, 71
DeFore, Don 236
DeHaven, Gloria 218
Dehner, John 103
DeJesus, Wanda 22, 39
Delaney, Kim 22
Delany, Dana 188
Delfino, Marieh 87
Delia, Joe 25
DeLisle, Christine 156
DeLuise, Michael 131
DeLuise, Peter 131
DeMay, Janet 101
Dennehy, Brian 12
Denning, Richard 77, 79
Denton, Donna 78
Depp, Johnny 131
D'Errico, Donna 3
DeSales, Francis 79
Desiderio, Robert 51, 228
Devane, William 159
DeVine, Loretta 273
Devlin, Joe 28
Devon, Laura 93
DeVorzon, Barry 30
DeWindt, Sheila 4
DiAquino, John 49
Diaz, Cameron 14
Dickinson, Angie 96
Diehl, John 76
Dierkop, Charles 96
Dillman, Bradford 119
Dishy, Bob 139
Dobson, Kevin 63, 78
Dohrman, Angela 88
Dollivaine, Dorothy 86
Dolman, Nancy 49, 193
Donahue, Patricia 77, 125
Donahue, Teresa 8
Donahue, Troy 50, 120
Donnell, Jeff 72

Douglas, Shirley 48
Dourdan, Gary 22
Downing, Sara 49
Doyle, David 14
Dryer, Fred 16, 54
Dubov, Paul 133
Duell, William 95
Dugan, Dennis 83, 105
Duggan, Andrew 7
Duncan, Archie 269
Dunford, Christine 53
Duning, George 86, 127
Dunlap, Robert 244
Dunn, Carolyn 121]
Dunne, Steve 9
Durning, Charles 35
Dusenberry, Ann 197
Dzundza, George 42

Eades, George 22
Easton, Sheena 76
Ebsen, Buddy 73
Edelman, Herb 117
Eden, Barbara 283
Eggert, Nicole 128
Eilbacher, Lisa 45, 75
Eisley, Anthony 50, 92
Elerick, John 175
Elfman, Danny 111
Elliott, David 133
Elliott, Dick 28
Elliott, Jack 14
Ellis, Herb 32
Emerson, Hope 93
English, Deven 45
Englund, Robert 31
Ericson, John 42
Erikson, Kaj-Eric 18
Erwin, Jhene 87
Estes, Rob 78, 110
Estrada Eric 16
Evans, Debbie 16
Everhard, Nancy 119, 133
Evigan, Greg 4, 98

Fabares, Shelley 287
Fabiani, Joel 26
Facinelli, Peter 36
Fahey, Jeff 247
Falk, Peter 17
Faracy, Stephanie 35

Farentino, Debrah 129
Fargas, Antonio 115, 145
Farina, Dennis 10
Farr, Diane 58
Farrell, Terry 226
Faustino, David 55
Fawcett, Farrah 14, 46
Feinstein, Alan 288
Feldman, Corey 109
Feldshuh, Tovah 49, 235
Fennelly, Parker 137
Fenneman, George 32
Ferguson, Allyn 14
Fernandez, Abel 133
Fernetz, Charlene 116
Ferrer, Miguel 8, 21, 54
Field, Todd 23
Fielding, Jerry 74
Finkel, Fyvush 94
Finley, Pat 105
Firestone, Eddie 133
Fitzgerald, Ella 92
Flanery, Sean Patrick 118
Fluegel, Darlanne 54, 78
Fong, Brian 15
Foray, June 183
Ford, Glenn 213
Ford, Ruth 20, 138
Forrest, Frederic 131
Forster, Robert 173
Forsythe, John 14
Forsythe, William 59, 133
Foster, Meg 12
Fountain, Suzanne 98
Fox, Bernard 270
Fox, Crystal 56
Fox, Jorga 22
Fox, Matthew 49
Frakes, Jonathan 156
Franciosa, Anthony 72
Francis, Anne 11, 52
Franciscus, James 86, 119
Franke, Christopher 100
Frann, Mary 78
Frazer, Dan 63
Frazer, Jayne 98
Freed, Bert 17
Frees, Paul 28
Frontiere, Dominic 73, 117
Frost, Warren 71
Fry, Glenn 278

Fry, Taylor 57
Fuller, Penny 150
Fuller, Robert 212
Fulton, Bill 32

Gabel, Martin 204
Gail, David 104
Galasso, Frankie J. 53
Gammon, James 88
Garber, Victor 55
Gardner, Craig 15
Gargan, William 70
Garland, Beverly 24
Garner, James 105
Garner, Mousie 120
Garwood, Kelton 7
Gates, Rick 45
Gay, Gregory 103
Gayle, Tina 16
Gellar, Pat 82
Gelman, Larry 289
Gemignani, Rhoda 40
Genesse, Bryan 116
George, Anthony 133
Georgiade, Nicholas 133
Gerard, Gil 119, 215
Gershon, Gina 112
Getz, John 68
Giambalvo, Louis 187
Gibb, Cynthia 27
Gibney, Hal 32
Gibson, John 20, 138
Gilbert, Edmund 45
Gilbert, Herschel Burke 11
Gilborn, Steven 53
Gillespie, Ann 268
Gillette, Anita 99
Gilyard, Jr., Clarence 71, 134
Givens, Robin 1
Glaser, Paul Michael 115
Glenn, Louise 103
Gless, Sharon 12, 122, 246
Goldberg, Barry 31
Goldblum, Jeff 123
Goldenberg, Billy 17, 46, 63
Goldman, Danny 78
Goldsmith, Joel 133
Gomez, Jaime P. 88
Gomez, Jesse 257
Goodwin, Michael 117
Gordon, Phil 92

Index (to entry numbers)

Gordon, Richard 137
Gorrell, Ashley 126
Gossett, Louis, Jr. 198, 258
Gossett, Robert 110
Goulet, Robert 95, 140
Gower, Andre 128
Granger, Stewart 270
Grant, Lee 248
Grant, Sarina 211
Granville, Bonita 87
Graves, Gayla 103
Graves, Peter 219
Graves, Teresa 39
Gray, Bruce 85
Gray, Colin 45
Grayden, Sprague 59
Greene, Angela 28
Greene, Johnny 125
Greene, Lorne 41, 95
Grieco, Richard 131
Grier, Rosey 63
Griffith, Andy 71, 141, 142
Grusin, Dave 17
Gruska, Jay 40
Guardino, Harry 157
Guilbert, Ann 94
Guilfoyle, Paul 22
Guillaume, Robert 200
Gunn, Janet 110
Gunn, Moses 114

Hack, Shelley 14
Hagan, Molly 49
Hagen, Earle 78
Hager, Jim 295
Hager, Jon 295
Haggerty, Don 13
Hagman, Larry 186
Hahn, Kathryn 21
Hallahan, Charles 54, 78
Hamilton, Bernie 115
Hamilton, Murray 4
Hammer, Jan 76
Hammond, Earl 292
Han, Maggie 85
Hancock, John 111
Hanks, Steven 2
Harden, Marcia Gay 114
Hardy, Craig 19
Harewood, Dorian 117, 207
Hargitay, Mariska 31, 124

Harmon, Angie 3
Harmon, John 28
Harmon, Mark 83, 119, 124
Harris, Johnny 31
Harris, Ricky 23
Harris, Stacy 86
Harrold, Kathryn 68
Hart, David 56
Hart, Richard 34
Hartley, Mariette 27
Hartman, David 208
Hasseloff, David 3
Haskell, Jimmie 35
Hathaway, Noah 170
Hauser, Fay 69
Haydn, Lili 62
Hayes, Isaac 203
Hayworth, Vinton 79
Heckart, Eileen 91
Hector, Louis 135
Helgenberger, Marg 22
Heller, Ken 91
Henderson, Florence 95
Hennessy, Jill 21
Hennings, Sam 54
Henry, Gregg 163
Hensley, Pamela 73
Henstridge, Natasha 108
Herd, Richard 128
Herman, Randy 279
Hetrick, Jennifer 132
Hill, Carol 292
Hill, Richard 156
Highet, Fiona 45
Hillerman, John 34, 69
Hingle, Pat 170
Hobbs, Heather 109
Hoenig, Michael 29
Hoffman, Paula 174
Hogan, Robert 105
Hogan, Terry "Hulk" 126
Holdridge, Lee 90
Holland, Amy 75
Holliday, Kene 71
Holliman, Earl 96, 98
Holly, Lauren 94
Hooks, Robert 297
Horan, Barbra 4
Hornsby, Russell 49
Horse, Michael 133
Horsley, Lee 73, 89

Horton, Michael 291
Howard, D.D. 196
Howard, Ken 21
Howard, Meredith 92
Howard, Ronald 269
Howell, Arlene 7
Hudson, Ernie 8, 65, 114
Hudson, Rock 74
Hughes, Barnard 37
Hurst, David 89
Hutton, Jim 34
Hutton, Timothy 89

Ihnat, Steve 254
Inwood, Steve 114
Ito, Robert 99

Jackson, Kate 14, 151
Jacott, Carlos 108
Jaeckel, Richard 114
Jaffe, Taliesin 109
Janssen, David 46, 102
Jarreau, Al 83, 85
Jenco, Sal 131
Jeter, Michael 94
Jobson, Eddie 88
Johnson, Adrienne-Joi 274
Johnson, Anne-Marie 56
Johnson, Artie 169
Johnson, Don 76, 88, 173, 296
Johnson, Janet Louise 87
Johnson, Jay 8
Jones, Cherry 67
Jones, Clayton Barclay 76
Jones, Henry 62
Jones, James Earl 75, 97
Jones, John Marshall 59
Jones, Judy 119
Jones, L.Q. 175
Jones, Sam 280
Jurasik, Peter 93

Kahn, Dave 130
Kallis, Nicole 96
Kamekona, Danny 11
Kamel, Stanley 81
Kaminski, Dana 5
Kane, Byron 45
Kapture, Mitzi 110
Karlen, John 12
Karling, Reed 45

Kaye, Caren 262
Kayzer, Beau 203
Keach, Stacy 78
Keane, Charlotte 34
Keane, Kerrie 187
Keats, Steven 288
Keehoe, Virginia 170
Keith, Brian 44, 286
Keith, Byron 107
Kelly, Brian 130
Kelly, Daniel Hugh 44, 235
Kelly, Jack 39, 45
Kennedy, George 37
Kennedy, Jayne 231
Kerr, Edward 112
Kersch, Stan 286
Kiley, Richard 40
Kilpatrick, Lincoln 73
Kind, Richard 132
King, David 299
Kinsella, Walter 70
Kirk, Phyllis 125
Kirk, Tommy 45
Kiser, Terry 158
Klugman, Jack 99
Knotts, Don 71
Kooch, Guich 109
Kokotakis, Nick 110
Komant, Carolyn 103
Kopins, Karen 14
Kovacs, Ernie 209
Kove, Martin 12
Kramer, Stepfanie 54, 196
Kroeger, Lee 229
Krueger, Regina 37
Krushen, Jack 92
Kurtzman, Katy 147
Kuzak, Mimi 207

Labine, Tyler 49
LaChance, Devon 116
Ladd, Cheryl 14, 21
Landers, Judy 4
Lane, Lauren 54
Langenkamp, Heather 287
Lankford, Kim 85
Lannon, Les 46
Lansbury, Angela 84
Lansing, Robert 178, 262, 267
Larson, Glen A., Jr. 87, 99, 122
LaTorre, Tony 12

Index (to entry numbers)

Lauren, Jane 137
Lauter, Ed 4
Lawford, Peter 34, 125
Lawson, Maggie 87
Layton, Tyler 110
Leary, Brianne 16
Leary, Denis 58
Lee, Alexondra 94
Lee, Bruce 119
Lee, Peggy 92
Leeds, Peter 133
Leeson, John 124
Leibman, Ron 152
Leigh, Barbara 46
Lemmon, Chris 126
Lenrow, Bernard 20
Lenz, Kay 37, 51, 119
Leonard, Herbert B. 86
Leoni, Tea 14
Levin, Stewart 94
Levine, Ted 81
Lewis, Charlotte 8
Lightfoot, Leonard 109
Linden, Hal 230
Lipton, Peggy 80
Litel, John 87
Liu, Lucy 14
Livingston, Jerry 7, 50, 103, 107, 120
Lizer, Kari 71
Lloyd, Kathleen 69
LoBianco, Tony 230
Locklear, Heather 128
Logan, Robert 107
Loggia, Robert 244
Lohman, Rick 49
Long, Richard 7, 107
Longden, John 269
Longo, Tony 16
Lontoc, Leon 11
Lopinto, Dorian 119
Loudon, Steve 133
Loughlin, Lori 45, 53
Lovejoy, Frank 214
Luke, Keye 46
Lumbly, Carl 12
Lundy, Jessica 90
Lupton, Heather 111
Lupus, Peter 95
Lux, Danny 59
Luz, Franc 54
Lynch, Ken 137

Mac, Bernie 14
MacDonnell, Ray 28
Macnee, Patrick 126
MacRae, Michael 96
Mahaffey, Lorrie 4
Maharis, George 233
Mahmud-Bey, Shiek 114
Mahoney, Jock 4, 272
Maitland, Arthur 135, 136
Majors, Lee 100
Malone, Nancy 86
Maloney, James 130
Manetti, Larry 69
Mancini, Henry 17, 93, 101
Mancinia, Mark 118
Mancuso, Nick 194
Mandylor, Costas 94
Manoff, Dinah 273
Mantegna, Joe 114
Mara, Mary 191
Margolin, Janet 37
Margolin, Stuart 37, 105
Marin, Cheech 88
Marinaro, Ed 291
Marinelli, Anthony 1
Markowitz, Richard 66
Marlowe, Hugh 34
Marshall, Paula 112
Martin, Anne-Marie 111
Martin, Dean Paul 163
Martin, Mary 44
Martin, Millicent 31
Martin, Pamela Sue 87
Martin, Ross 259
Maruzzo, Joe 132
Marvel, Elizabeth 29
Masak, Ron 84
Mason, Marlyn 119
Mason, Tom 89
Matheson, Tim 45
Matlin, Marlee 94, 119
Maunder, Wayne 15
Maxwell-Reid, Daphne 112
May, Billy 86
May, Donald 103
Mayo, Whitman 37
McAndrew, Marianne 227
McBain, Diane 120
McCall, Mitzi 110
McCann, Sean 253

McCarthy, Tripper 174
McClung, Susan 128
McClure, Doug 243
McCord, Kent 132
McCormick, Pat 261
McCullough, Julie 104
McCullough, Linda 4
McDonald, Seven Ann 33
McDormand, Frances 67
McGavin, Darren 20, 78
McGillin, Howard 226
McGillis, Kelly 184
McGuire, Biff 89
McGuire, Dorothy 136
McGuire, Michael 37
McIntire, John 86
McKay, Robert 124
McKenna, Alex 21
McKenna, Wendy 58
McKennon, Dallas 45
McMahon, Horace 86
McQuade, John 79
McWilliams, Caroline 109
Meek, Jeffrey 100
Melvin, Wendy 21
Mendoza, Mauricio 14
Mettey, Lynnette 99
Michell, Keith 84
Miller, Allan 89
Miller, Bruce 109
Miller, Kristen 108
Miller, Mark 265
Miller, Mindi 122
Mills, Donna 154, 168
Mills, Judson 134
Mimieux, Yvette 241
Miner, Jan 20
Minns, Byron Keith 25
Mitchell, Shareen 53
Montgomery, Belinda J. 76
Moore, Mary Tyler 102
Moreno, Rita 5
Morgan, Charlie 296
Morgan, Cindy 231
Morgan, David 44
Morgan, Dennis 130
Morgan, Harry 32, 34
Morisette, Billy 23
Morison, Patricia 13
Morita, Pat 200
Morris, Garrett 54

Morrow, Don 70
Morrow, Vic 2, 14, 251
Morse, David 42
Moses, William R. 143
Mosley, Roger E. 69
Mostel, Josh 85
Moxey, Dawn 113
Mulgrew, Kate 62
Mullavey, Greg 4
Mullendore, Joseph 52
Mulky, Chris 124
Murphy, Ben 41
Murphy, Donna 42
Murphy, M.P. 4
Murray, Bill 14

Nader, George 34
Nagulich, Natalija 94
Narvanna, Yana 65
Natwick, Mildred 44
Naughton, James 19
Needham, Tracey 129
Nelson, Craig T. 29
Nelson, Oliver 15
Nelson, Portia 45
Nelson, Tracy 37, 71, 143
Nettleton, Lois 21, 56
Newborn, Ira 95
Newman, Robert Conner 54
Newton, John Haymes 133
Nguyen, Dustin 131
Nicholas, Denise 56
Nichols, Roger 47
Nicols, Rosemary 26
Nielsen, Leslie 95
Noble, Trisha 117
Nolan, Lloyd 70
Nordstrom, John E. 104
Norris, Chuck 134
North, Alan 95
North, Sheree 69
Nouri, Michael 31, 124, 281
Nucci, Danny 112
Nunn, Bill 58

Oakes, Randi 16
O'Brien, Edmond 60
O'Connor, Carroll 56
O'Hanlon, George, Jr. 87
O'Keefe, Jodi-Lynn 88
Okuma, Enuka 119

Index (to entry numbers)

Olkewicz, Walter 91
Olms, Edward James 76
O'Loughlin, Gerald S. 189
Olsen, Ashley 143
Olsen, Mary Kate 143
Olvis, William 97
O'Neill, Dick 193
O'Neill, Ed 32, 255
O'Neill, Eileen 11
Orbach, Jerry 66, 84
Orth, Frank 6
Osterhage, Jeff 32, 289
Osterlich, Robert 133
O'Toole, Annette 88
O'Toole, Matt 22
Owen, Ethel 137
Oxenberg, Catherine 124

Pagan, Anna L. 211
Page, Harrison 111, 145
Page, LaWanda 2
Paige, Janis 37
Pare, Michael 191
Paris, Jerry 77, 133
Parker, Paula Jai 112
Parsons, Karyn 58
Patterson, Lee 120
Paul, Don Michael 48
Pearson, Billy 176
Peeples, Nia 134
Penny, Joe 57, 264
Peppard, George 71
Perez, Jose 210
Perry, Felton 198
Perry, Jeff 88
Peters, Dennis Alaba 26
Petersen, William 22
Petrie, George O. 82
Petrie, Howard 137
Pfeiffer, Michelle 2
Pflug, Jo Ann 125, 182
Phillips, Barney 32
Phillips, Michelle 217
Phillips, Stephen H. 42
Phillips, Wendy 33
Picerni, Paul 133
Pickens, Slim 4
Pickett, Cindy 78
Piland, Sheryl Lynn 56
Pine, Robert 16
Plana, Tony 129

Plank, Scott 202
Playten, Alice 19
Pleshette, Suzanne 63
Plumb, Eve 28
Podmore, William 135
Ponce, Poncie 50
Popowich, Paul 45
Post, Mike 8, 17, 18, 41, 48, 54, 63, 65, 69, 105, 110, 123, 124, 129, 132
Potter, Carol 256
Potter, Chris 110
Powers, Alexandra 131
Powers, Stefanie 47
Pratt, Mike 49
Prescott, Robert 37
Prestidge, Mel 50
Procter, Emily 22
Provall, David 94
Provine, Dorothy 103
Purcell, Dominic 59
Purcell, Lee 277
Purl, Linda 71, 104

Quinn, Louis 107

Ragin, John S. 99
Rambo, Dack 299
Ramin, Ron 78
Ramsay, Ann 25
Rappaport, David 93, 249
Rasalala, Thalmus 32
Rasche, David 111
Rasey, Jean 87
Rawls, Lou 3
Raye, Martha 74
Read, James 101
Reason, Rex 103
Reece, Brian 70
Regan, Ellen 294
Regan, Margie 77
Reid, Kate 234
Reid, Shanna 55
Reid, Tim 112
Reilly, John 195
Reilly, Tom 16
Remar, James 129
Reynolds, Burt 5
Reynolds, Madison 22
Reynolds, Rebecca 4
Richards, Lou 109
Richards, Michael 276

Index (to entry numbers)

Richman, Peter Mark 119
Richmond, Branscombe 51
Riddle, Nelson 86, 133
Rispoli, Michael 40
Richie, Jill 87
Ritchote, Kane 81
Road, Mike 103
Robbins, Bruce 48
Roberts, Doris 101, 218
Roberts, Lynn 13
Roberts, Mark 9
Roberts, Tanya 14, 78, 217
Robertson, Dale 160
Robins, Laila 97
Robinson, Bumper 280
Robinson, Christina 1
Robinson, Holly 131
Roche, Eugene 69, 190
Rocket, Charles 85, 124
Rodriquez, Adam 22
Roebuck, Daniel 71
Rogers, Mimi 119
Rolle, Esther 232
Rollins, Howard 56
Romano, Andy 8, 39
Romanus, Richard 117
Rooney, Mickey 245
Rose, Christine 94
Rose, Jamie 64
Rose, Nicky 109
Rosenberg, Arthur 54
Ross, Chelcie 82
Rossovich, Rick 124
Rowell, Victoria 27
Rubes, Jan 1
Rubin, Benny 28
Rubinek, Saul 189
Rubinstein, John 229
Rudley, Herbert 77
Rugolo, Pete 102, 125
Russell, Mark 63
Rutherford, Kelly 40
Ryan, Mitchell 15
Ryan, Steve 246
Ryan, Tracy 87

Saint James, Susan 74
Saldana, Theresa 18
Samuda, Jacqueline 253
Samuels, Ken 45
Sanchez, Mario 113

Sanders, Brad 124
Santiago, Saundra 76
Santos, Joe 105
Sassover, Nathan 91
Savage, Elizabeth 85
Savalas, George 63
Savalas, Telly 63
Sawatsky, Sarah 85
Scalia, Jack 124
Schallert, William 87
Schifrin, Lalo 115
Schlatter, Charlie 27
Schram, Bitty 81
Schuck, John 74
Schumann, Walter 32
Scott, Simon 80
Seagren, Bob 14
Segal, George 85
Selby, Sarah 45
Sellecca, Connie 98
Selleck, Tom 69, 105, 168
Serrano, Nestor 48
Server, Eric 4
Seymour, Carolyn 67
Shalhoub, Tony 81
Sharkey, Ray 225
Shatner, William 95, 128
Sheen, Martin 46
Shenkarow, Justin 94
Shepherd, Cybill 83, 284
Sheridan, Nicollette 65
Shimoda, Yuki 60
Shipp, John Wesley 183, 199
Shortridge, Stephen 14
Shragge, Courtney 116
Shutan, Liz 28
Sierra, Gregory 76
Sierra, Margarietta 120
Sikes, Cynthia 96
Simcox, Tom 164
Sinclair, Madge 97
Singer, Campbell 269
Singer, Marc 181
Sirgo, Louis J. 86
Skerritt, Tom 94
Sladen, Elisabeth 124
Slaten, Troy 12
Sloane, Everett 28, 206
Sloyan, James, Cotter 185
Smith, Everett 1
Smith, Jaclyn 14, 122

Index (to entry numbers)

Smith, Lewis 221
Smith, Roger 107
Smitrovich, Bill 89
Snow, Mark 49, 128
Snyder, Liza 274
Solomon, Bruce 37
Somers, Suzanne 109
Sorvino, Paul 148
Soul, David 115, 132
Spang, Laurette 4
Speedman, Scott 87
Springfield, Rick 87, 104
Stack, Robert 117, 133
Stafford, Nancy 71
Stahl, Lisa 3
Staley, Joan 107
Stander, Lionel 47
Stanwyck, Barbara 14, 38, 133
Stauffer, Jack 124
Stephens, James 37
Stephens, Laraine 72
Stevens, Connie 50
Stevens, Craig 93, 125
Stevens, Leith 77
Stevens, Mark 70, 77
Stevens, Morton 72
Stevenson, Parker 45
Stewart, Bob 121
Stewart, Mel 46
Stich, Patricia 41
Stiers, David Ogden 14
Stiteler, Elena 124
Stock, Barbara 16, 114
Stone, Christopher 301
Stone, Sharon 128, 228
Storm, Gale 236
Storrs, Suzanne 86
Strand, Robin 156, 239, 291
Strassman, Marcia 131, 242
Strauss, Peter 93
Stroud, Don 32, 62, 78, 96
Stuart, Maxine 79
Stuart, Randy 107
Surovy, Nick 282
Susman, Todd 195
Swit, Loretta 12
Swofford, Ken 33, 34
Sylvester, Harold 96

Tagawa, Cary Hisoyuki 100
Talbot, Nita 7, 125
Tanner, Joy 87
Tayback, Vic 41
Taylor, Holland 75
Taylor, Jeff 45
Taylor, Kent 6
Taylor, Mary Lou 79
Taylor, Robert 238
Terris, Tom 136
Terry, John 222, 263
Thayer, Brynn 71
Theroux, Justin 29
Thiessen, Tiffani 36
Thigpen, Lynn 29
Thinnes, Roy 80
Thomas, Frank M. 70
Thomas, Frank, Jr. 87
Thomas, Heather 4
Thomas, Philip Michael 76
Thomas, Richard 61
Thomas, Scott 178
Thomas, Sean Patrick 29
Thomas, Serena Scott 88
Thomerson, Tim 158
Thompson, Bob 107
Thor, Jerome 149
Thorndike, Oliver 20, 138
Thorne, Geoffrey 56
Thornton, Noley 124
Todd, Hallie 84
Tolkan, James 48, 101
Tomita, Tamlyn 21
Toomey, Regis 11, 102
Torry, Guy 118
Toussant, Beth 54
Townsend, Pete 22
Townsend, Trisha 16
Tracy, Lee 70
Tremayne, Les 34
Tucci, Michael 27
Tuck, Jessica 94
Tucker, John 87
Tulley, Paul 4
Turman, Glynn 109
Turton, Kett 49
Tyson, Richard 43

Underwood, Blair 31
Urecal, Minerva 93
Urich, Robert 114, 168

Valentine, Steve 21

Valenza, Tasia 257
Vandis, Titos 39
Van Dusen, Granville 49
Van Dyke, Barry 27
Van Dyke, Dick 27
Van Dyke, Stacey 27
Vaughn, Robert 23, 162
Venuta, Beany 176
Vereen, Ben 110, 123
Vida, Christina 18
Vidal, Lisa 18
Vidal, Sandra 14
Vigoda, Abe 5
Vilan, Mayte 104
Vinson, Gary 103
Viscusso, Sal 114
Visitor, Nana 197
Viterelli, Joe 118
Von Eltz, Theodore 17
Voskovec, George 89

Wagner, Robert 47, 122
Walberg, Garry 99
Walker, Ally 82
Walker, Arnetia 64
Walker, Nancy 74
Wallace, Dee 287
Walsh, M. Emmet 132
Walsh, Sydney 67
Walston, Ray 94
Walter, Tracey 88
Ward, Jonathan 51
Warden, Jack 301
Warlock, Billy 48
Washington, Ned 86
Watkin, Pierre 28
Watson, James A., Jr. 96
Waxman, Al 12
Waterman, Felicity 126
Wayland, Len 124
Wayne, David 34
Weathers, Carl 56, 116, 165
Weaver, Dennis 200
Webb, Jack 32, 92
Webb, Jane 45
Weisman, Robin 126
Wells, Rebecca 9
Wells, Tom 109
West, Adam 23, 65, 223
Westerman, Floyd 134
Wever, Ned 136

Whaley, Frank 10
Wheeler, Ellen 54
Whirry, Shannon 78
White, Bernard 32
Whitfield, Lynn 19
Wicek, Jimmy 113
Wickes, Mary 37
Wilcox, Larry 16
Willcox, Pete 65
Williams, Barbara 93, 114
Williams, Bill 133
Williams, Clarence, III 80
Williams, Cress 88
Williams, Dick Anthony 51
Williams, Ed 95
Williams, Grant 50
Williams, Greg Alan 3
Williams, Jo Beth 49
Williams, Josh C. 100
Williams, Kent 78
Williams, Natashia 108
Williams, Patrick 51
Williams, Paul 261
Williams, Steven 131
Williams, Van 7, 120
Willingham, Noble 134
Willis, Bruce 83
Wilson, Flip 172
Wilson, Sheree J. 134
Wilson, Tom 124
Windom, William 45, 49, 84
Winters, Shelley 161
Wolff, Jonathan 53
Wolter, Sherilyn 4
Wong, Anna May 38
Woodward, Edward 90
Wuhl, Robert 124
Wylie, Adam 94
Wyner, George 73, 109
Wyngarde, Peter 26
Wynn, Keenan 65, 133
Wyss, Amanda 45, 109

Yagher, Jeff 131
Yarborough, Barton 32
Yarlett, Claire 14, 104
Yohn, Erica 94
Young, Leigh Taylor 94
Yune, Johnny 266

Zada, Ramy 38

Index (to entry numbers)

Zal, Roxanne 82
Zapata, Carmen 45
Zerbe, Anthony 45

Zimbalist, Efrem, Jr. 101, 107, 193
Zimbalist, Stephanie 101
Zmed, Adrian 12

www.ingramcontent.com/pod-product-compliance
Ingram Content Group UK Ltd.
Pitfield, Milton Keynes, MK11 3LW, UK
UKHW041957140426
5217IPUK00015B/853